INTENTIONAL PRACTICE
FOR MUSEUMS

INTENTIONAL PRACTICE FOR MUSEUMS

A Guide for Maximizing Impact

RANDI KORN

ROWMAN & LITTLEFIELD
Lanham • Boulder • New York • London

Published by Rowman & Littlefield
An imprint of The Rowman & Littlefield Publishing Group, Inc.
4501 Forbes Boulevard, Suite 200, Lanham, Maryland 20706
www.rowman.com

6 Tinworth Street, London SE11 5AL

British Library Cataloguing in Publication Information Available

Library of Congress Cataloging-in-Publication Data
Names: Korn, Randi, author.
Title: Intentional practice for museums : a guide for maximizing impact / Randi Korn.
Description: Lanham : Rowman & Littlefield, [2018] | Includes bibliographical references and index.
Identifiers: LCCN 2018028876 (print) | LCCN 2018043325 (ebook) | ISBN 9781538106372 (electronic) | ISBN 9781538106358 (cloth : alk. paper) | ISBN 9781538106365 (paperback : alk. paper)
Subjects: LCSH: Museums—Management. | System theory.
Classification: LCC AM121 (ebook) | LCC AM121 .K67 2018 (print) | DDC 069/.068—dc23
LC record available at https://lccn.loc.gov/2018028876

∞™ The paper used in this publication meets the minimum requirements of American National Standard for Information Sciences—Permanence of Paper for Printed Library Materials, ANSI/NISO Z39.48-1992.

Printed in the United States of America

To Jack and Lucas
May you embrace life's journey with great purpose and intentionality

CONTENTS

FIGURES

TABLES

TEXTBOXES

Acknowledgments

EXPERIENCING THE WORLD through incredible objects, artifacts, and specimens has been rewarding in so many personal ways. Thank you to the many colleagues who have welcomed me into your museums for meaningful discussions and important work; I am grateful. Part of my museum work took place in the public spaces of museums, where I had the honor of meeting and talking with hundreds of visitors who agreed to share their insights and experiences so we—those of us who work on their behalf—could work harder to make a positive difference in the quality of their lives (a phrase attributed to scholar Stephen Weil that you will see throughout the book). I am thankful that so many visitors agreed to talk with a stranger about their personal reflections. While I don't remember any of their names, I recall many of their stories, reactions, and heartfelt experiences.

When the ideas associated with intentional practice were in my head, I needed someone to ask me questions so I could begin to see them, think about them, and develop them. I am indebted to Ann-Clayton Everett (ACE), who was able to bring just the right kind of thinking to the table; she asked me hard questions in the gentlest way possible and persisted until I found clarity of thought. We field-tested ideas together, collecting feedback from colleagues, and learned a great deal along the way. After two years of research and development, we were delighted to receive our first intentional-practice project. ACE was my thought partner in creating much of the work in this book; she deserves considerable credit. Thank you, ACE, for encouraging me and for wanting to pursue these ideas without knowing where the adventure would lead.

So many colleagues and friends helped me through the book-writing process—from fact checking, quotation checking, editing, and reference formatting to preparing graphics so they were camera-ready—the list goes on! Thank you all. Specifically, thank you, George Hein, Andrea Herrick, Wendy Luke, Marsha Semmel, Dave Ucko, and staff at RK&A who worked with me on several intentional practice projects, including Stephanie Downey, Amanda Krantz, Katie Chandler, Cathy Sigmond, Erin Wilcox, and Samantha Theriault—who deserves a special callout. Sam attended to the many organizational details that are part of preparing a manuscript, including securing copyright permissions for graphics, double-checking the many quotations in the manuscript and their accompanying references, organizing all the figures, tables, and so on according to the publisher's guidelines, and attending to so many other details so I didn't have to. Thank you, Sam.

Thank you to all the authors appearing in chapter 6 who agreed to support this project by sharing their personal intentional-practice experiences. Case-study authors, in their order of appearance, are Henry Schulman and Shannon Johnson; Cathy Sigmond and Laurel Zhang; Tim Grove; Danielle Amodeo, Eileen Smith, and Jocelyn Edens; Franny Kent and Stephanie Downey; Shari Werb; Wendy Lovelady; Barbara Bassett and Amanda Krantz; Stephanie Ratcliffe; and Kathryn Potts. I know that finding one's voice when writing is a process onto itself. Thank you all.

Several people pushed me toward that sometimes-elusive element I call clarity. Charles Harmon of Rowman & Littlefield provided support for the idea of this book, offered insights after reading all the chapters as they were completed, and gently nudged me along. I am deeply appreciative of Kris Morrissey, Stephanie Ratcliffe, and Beverly Serrell who read significant parts of the manuscript and provided concrete, directive feedback. Their comments and questions helped me find my voice and the clarity I was seeking. I thank them for their honesty and forthrightness. And speaking of honesty, my husband, John Daniel Rogers, the curator in chapter 2 who so eloquently explains the essence and purpose of natural history museum collections, read nearly every chapter. He always noticed when I had veered off track, which ultimately diluted what I wanted to say. Thank you for challenging my thinking and saving me from myself, Dan. You have a way of zeroing in on the essence of ideas, and I am grateful for having such a clear, deep thinker in my life.

Preface

MY VERY FIRST MUSEUM VISIT was as a first grader when my class took a field trip to the Metropolitan Museum of Art. I vividly recall sitting cross-legged on the floor inside an Egyptian tomb with my classmates in complete awe of my surroundings. I felt so tiny and insignificant surrounded by large pieces of stone with intricate mysterious carvings. They mesmerized me. Some ten years later I visited the museum again—this time by myself in search of another awe-inspiring experience. I was not disappointed. I was taken with a very small work of art from the Cyclades that I consider to be my very favorite piece to date—in part because of how it affected me. A few years ago, a colleague was collecting museum stories for a presentation she was to deliver, and I sent this recollection, written from the perspective of an adult reflecting back:

> It is easy to say that I love the simplicity of the form. It is much harder to think about why I so loved this piece when I first saw it at the age of 16—on my first visit to NYC by myself. Alone in the city, the world felt large and loud, and I, like many teens, was searching for who I was. In this small, unassuming piece I saw a harp player exuding pride and confidence as he played his harp, which was one with his body, and he looked so pleased with the sounds he was creating. I wondered, "Will I be able to find the one thing I love?" (see figure P.1)

Although it took me several years, I realized that museums represented a fairly significant thing I love, and I am fortunate to have been able to build a career that allowed me to visit them all the time. I care deeply about museums and their future. This book comes from that place—I want to

Figure P.1.   Marble Seated Harp Player, ca. 2800–2700 BC
Courtesy of the Metropolitan Museum of Art

help museums have a long and prosperous future so others can experience awe and find pleasure and solace in them.

A Way of Thinking

Intentional Practice for Museums: A Guide for Maximizing Impact uses intentional-practice thinking and strategies to help museums maximize their ability to achieve impact on audiences. It presents a methodical planning approach to achieving impact because *planning* for impact is a prerequisite to *measuring* impact. Without a strong plan, impact is not likely to happen—at least not in the way the museum intended. Intentional practice is a holistic way of thinking and working that includes collaborating with colleagues from across the organization to articulate the organization's intended impact so it can plan the organization's work; evaluate the ways in which it is achieving impact; reflect on evaluation results for the purpose of learning and improving; and strengthen alignment between what it does and its intended impact. I adopted museum scholar Stephen Weil's definition of impact: making a positive difference in the quality of people's lives.[1] A museum's intended impact is at the center of a museum's work; it, along with planning, evaluating, aligning, and reflecting, constitute the Cycle of Intentional Practice, which is fully deconstructed herein. Staff participation in intentional practice is vital; all employees create a force that keeps the museum engine moving forward with great intentionality toward achieving impact.

Culture and sustainability specialist Doug Worts recently wrote, "Among the biggest challenges for museums is the planning for and measurement of cultural outcomes within the larger world."[2] This book responds to his observation and provides an impact- and audience-driven approach to museum planning with the goal of guiding museums to articulate the benefits of their organizations on audiences. Developed through collaborative workshops strategies, an impact statement and associated visitor-experience outcomes serve as the gauge of success from a visitor-benefit perspective. Similar to how audience outcomes are needed to conduct program or exhibition evaluation, an impact statement and associated outcomes are a prerequisite for conducting impact evaluation. Without a clear notion of what the museum intends to achieve, evaluation is moot. How would the museum know if the exhibition, program, or museum is achieving what it set out to achieve? What would the evaluator use to frame and design the evaluation? What criteria would guide the analysis?

An impact statement is one sentence that describes the overall effect of a museum visit on target audiences. It balances aspiration with realism, and by design, it reflects staff members' passion for their work, the museum's distinct qualities, and what is relevant to audiences. Outcomes are explicit measurable results on specified audiences that support the impact statement. Without a clear vision of the end result, museums may not know how to organize their work and which actions to take to achieve those ends. Planning and evaluation are inextricably linked, and if a museum hasn't articulated its intended results and doesn't have a sound plan for how to achieve them, the museum isn't ready to conduct an impact evaluation. If your museum does not have an impact statement and associated outcomes that describe how the museum wants to affect audiences, this book can guide you through the necessary steps.

The Intended Audience

While writing this book accommodates my desire to share an impact-driven way of thinking and working, I also hope to inspire professionals to want to create their own intentional practice so they can support their organization in achieving impact. Whether you are a seasoned or midcareer practitioner or just starting out, you can apply intentional-practice ideas in a multitude of ways. For example, when an organization's intentional practice is pursued from the top of the organization, impact is maximized. However, a department head can also apply intentional-practice concepts and exercises to strengthen a section in the middle of the organization, which may very well garner attention from other departments, eventually evolving into a larger intentional-practice movement. And individuals also can quietly apply holistic thinking and practices to their daily work and slowly begin to invite others to do the same. Intentional-practice strategies are designed to support museums as they zero in on achieving impact because achieving impact on audiences is a museum's ultimate purpose; achieving impact is the answer to the "so what?" question that some organizations—especially museums—often face.

I also hope to affect how museum professionals think and talk about impact. Sometimes, individual museums talk about and describe impact using numbers and measure their successes by counting—for example, numbers of people, numbers of exhibits and programs, and numbers of new acquisitions. Research conducted on behalf of the museum community describes the impact of museums in economic terms, such as how many jobs museums create in a community or how many dollars a museum contributes

to the local economy.[3] While the economic value of museums is important—especially to local politicians and lawmakers—discussing the value of
museums solely from an economic viewpoint doesn't fully express what is
truly unique about museums and what they afford people and communities.

Coming face-to-face with works of art, specimens from the natural
world, and objects from other cultures offers opportunities unique to museums. Hearing ancestors share their stories, having interactive experiences
that demonstrate an idea or phenomenon, participating in conversations
about American democracy, or discussing contentious contemporary social
challenges all demonstrate that museum collections, though from times
past, have meaning in today's world. I believe that such experiences can
make a positive difference in the quality of people's lives. Museums contribute important economic benefits to cities, states, and the country, *and*
they provide deeply meaningful experiences to people; both results deserve
the same attention and recognition from the museum community.

What to Expect

The book is organized methodically. The first chapter explains how I came
to a philosophy of intentional practice by highlighting thinkers who influenced me throughout my career. You will read about six people in three
fields (philosophy, museums, and evaluation) who played a role in my professional evolution and affected my intentional-practice thinking. Chapter
2 recounts historic moments, landmark publications, museum visitation
trends, and personal observations of the museum and evaluation fields that
led to the concept of intentional practice, the Cycle of Intentional Practice,
and a suite of intentional-planning workshops. As I explored these events
and ideas, I slowly came to understand that my work with museums would
evolve from studying visitors' experiences in programs and exhibitions to
guiding the *whole* museum to intentionally plan its work to achieve impact
on the audiences it serves.

Chapters 3, 4, and 5 are devoted to deconstructing, defining, and
explaining intentional-practice work. Two threads tie these three chapters together: the central piece in the middle of the Cycle of Intentional
Practice and the four quadrants that surround it, and the idea that learning—personal, professional, and organizational—is the primary benefit and
result of intentional practice. Chapter 3 introduces the Cycle of Intentional
Practice, starting with the center of the cycle, impact. Included in the discussion about impact is the need for a museum to identify three or four target audiences that will become the focus of its intentional-practice work.

Chapter 3 prepares readers for chapter 4, which delves a bit deeper into the concepts that the cycle embodies. It introduces and describes the seven principles of intentional practice, shares guidelines for participating in intentional-practice workshops, and identifies two fundamental beliefs that underlie intentional-practice thinking. The seven principles can be thought of as values, as they are the pillars of intentional practice, and all are needed at one time or another to sustain one's intentional work (see textbox 4.1 on page 78 for a complete list). The first five principles follow the Cycle of Intentional Practice, and the last two represent the primary approaches that can support museums as they move around and across the cycle. After reading chapters 3 and 4, you will have garnered considerable knowledge about the underpinnings of intentional-practice thinking and working, and you will be anxious to begin applying intentional-practice strategies. The exercises in chapter 5 will help you begin your intentional-practice journey.

These exercises are unencumbered; that is, they do not include museum-specific customizations. There are exercises for all four quadrants, and they include implementation instructions, questions for the facilitator to ask participants, and exercises for small working groups. To sustain your intentional practice, you can recycle the exercises, interjecting your own questions as needed. As you become proficient in impact-driven thinking, you will want to customize the exercises to respond to your changing museum and public.

Chapter 6 presents ten case studies written by museum professionals who participated in intentional-practice workshops. Projects were selected because the organizations, and in some cases, the authors, took an intentional-practice idea and made it their own. These stories give a personal voice to intentional practice and impact-driven decision making. Chapter 7 is the conclusion where I reinforce the two most important purposes of intentional practice: to create an impact-drive plan to maximize the museum's ability to achieve impact, and to benefit from ongoing learning—yours (i.e., personal and professional) and your museum's. Both purposes are continual evolutions because planning for impact and achieving impact are interactive forces that are in constant motion.

My hope is that *Intentional Practice for Museums: A Guide for Maximizing Impact* deepens your interest in pursuing intentional practice for the purposes of achieving impact on museum audiences. Because the underlying goal is learning, I also hope your museum practice continually improves—along with your fellow colleagues and your museum—for the ultimate purpose of making a positive difference in people's lives.

Toward a Philosophy of Intentionality **1**

The real voyage of discovery comes not in seeking new landscapes but in having new eyes.

—MARCEL PROUST

INTENTIONALITY, AS A CONCEPT and professional practice, was slow-growing in my mind and at times barely recognizable as a worthwhile notion to continue pondering. Yet I was not able to let go. My desire to connect my past work to what would be my future work pulled me forward, but not without the help of others. Little by little, amorphous, disparate ideas joined as one solid, well-formulated concept. Friends and colleagues offered words of encouragement, so I continued thinking about intentionality and how to apply such thinking to museums.

No one works or thinks in a vacuum; a long significant history of thought and practice precedes us, and I, like many others, have benefited from past thinkers and practitioners of our time and past times—from museum scholars to evaluation theorists. This book begins by recognizing those who have unknowingly helped me frame, shape, build, and clarify ideas about intentionality and the role intentional practice plays in museum work. I have learned a great deal while journeying toward a relevant philosophy of intentionality—and if I have learned anything at all, it is that my learning will continue, creating one draft after another of intentional practice. To those great thinkers who came before me, "If I have seen further, it is by standing on the shoulders of giants" (a quotation attributed to Isaac Newton, see figure 1.1).

Figure 1.1. "Orion the Giant." Cedalion sits on the shoulders of Orion, the blind giant, to serve as the giant's eyes.

Courtesy of the Rosenwald Collection, Rare Book and Special Collections Division of the Library of Congress, Washington, DC.

The thought leaders featured below were selected because their ideas affected my thinking and actions. As such, in presenting their thoughts, I also simultaneously introduce intentional-practice ideas. Full explanations of intentional practice, though, are in subsequent chapters. This chapter introduces the Cycle of Intentional Practice (see figure 1.2) and throughout the book you will be reading about it in different ways depending on the topic under discussion. On the surface, it looks like a simple graphic; further into the book you will learn about its layers of complexity. This chapter also presents the philosophical underpinnings of intentional practice; proposes that museums need impact statements and associated outcomes that clearly articulate the positive difference they want to make in people's lives; advocates for museums to undertake deliberate actions to achieve their intended impact; and illustrates that intentional practice stems from having an evaluative mindset where staff ask questions and explore challenges together with the purpose of continually learning and improving as they pursue achieving impact. Finally, this chapter suggests that achieving impact through intentional practice requires the effort of the entire museum, which may necessitate organizational change—a concept implicit in intentional practice work and discussed in the conclusion of the book.

Figure 1.2.   The Cycle of Intentional Practice.

Philosophers

When intentionality first emerged in my thinking, I wondered in which field of study the concept lives. Not surprisingly, philosophers have, over time, written extensively about intentionality. Appropriately, Franz Brentano, the father of intentionality, is presented first, followed by John Dewey, an important thinker about progressive education and democracy.

Franz Brentano

Franz Brentano revitalized the concept of intentionality in 1874, and it is he whom most philosophers, past and present, credit when discussing intentionality. There are many ways to discuss intentionality, and among them are a few that illustrate how intentionality applies to museums. Intentionality is a philosophical term from the Medieval Latin *intentio,* a word for "the ideas or representations of things *formed by the mind*"[1] (emphasis mine), and *intentio* derives from the verb *intendere,* which means "being *directed toward some goal* or thing"[2] (emphasis mine). Brentano's thesis (as it is called), considered as the most influential of all contemporary philosophy,[3] is expressed by saying that "one cannot believe, wish, or hope without believing or wishing something."[4] The connection between Brentano's idea of intentionality and the application of intentionality concepts to museums is through the meaning of *intendere* noted above: a museum might develop an impact statement (meaning that staff articulate their beliefs and wishes for the results they would like to achieve on audiences) and then use the impact statement to *direct* their decisions and actions *toward some goal or thing.* More specifically, staff use the impact statement, which they developed through facilitated exercises, to guide them as they make decisions and take actions to achieve a particular end.[5] While the original concept of *intentio* focuses on the power of the mind to pursue a goal, I push that power, as it were, a step further by helping museums determine the actions they need to take to achieve their intent—the ideas that originated in their mind.

A decade ago museum literature did not include "intentionality." The word and the concept were absent—at least explicitly—but now intentionality has become part of museum practitioners' lexicon (see textbox 1.1).

John Dewey

I am indebted to George Hein, professor emeritus of Lesley University, for the depth with which he has studied Dewey as well as his ability to translate, clarify, and weave together Dewey's complicated ideas about ed-

Textbox 1.1.

Intentionality: When an idea formed in the mind through careful deliberation and reflection directs a person/entity toward some goal or thing. (In a museum context, the goal or thing is the contents of an impact statement, supporting outcomes, and specified audiences as the recipients of the museum's impact.)

Intentional practice: a holistic way of thinking and working that includes collaborating with colleagues from across the organization to articulate the organization's intended impact so it can do the following: plan the organization's work to achieve impact; evaluate the ways in which the organization is achieving impact based on its intentions; reflect on the results of the evaluation and the organization's actions for the purpose of learning and improving; and analyze its work with the goal of strengthening alignment between what it does and its intended impact.

ucation and democracy into understandable prose.[6] Reading Hein's most recent book, *Progressive Museum Practice: John Dewey and Democracy*, provided a new and deeper understanding of Dewey's ideas and reinforces the importance of intentional thinking. There are three philosophical points important to Dewey that are particularly meaningful and aligned with intentionality. Below, you will see Dewey's idea, as per Hein's explanation, followed by how the idea is applied in intentional practice.

1. Social problems in our democratic society will not solve themselves; they require social and political action.[7]

Application: Achieving impact requires determination and the full force of the museum, meaning that staff members from across the entire organization will want to collaborate to determine the actions they will take if they are to make a discernable difference in people's lives. Before taking actions, though, the museum will need to first articulate the impact it would like to achieve on audiences and then align its actions and resources to achieve that end. Impact will not happen without deliberate actions. These ideas (articulating impact and aligning actions and resources) are discussed in chapter 3.

2. Dewey believes in the possibility of continual societal progress and improvement. One can see how this belief connects to progressive education and democracy—the focus of Dewey's work throughout his life.[8]

Application: When a museum focuses on achieving impact, as per the impact statement in the center of the Cycle of Intentional Practice, staff continually navigate around and across the cycle in pursuit of impact. Visualizing the cycle spiraling upward in infinity suggests continual improvement as well as the possibility that a museum always may be striving to reach its intended impact, which also relates to the third point below.

3. Hein points out that

> Dewey's philosophical system pivots around *the process of thinking* . . . [which] commits Dewey to a *process* philosophy. . . . By relinquishing any claim to the existence of an ideal (or absolute) state of being, and denying the possibility of achieving a final goal, Dewey's philosophy leaves us in a state of uncertainty about how far we have advanced towards achieving a desired goal. . . . And based on analyzing our experiences, we always need to ask whether the consequences of a particular action are leading us in the direction we desire.[9]

Application: As noted above, the Cycle of Intentional Practice spirals upward. In reality, a museum's impact statement reflects its most current iteration of what it would like to achieve, which includes what is relevant to the public; both the museum and the public are in constant states of change, and as such, achieving impact is always just beyond a museum's reach. In that way, "the possibility of achieving a final goal" is denied; however, rather than dwelling on that point, museums need to maintain focus on continual learning and improvement while pursuing impact, which is the essence of intentional practice. Also relevant here is Hein's point that "Dewey's philosophy leaves us in a state of uncertainty about how far we have advanced towards achieving a desired goal." And while philosophically true, the Cycle of Intentional Practice includes an evaluation quadrant (refer to figure 1.2) where one can explore and study progress toward a final goal. That said, the intent of the evaluation process, from an intentional practice perspective, is not to judge but to learn. While evaluation might produce concrete products (reports with data) and provide results that symbolize an end point, especially if it is a summative evaluation, someone who lives on the Cycle of Intentional Practice will use evaluation and reflection as learning opportunities to affect future work.

Even though intentionality has philosophical roots, I do not draw attention to them when working with museums because museums exist to serve a pragmatic purpose—to make a difference in the quality of people's lives. If intentional practice is to be relevant and useful to museums, pragmatism will need to prevail in all discussions, along with a bit of idealism to carry museums forward.

Past Museum Provocateurs

As a graduate student in museum studies, fortunately I was required to read the works of many great museum thinkers who helped solidify museum practice as a profession. While I may not have gleaned their true value at the time, I now see the strength of the platform they built. Many people's ideas are so ingrained in how I think that sometimes I have difficulty knowing where their ideas end and mine begin. Suffice it to say, I have learned a great deal from books, professionals I have known and worked with over the years, and museum visitors I have had the pleasure of meeting; all have made their mark on how I think about museum practice.

This section presents two thought leaders—John Cotton Dana and Stephen Weil. Dana was extraordinarily practical and a champion of the people—two ideas that are important in intentional-practice work. Stephen Weil's influence is quite direct and concrete; in short, his readings clarified what museums ought to be concerned with and helped me move toward a new pursuit. His writings highlighted gaps in museum practice that I heard as calls to action, and they continue to be a source of inspiration. I often reread the same pieces again and again, always learning something new or seeing a familiar idea in a new way with each read.

John Cotton Dana

Many museum professionals are most familiar with John Cotton Dana as the founding director of the Newark Museum in Newark, New Jersey (see figure 1.3). His thoughts are provocative and important to the history of museums. The most meaningful quotation that well explains his important contribution in just a few words is this: "A museum is good only in so far it is of use."[10] "Use" for Dana specifically meant doing work for the public good—an extremely important idea in intentional practice. Museums must create public value,[11] and for that reason, museums need to relentlessly focus on "use" by clarifying what they want to achieve in the public domain and in determining how to achieve it. Remarkably, Dana voiced this opinion in 1916, in an address to the American Association of Museums (now American Alliance of Museums). Dana's vision was that museums would reach out to people and enrich their lives, particularly those in underserved communities, and importantly, he rejected that a museum's purpose was to collect and preserve objects. Dana believed that museums' efforts to collect, preserve, and educate are a means to an end. For a museum to be useful, at the very least, it should work on behalf of the public. His ideas beg the question "To what end?" To what greater end do museum practitioners do

Figure 1.3.   Newark Free Public Library, the first home of the Newark Museum, ca. 1910.
From the postcard collection of Randi Korn.

their work? The intentional-practice exercises (provided in chapter 5) will guide museums through the steps to answer that question.

Dana's book, *The New Museum,* was first published in 1917 and the Newark Museum reproduced and republished it in 1999. This book presents Dana's thoughts about museums serving their community, a powerful idea that resonates with contemporary museum practitioners, although exactly what "serving their community" means and how museums discuss and actualize it has changed and evolved over time. For example, at the turn of the twenty-first century, staff talked about museums becoming centers in their communities,[12] and today, fifteen years later, relevance and social justice are topics of conversation.[13] Often attendance numbers, particularly of schoolchildren from underserved communities, are cited as evidence that a museum is serving its community. While attendance may suggest "use," it does not indicate use*fulness* or meaningfulness to the visitor. If a museum is going to be useful and meaningful, it should first articulate—in the form of an impact statement and supporting outcomes—the ways it intends to be useful and meaningful to the communities it serves.[14] The impact statement and outcomes specify in concrete terms what usefulness and meaningfulness look like and sound like. Such specificity serves two purposes: it guides planning and becomes the gauge for success during the evaluation process. Dana did not address accountability in detail in his writings, as the museum profession was quite young at the time, but this one passage suggests he believed that museums should be held accountable to the public:

> All public institutions, and museums are no exceptions, should give returns for their cost, and those returns should be in good degree positive, definite, visible, measurable. . . . Common sense demands that a publicly supported institution do something for its supporters, and that some part at least of what it does be capable of clear description and downright valuation.[15]

Dana's idea of a useful museum for the public good was the start of museums' negotiation of their relationship with the public, which, one century later, continues to evolve. The concept of "use" is meaningful and can be applied to a variety of situations; for example, "data is good only insofar it is of use," "an evaluation report is good only insofar it is of use," and "a meeting is good only insofar as it is of use." Those mantras all point to pragmatism, and they clarify the purpose of intentional practice—museums working to improve their organizations so they can achieve public value.

Stephen Weil

Stephen Weil, noted museum thought leader and scholar, has significantly influenced many people who work in museums. He was a theoretician and sought-after presenter who was willing to address thorny issues, and he did so with intelligence, humor, and grace. His many papers can be found in three books, *Making Museums Matter* (2002), *A Cabinet of Curiosities: Inquiries into Museums and Their Prospects* (1995), and *Rethinking the Museum and Other Meditations* (1990), and numerous journal publications. A few chapters in *Making Museums Matter* as well as his last published article titled "A Success/Failure Matrix for Museums," which appeared in *Museum News,* were particularly influential. A few essential ideas from those works are highlighted below.

The first piece, "Museums: Can and Do They Make a Difference?" is a chapter that prompts one to think about a museum's purpose. Weil clarifies a problem that museums need to address:

> So what difference did it make that museums were ever here? So what difference would it have made if they hadn't been? Posed in a variety of ways . . . these are also the in-your-face, bottom-line, hard-nosed questions that the museum community has, for the past several decades or more, struggled mightily to keep safely locked in the closet and out of public view. . . . That time is gone. Those ultimate "so what" questions

are finally here and with us. With us as well are some postultimate questions that must invariably follow in their wake. If museums do matter, if
they can make a difference, to whom do they matter, and what are the
differences that they might make?[16]

Further into the chapter, Weil unequivocally states the need for a museum
to establish a clear institutional purpose when he notes that "the good
museum is a purpose-driven institution,"[17] and he tries to help museums
move forward by further suggesting that good museums "make a positive
difference in the quality of people's lives."[18] The parallel between the latter
idea and Dana's idea of usefulness is clear. Weil credits the United Way as
the organization that coined the above phrase, writing:

> I would . . . argue that United Way's cornerstone—to make a positive dif-
> ference in the quality of people's lives—ought to be consciously adopted as
> our cornerstone as well. And I would argue still further that, at least at their
> best, museums operate today in the hope and expectation that they will
> make a positive difference in the quality of people's lives. And I would ar-
> gue finally that we form, preserve, and study collections today not because
> we think those activities are appropriate ends in themselves but because we
> hope and expect that those collections will be used in ways that will, to
> quote United Way, "provide benefits . . . for individuals or populations."[19]

Also, the above quotation clarifies Weil's belief that museums are a
means to an end—an idea he fully explains in a chapter appropriately titled
"From Being about Something to Being for Somebody."[20] In that chapter
Weil again mentions museums' inability to articulate their purpose:

> The work that needs to be done is daunting. In many instances, it may start
> with something so basic as getting a museum's leadership to articulate what
> it hopes or expects its institution to accomplish. That so many museums
> continue to be so unfocused about their purpose—avoiding any reference
> to outcomes at all . . . —is only the beginning of the problem.[21]

I read the two ideas reflected in the above quotations as calls to action,
as I, too, saw a deficit in museum practice, albeit from an evaluator's
perspective: If a museum did not articulate a clear purpose (whether for a
program or an entire organization), how could it know where it wanted
to go, what actions to take, and whether it was successful? Though Weil
was not a practicing evaluator, he knew that establishing a clear institutional purpose is the first step to being able to assess an institution's effectiveness in achieving that purpose. Evaluators have always known about

the importance of articulating experience outcomes as part of the planning process; why wouldn't an entire organization follow the same strategy? He notes in another chapter titled "Romance Versus Realism"[22] that museums are familiar with and comfortable creating institutional mission statements that describe what their organization does, such as "educate" and "preserve," but they are unfamiliar with thinking about outcomes or impact. Weil notes,

> For institutional purposes to be recast in terms of intended outcomes, those responsible . . . will have to . . . ask themselves fundamental questions as to just why that work is being done, and for whom. How will the community we serve be positively different as a result of our effort? How much difference would it make if we had never undertaken such an effort to begin with?[23]

Weil asked another important question when he wrote, "As for making a difference, will any differences do, or is it only intended differences with which we are concerned?" He answers his question by stating: "In terms of accountability, it must surely be the latter."[24] The fact that museums have mission statements that describe what they do—but do not have companion statements that describe the result of what they do on audiences served—became another call to action.[25] Before a museum can achieve impact, first it needs a statement that describes its intended impact to guide its actions; a museum's intended impact reflects staff members' deepest aspirations for what they want to achieve in the public domain. The same evaluation skills that are used to help museums craft outcomes for individual programs can be applied to developing impact statements and supporting outcomes for the whole museum. Using evaluation approaches, such as asking probing questions, collecting information from staff and outside stakeholders, and analyzing responses, a collective voice could emerge, representing the museum and the impact it wanted to achieve on audiences. The next step would be helping staff develop concrete outcomes, followed by helping them move toward those ends, and so on, and so on. In short, Weil inspired me to extend my evaluative thinking[26] and practice to work with museums to plan for and pursue impact.

In "A Success/Failure Matrix for Museums," Weil recognized that even after a museum determines its purpose, its work is just beginning: "Once a purpose has been established, however, the museum is still unable to move forward until either (a) all of the necessary resources can be identified and secured, or (b) the purpose has been scaled back to match the available resources."[27] This article is important in intentional practice

because it highlights the necessity of alignment—between purpose and resources (dollars and staff time, an often-overlooked resource), and between
purpose and programming. He notes:

> What makes a well-run museum well run is that its efforts are channeled
> exclusively into the pursuit of its purpose and not scattered elsewhere. Ef-
> forts directed elsewhere are a waste of institutional resources. . . . The only
> activities in which the museum can legitimately engage are those intended
> to further its institutional purpose.[28]

There are other useful discussions in this piece; for example, Weil clarifies
the difference between outputs and outcomes, as the museum community often confuses the two. Outputs are products such as an exhibition
or how many people attended, and outcomes are "positive changes in its
targeted audiences— . . . those hearts and minds differences—that are the
museum's ultimate goal. Outcomes are the realization of its institutional
purpose."[29] And finally, he suggests, and the evaluator in me agrees, "care
must be taken not to muddle quantitative measures of efficiency appropriate for evaluating outputs with the qualitative estimates of effectiveness
required for evaluating outcomes."[30] Intentional-practice work includes
helping museums articulate their purpose (impact), develop associated
outcomes, evaluate their effectiveness in achieving outcomes and impact,
align their actions and resources to support achieving impact, and reflect
on results as well as their work to enhance their professional learning. The
most difficult process for museums to engage in is analyzing their actions
and determining whether they are leading the museum toward its intended
direction—the impact it wants to achieve. This alignment process and its
complications in practice are discussed in chapters 3, 4, and 5, and practitioners' thoughts are presented in a few of the case studies in chapter 6.

Stephen Weil's writings clarified a need among museums. The purpose and accountability deficit in museums was deeply troubling, and I
wanted to create planning strategies to address them head-on using my
experience as an evaluator. I could no longer shake my interest in pursuing
intentional-practice strategies with the entire museum.

Evaluation Provocateurs

Evaluation, as a field of study, is enormous. Most practicing evaluators work
in the social service and health sectors, some work in formal education, and
a few, relatively speaking, work in museums and other informal learning
organizations, including the performing arts. Learning how evaluators from

outside the cultural sector address problems can provide insight, as evaluators often face similar challenges, such as the universal aversion to writing
outcomes. As intentional-practice ideas began to solidify, I realized that
intentional practice, when viewed from a high vantage point, is really about
organizational learning and change. In fact, early on, the Cycle of Intentional Practice was titled the Cycle of Learning, in part because learning is
immediately understandable to people. Certainly, there are plenty of dots
to connect between the Cycle of Intentional Practice and organizational
learning and change, and while the remainder of this book clarifies the relationship, for now, suffice it to say, learning about organizational learning
and change[31] from evaluators was gratifying and reassuring. Hallie Preskill
and Rosalie T. Torres led the way with their seminal book discussed below.

Dr. Preskill was a professor at Claremont Graduate University, where
she published widely on topics such as evaluation capacity building, appreciative inquiry, and using evaluation as the catalyst for organizational
learning and change. Now at FSG, a global, not-for-profit strategy, evaluation and research consulting firm started by Michael Porter of Harvard, she
continues to publish groundbreaking work. *Evaluative Inquiry for Learning
in Organizations*, by Preskill and coauthor Rosalie T. Torres, president of
Torres Consulting Group, published in 1999, provides continued inspiration and learning for my intentional-practice pursuit. Their impetus for
the book grew from realizing that "traditional evaluation practice" was not
doing all it could to support organizations in today's complicated world.[32]
They, like many other evaluators, noticed that evaluation reports were
lying dormant when their information could be used to stimulate professional and organizational learning and action. They came to realize that
one-off program evaluations were not supporting the ongoing learning of
the whole organization,[33] and they wanted to apply evaluation processes
(or in their words—evaluative inquiry) to support individual, team, and
organizational learning.

> Evaluative inquiry . . . is an approach to learning that is fully integrated
> with an organization's work practices, and as such, it engenders (a) or-
> ganization members' interest and ability in exploring critical issues using
> evaluation logic, (b) organization members' involvement in evaluative
> processes, and (c) the personal and professional growth of individuals
> within the organization. Evaluative inquiry represents an emphasis on
> understanding each other in order to understand larger organizational chal-
> lenges. . . . In essence, evaluative inquiry is about practical wisdom and
> organization members deliberating about what is good and expedient, with
> an emphasis on using data to inform learning and action.[34]

As confessed earlier in this chapter, sometimes I do not know where another person's ideas end and mine begin, and in a million ways, this is true with all that Preskill and Torres wrote. Their evaluative inquiry strategies echo intentional-practice ideas, as in the following:

> Evaluative inquiry [intentional practice] offers organizations [museums] a process for collaborating on issues that challenge success. Through the collective action of dialogue, reflection, asking questions, and identifying and clarifying individuals' values, beliefs, assumptions, and knowledge, evaluative inquiry provides organization members with an approach to inquiry that results in learning about significant organizational issues. . . . Inquiry becomes the catalyst not only for continuous growth and improvement toward meeting the organization's goals [achieving impact] but also for the organization's employees—those individuals who make up the lifeblood of all organizations (brackets mine).[35]

I came to intentional practice through personal experiences as a cultural consumer; professional experiences as an exhibition designer and evaluator in museums spanning several decades; interactions with museum professionals ranging from educators, to designers, to directors; observations of how museum staff actualize their work; and my intuition. Preskill and Torres came to evaluative inquiry through their personal and professional experiences, too. Reading their well-referenced book bolstered my confidence and helped me know that I should continue exploring intentional-practice ideas for museums.

One of the underlying messages in their book that intentional practice fully embraces is that absolute knowing is an impossibility in process work and no matter how one moves through the process, no one knows where the work will lead as situations and challenges are explored. Intentional-practice work and processes are messy. Not knowing and messiness are prerequisites to real learning, and so is having an open mind during discussions with colleagues, feeling completely comfortable in a naive state, listening to understand, asking questions to seek clarity, and reflecting on observations, conversations, and data. "Learning from others is an integral part of evaluative inquiry"[36] and of intentional practice. Personal learning may take place privately, away from colleagues, while team learning is integrated into intentional-practice workshops by having museum staff work in interdisciplinary breakout groups, which for some museums is a different way of working.

Evaluative Inquiry for Learning in Organizations is an inspirational and aspirational book filled with practical advice, strategies, and suggested questions. In the last chapter, Preskill and Torres identify four characteristics of evaluative inquiry (to distinguish it among other types of evaluation); they appear below with descriptions of how they connect to intentional practice.

1. "Evaluative inquiry is integrated into the organization's work processes and performed primarily by organization members."[37] Intentional practice is meant to be integrated into an organization's work processes and achieving integration is an ongoing goal. Often people have trouble changing their habits, and organizations have trouble changing their systems, so intentional-practice strategies are designed to help museums take small steps. To their second point about who does the work: staff members do the work. As indicated in the third point below, intentional practice uses inquiry as a primary facilitation strategy because asking questions helps people realize what they think. When staff members come to an understanding in their own time, they can accept needing to change how they do their work (e.g., integrating intentional-practice processes into their organization).

2. "Evaluative inquiry for organizational learning and change is ongoing; . . . it is used to nourish continuous individual, team, and organizational learning."[38] The Cycle of Intentional Practice represents this idea. Achieving impact is ongoing, and so is the learning that emerges—whether for the individual, team, or museum.

3. "Evaluative inquiry for learning in organizations strongly relies on the democratic process of asking questions and exploring individuals' values, beliefs, assumptions, and knowledge through dialogue and reflection."[39] Inquiry is the primary intentional-practice approach because of its invaluable neutralizing effect. It is a useful strategy for all staff to adopt as they move around the Cycle of Intentional Practice working with their colleagues.

4. "Evaluative inquiry contributes to a culture of inquiry and occurs within an infrastructure that values continuous improvement and learning."[40] Pursuing both—a culture of inquiry and an infrastructure that values continuous learning—requires ongoing work, and this is where the Cycle of Intentional Practice lives up to its cycle characteristic. Continuous learning and improvement is also built into the cycle, and once learning is realized as the perpetual goal, exhilaration prevails.

Like Weil, Preskill and Torres gave me confidence to pursue intentional practice with museums. I found tremendous comfort knowing that their ideas emerged from their evaluation experience. Their evaluation roots are reminders that evaluation can evolve into a very valuable catalyst for learning and change.

Six leaders from three fields of study—philosophy, museum studies, and evaluation—clarified a way of knowing intentionality and supported my pursuit of intentional practice with museums. Philosophers Franz Brentano and John Dewey clarified two things: intentionality is about deep, unrelenting focus of the mind and heart on a goal that requires deliberate actions to move toward that goal—even though the goal may be continuously slightly out of reach. Without the initial thought that clarifies a destination, actions will be directionless. Museum thought leader John Cotton Dana boldly stated that "a museum is good only in so far it is of use," thereby initiating museums' ever-changing relationship with its publics; Stephen Weil picks up where Dana left off, noting the need for museums to establish a clear institutional purpose if they are to assess their effectiveness. Weil puts forth that a good museum channels all of its efforts and resources exclusively into the pursuit of its purpose and says, "the only activities in which the museum can legitimately engage are those intended to further its institutional purpose."[41] Hallie Preskill and Rosalie T. Torres—evaluators by training—raise evaluative thinking and evaluation practice from the program level to the organizational level by applying evaluative inquiry to pursue personal, team, and organizational learning. All have contributed to how I practice intentionality.

The next chapter chronicles how the ideas that form the Cycle of Intentional Practice emerged. National politics played a role, as did a landmark publication. The chapter also discusses the intrinsic benefits of art museums, science-focused institutions, and history museums and historic sites. And, after discussing personal observations of museums in the cultural landscape, these disparate occurrences that spanned more than twenty years are synthesized, thereby clarifying my intentional practice.

Origins of the Cycle of Intentional Practice

2

> *The questions I ask about our culture are questions about our general and common purposes, yet also questions about deep personal meanings.*

—RAYMOND WILLIAMS, 1958

M USEUMS, LIKE SO MANY OTHER types of organizations, are affected by social and political events and trends, and by extension, those of us who work with museums are also affected. This chapter recounts landmark events, museums' responses to those events, and observations of the cultural landscape. All played a role in developing a holistic organizational model of impact-based thinking and planning that would ultimately expand my work from understanding visitors' experiences in programs and exhibitions to helping the *whole* museum intentionally plan its work to achieve impact.

Contextual Events

There were three interrelated events that would affect museums and evaluation practice. The first, activated by a political change in the U.S. House of Representatives, signified a turning point in America's cultural history. It will sound strangely familiar as, at the writing of this, there are plans, once again, to defund government agencies that support museums. The second is not an event, per se, and if this was a musical score you would hear the ever-increasing crescendo calling for museums to be accountable to themselves, the public, and their funders—whether government or private. The third event—the publication of *Gifts of the Muse,* a book that thoughtfully examines the intrinsic value of the arts—confirmed that the cultural sector, including museums, needed two things to defend their value to those outside their inner spheres: language that clearly articulates museums' value to enable staff to make a case for themselves; and rigorously collected data about the intrinsic value of museums to provide evidence of how museums benefit communities.

The 1994 Election

In 1994, for the first time in forty years, Republicans had taken control of the House, and House Speaker Newt Gingrich wrote the Contract with America. This contract included defunding the National Endowment for the Arts (NEA) and the National Endowment for the Humanities (NEH) and Institute of Museum Services (IMS)—the precursor to the Institute of Museum and Library Services (IMLS). Defenders of these agencies noted that the agencies cost Americans relatively little in terms of tax dollars compared to other government functions, so placing them on the chopping block was ideological rather than economical. Threats to defund these programs cycle in and out of political conversations, depending on who is in power.[1]

Typically, the museum community's response to potential political action includes mobilizing people to advocate for museums and continued agency funding as well as searching for data to prove that these government-funded programs are worthwhile—all in an effort to suggest that doing away with the agencies would adversely affect Americans and their lives. Today, the internet affords advocates and activists the ability to mobilize instantly; such was not the case in 1994. Even so, advocacy was robust, and all three agencies survived. As for studies about the value of these programs, there were no known national studies about the benefits of museums at that time.

There were two significant responses to the threat of cutting government agencies that fund museums. The first took place a few years later, in 1997, when NEH, NEA, IMLS, and the National Science Foundation (NSF) collaborated to fund the Museum Learning Collaborative. This five-year research project, designed to study elements in museum environments and visitor contexts that influence museum learning, was conducted by the University of Pittsburgh and several collaborating museums. A 2003 *Journal of Museum Education* article notes that while the museum community had been increasingly interested in understanding the nature of museum learning, the project was also a response to the "increasing pressure on museums to show that they were deserving of financial support from governmental agencies."[2]

The second response was from IMLS, independent of other government agencies. Diane Frankel, director at the time, initiated a study that explored the ways in which museums support schools in educating America's youth. Study results, based on 376 responses from museums, provided important contextual information about the benefit of museums in formal education—a concern that resonated with most politicians and families.[3]

Museums and Accountability

In 1993, the U.S. government planted the accountability seed with the introduction of the Government Performance and Results Act (GPRA), which became law in 1999. Before then, "accountability" did not appear in museum literature, as the word was not in the indexes of a number of books on museum leadership, museum evaluation, and the history of museums. Then in 1997, Stephen Weil delivered a keynote address at the fiftieth anniversary of the Mid-Atlantic Association of Museums where he talked about accountability in the context of making a positive difference in the quality of people's lives. "Accountability" started appearing in museum books starting in 2006, as noted below, with increasing frequency thereafter.[4]

After GPRA became law, things started to change, slowly. According to the law, which was updated in 2010, government agencies are required to follow standard performance management procedures, which include identifying goals, measuring results, and reporting the ways in which they progress toward those goals.[5] The government's actions affected agencies that fund museums, and some responded. In 2000, IMLS produced *Perspectives on Outcome Based Evaluation for Libraries and Museums,* explicitly noting the "increasing demands for accountability" and the "legislative reality" of the GPRA.[6] In 2008, NSF produced an edited volume titled *Framework for Evaluating Impacts of Informal Science Education Projects,* which focused exclusively on conducting summative evaluation.[7] Part 1 of the report introduces an impact framework (different from the one associated with intentional practice introduced later) with specified impact categories that then consistently appear throughout part 2 in chapters by different evaluators.

The intent behind NSF's impact framework was twofold: (1) NSF recognized that grantees needed a tool to support outcome-based planning that promoted methods beyond randomized controlled trials, which were being advocated at the time as the only meaningful design (according to my email correspondence with David Ucko on June 7, 2017). Needless to say, evaluators were elated, because as much as they tried to move planning teams in the direction of outcome-based planning, when a funder says, "This is required," it gets done—with the help of an evaluator. NSF also recognized that project planners might need guidance in outcome-based thinking and strongly suggested that teams include an evaluator. Ideally, a completed framework, which would be embedded in NSF proposals, would also become the planning tool for project teams. (2) A completed impact framework would serve as the gauge of success for the evaluation and "facilitate the capture, synthesis, and analysis of project outcomes and impacts"—all of which would populate the online Project Monitoring System that NSF developed.[8] In other words, the framework became part of NSF's larger accountability system that enabled NSF to report its impact to Congress. The categories in the impact framework are generic and applicable to any type of museum that creates programs and exhibitions for the public (see table 2.1).

John Falk and Beverly Sheppard note the increasing importance of accountability in their book *Thriving in the Knowledge Age*: "Accountability promises to become one of the largest challenges of this new age. . . . If museums are not proactive about accountability, if they do not seize the initiative and define for themselves the criteria of success, then . . . external forces will sooner or later impose criteria upon them."[9] The increase in concern about accountability goes beyond the government sector, as private foundations also started asking museums to demonstrate that the dollars they receive are achieving what the museum set out to achieve. However, some foundation staff and museum grant recipients may not have a clear and unified understanding of what evaluation is and that conducting evaluation requires methodological knowledge and analytical skills. Professional evaluators want to uphold the standards of practice set forth by the American Evaluation Association[10] and Visitor Studies Association,[11] and therein lies the tension. Professional evaluation often costs more than what most private foundations are willing to financially support, and accountability cannot happen without evaluation. While there may not be consensus around what criteria to set, what accountability means, and how to demonstrate it, museums were expected to respond to the call nevertheless.

Evaluators could support museums in addressing the proliferation of accountability requests, as they are skilled at helping museums clarify what they wanted to achieve in their exhibitions and programs and determining

Table 2.1. The NSF created this framework to help grantees think about and describe programmatic outcomes and impact on the public and/or professional audiences.

Impact category	Generic definition
Awareness, knowledge, or understanding	Measurable demonstration of assessment of, change in, or exercise of awareness, knowledge, understanding of a particular scientific topic, concept, phenomena, theory, or careers central to the project
Engagement or interest	Measurable demonstration of, change in, or exercise of engagement/interest in a particular scientific topic, concept, phenomena, theory, or careers central to the project
Attitude	Measurable demonstration of assessment of, change in, or exercise of attitude toward a particular scientific topic, concept, phenomena, theory, or careers central to the project or one's capabilities relative to these areas. . . . Attitudes refer to changes in . . . constructs such as empathy for animals and their habitats, appreciation for the role of scientists in society, or attitudes toward stem cell research.
Behavior	Measurable demonstration of assessment of, change in, or exercise of behavior related to a STEM topic. These types of impacts are particularly relevant to . . . environmental . . . or health science [projects] . . . since action is a desired outcome.
Skills	Measurable demonstration of the development and/or reinforcement of skills, either . . . new ones or . . . developing [ones]. These tend to be procedural aspects of knowing, as opposed to . . . declarative aspects of knowledge. . . . Although they can . . . manifest as engagement, typically observed skills include . . . engaging in scientific inquiry skills (observing, classifying, . . . predicting, [etc.]), as well as developing/practicing very specific skills related to [successfully using] scientific instruments and devices.
Other	Project specific

Source: Courtesy of the National Science Foundation; to see an unedited version of the NSF Impact Framework, please visit http://www.informalscience.org/framework-evaluating-impacts-informal-science-education-projects.

whether they have done so. Could evaluators apply the same results- and purpose-driven thinking toward the whole museum? Was it possible to bring staff and stakeholders together, including community stakeholders, around a core purpose and continue working from that vantage point? To reiterate Falk and Sheppard's insight: if museums do not develop their own criteria, others will do it for them.

The Intrinsic Benefits of Art Museums

Many believe that museums enlighten, inspire, and awe; if so, how do we know? In 2004, *Gifts of the Muse* was published.[12] The Wallace Foundation commissioned the Rand Corporation to explore the intrinsic value of the arts, which, according to the authors, was a direct response to twenty years of research that focused on demonstrating the instrumental benefits of the arts.[13] Instrumental benefits result when art is used as a means to an end and the end may have little to do with art—for example, outcomes like economic growth and cognitive gains. Intrinsic benefits, as the authors explain,

> refer to effects inherent in the arts experience that add value to people's lives. Obvious examples are the sheer joy one can feel in response to a piece of music or to movements in dance or to a painting. Beyond these immediate effects, there are personal effects that develop with recurrent aesthetic experiences, such as growth in one's capacity to feel, perceive, and judge for oneself and growth in one's capacity to participate imaginatively in the lives of others and to empathize with others. And some works go beyond such personal effects, providing a common experience that draws people together and influences the way the community perceives itself, thereby creating intrinsic benefits that accrue to the public.[14]

The purpose of the study had meaning, as arts organizations would benefit from having empirical evidence about what art, and museums in particular, affords people. The authors hoped to advance people's understanding of how the arts affects those who participated and investigate the ways in which the effects accumulate and spill over to the public and society at large. The timing of the commissioned study is noteworthy, too; it was ten years after the Contract with America and a few years after 9/11 and the recession when museums were still struggling financially. As noted earlier, in 1994, there was scant evaluation or research data available about the effects of programs funded by the NEA, NEH, and IM(L)S—a problem that is slowly improving. Increasingly, public and private funders are pressuring museums to conduct evaluations to demonstrate accountability, and government agencies are doing their share by studying the effects of specific grant programs.[15]

The analysis in *Gifts of the Muse* reported that there was ample evidence of the arts' economic benefits, observing that there were more economic benefit studies than any other type of study. They found a small number of studies with strong evidence supporting cognitive, attitudinal, and behavioral benefits of the arts, and while there were studies about health and social benefits, they were restricted by their methodological approaches and therefore inconclusive. The authors also point out that much of the empirical work on the arts' instrumental benefits was fraught with problems. For example, they note that the research is weak conceptually and methodologically, and they call out the studies' lack of specificity about "how the claimed benefits are produced, how they relate to different types of arts experiences, and under what circumstances and for which populations they are most likely to occur."[16] Thus, the authors had little confidence in the generalizability of the findings. They also pointed out an interesting flaw in the reporting of the arts' instrumental benefits in the reports that they reviewed, as explained here:

> The fact that the benefits claimed can all be produced in other ways is ignored [by researchers]. Cognitive benefits can be produced by better education (such as providing more-effective reading and mathematics courses), just as economic benefits can be generated by other types of social investment (such as a new sports stadium or transportation infrastructure). An argument based entirely on the instrumental effects of the arts runs the risk of being discredited if other activities are more effective at generating the same effects. . . . Because the literature on instrumental benefits fails to consider the comparative advantages of the arts in producing instrumental effects, it is vulnerable to challenge on these grounds.[17]

While the above quotation is critical of research that studied the instrumental benefits of the arts, the same can be said of museum research. Shouldn't research on the benefits of museums indicate museums' distinctiveness—that is, demonstrate what museums uniquely offer that no other place can? Do museums do themselves a disservice by focusing on their instrumental benefits, often to the exclusion of all other benefits—and not just in terms of what museum evaluators and researchers study but in how staff talk to others about the benefits of their museums? For example, education staff often explain the ways in which their museum's collection supports school curriculums; and museum directors report how many people visit their museum and how many dollars their museum contributes to the local economy. Similarly, when a museum adds a new building or wing, its advertising boasts that it is now the X-largest museum in the country.[18] However, when museum educators talk about their passion for their work, they never say they are driven by the joy they feel when teaching to the curriculum, and when museum directors talk about their passion, none has gushed about what it means to bolster the local economy. Yet often that is how champions of museums talk about the benefit and value of museums.

In *Beyond the Turnstile: Making the Case for Museums and Sustainable Values,* Selma Holo asks, "Must museum leaders meekly agree to be measured exclusively by the questions 'How many?' and 'How much?'"[19] Reporting the economic benefits of museums has resonance only when the economy is faltering, and wouldn't it be better to report data that has value regardless of the state of the economy? Is the museum community inadvertently belittling museums' intrinsic value by focusing the narrative on the instrumental benefits of museums? Are we embarrassed to exclaim and defend our belief about what art, art museums, or any type of museum can do for people?

Poignant descriptions of what art affords people exist in a few unpublished exhibition evaluations, but mostly they appear in books from those inside the art-museum circle—that is, people who have spent their careers in art museums and/or around original works of art.[20] These discussions in books do not include what the visiting public thinks—those who self-select to experience art—which was the focus of the analysis of *Gifts of the Muse;* instead they reflect the personal thoughts of specialists about what art does for them and, by extension, can do for others. As an example, psychologists Mihaly Csikszentmihalyi and Rick Robinson conducted qualitative research with museum curators to dissect and understand the aesthetic experience, and their book, *The Art of Seeing,* is filled with many accounts of what happens emotionally and/or cognitively when one experiences art objects. For example, the following quotation is from an anonymous curator:

> I think it [art] absorbs, it involves all of the senses in a unifying manner. Art is primarily visual, but it heightens your sense of the other, the outside, the thing experience, and in the process, heightens your awareness of yourself, and even though you're being fully absorbed and transported by an object perceived by the sense, you're losing yourself at the same time you become yourself.[21]

Others, specifically museum directors, have also written about the intrinsic benefit of original works of art from a viewer's perspective, all equally convincing as the above quotation.[22] If museum directors believe that the intrinsic benefit of art drives people to museums, why do they and other staff revert to talking about the instrumental benefits of their museums when talking with others?[23] That is not to say that reporting numbers, and especially numbers of schoolchildren who visit museums, is unimportant, and reporting data about the instrumental benefits of museums that museum associations collect and share (e.g., American Alliance of Museums, Association of Art Museum Directors) is unimportant; however, maintaining a singular focus on collecting visitation data, for example, and talking about the about instrumental benefits *to the exclusion of everything else* overlooks museums' distinctiveness, including their greatest asset (the collections and a knowledgeable staff to study and interpret them), and the essence of what museums can do for people.

While *Gifts of the Muse* authors intended to explore the full effects of the arts along the spectrum of benefits, they found painfully little when they searched for research on and public discourse about the intrinsic benefits of the arts. Their exploration included writings from other specialists, including philosophers, aestheticians, and art critics, and they presented their belief that "art is a unique form of communication, one capable of creating intrinsic benefits that enhance the lives of individuals and often contribute to the public welfare as well."[24] They also noted something else that had resonance based on volumes of visitor-experience data collected over the years. In the quotation below, "the arts" is replaced with "museums" because the essential idea is not only about the arts:

> People are drawn to [museums] not for their instrumental effects, but because [museums] can provide them with meaning and with a distinctive type of pleasure and emotional stimulation. We contend not only that these intrinsic effects are satisfying in themselves, but that many of them can lead to the development of individual capacities and community cohesiveness that are of benefit to the public sphere.[25]

Figure 2.1. Muses Sarcophagus represents the nine muses and their attributes: Calliope, the muse of epic poetry; Clio, the muse of history; Erato, the muse of love and poetry; Euterpe, the muse of music; Melpomene, muse of tragedy; Polyhymnia, the muse of sacred poetry and religious dance; Terpsichore, the muse of dance and lyric poetry; Thalia, the muse of comedy and idyllic poetry; and Urania, the muse of astronomy.
From Wikimedia Commons.

Given that *Gifts of the Muse* uncovered a fairly serious data gap, I harnessed some of my concern and searched for grant opportunities that might support intrinsic benefit research in the arts and humanities. Private foundations were more interested in funding programs for museums than in funding experience research in museums; art museum philanthropists and art collectors were more interested in purchasing art and donating it to museums than in funding research about how the art they purchased affected the public; and while NEA had consistently conducted research on arts participation (akin to visitation numbers) since 1982,[26] it had not studied the effects of participating in the arts or the intrinsic benefits of such participation, and it didn't appear ready to do so at that time. Two years after *Gifts of the Muse* was published, researcher Alan Brown, a strong advocate for assessing the intrinsic benefits of the arts, wrote an inspiring piece in response to *Gifts of the Muse* about the need to learn a "new language of value and benefits"; (again, "a museum" or "museums" replaces "the arts").

> It's not easy to talk about how [a museum] transforms or how we are different because of it. . . . Where is the language? . . . it's no one's job but everyone's job to find and to learn a new language of value and benefits. After all, if we can't communicate clearly and persuasively what [a museum] means to us, how can we expect others to gain a clearer sense of why they should get more involved and support [museums] at higher levels?[27]

So far, this chapter focuses on art and art museums, although occasionally "museum" replaces "art" because often museums and arts organizations, writ large, share similar challenges. Next, the intrinsic benefit of science-focused museums is discussed, followed by a discussion about the intrinsic benefit of history museums.

The Intrinsic Benefit of Science-Related Museums and Collections

Researchers have studied the instrumental benefits of museums that feature and teach science topics, and in particular they have studied science learning—whether among adults, schoolchildren, families, and preschool children, as is the case in children's museums. NSF deserves credit for generating knowledge about informal science learning, resulting from its long history of investing in and supporting research and evaluation of the projects it funds.[28] NSF has greatly affected science museum practice, too, by requiring evaluation of funded projects, and it advanced the informal science education field by (1) commissioning literature reviews;[29] (2) contracting third-party evaluators to conduct global assessments of grant programs in the Informal Science Education division;[30][31] (3) partnering with other federal agencies to fund the Museum Learning Collaborative, which in addition to researching and producing books on museum learning,[32] created a database of annotated literature that NSF still supports as well as an online repository of completed evaluation and research reports through the Center for the Advancement of Informal Science Education (CAISE); and (4) funding a synthesis of science learning research literature that produced *Learning Science in Informal Environments: People, Places, and Pursuits,* a publication that identified six strands of informal science learning,[33] prompting practitioners and researchers who work in art and history museums to consider strands of learning in their respective sectors—both of which are published in *Curator: The Museum Journal*[34] in a special edition. One can easily see the far-reaching effect of NSF's commitment to evaluation, museum learning, and research.

Upon careful examination of the six strands of informal science learning (see table 2.2), you may notice that the strands are on a continuum; that is, they appear to build on each other. The first of the six strands of

Table 2.2.   Six strands of informal science learning.

Strand 1:
Experience excitement, interest, and motivation to learn about phenomena in the natural and physical world.

Strand 2:
Come to generate, understand, remember, and use concepts, explanations, arguments, models, and facts related to science.

Strand 3:
Manipulate, test, explore, predict, question, observe, and make sense of the natural and physical world.

Strand 4:
Reflect on science as a way of knowing; on processes, concepts, and institutions of science; and on their own process of learning about phenomena.

Strand 5:
Participate in scientific activities and learning practices with others, using scientific language and tools.

Strand 6:
Think about themselves as science learners and develop an identity as someone who know about, uses, and sometimes contributes to science.

Source: Learning Science in Informal Environments: People, Places, and Pursuits. Reprinted with permission from the National Academies Press, copyright 2009, National Academy of Sciences.

informal science learning reflects an intrinsic benefit of science museums, and with some minor editing, it might describe an intrinsic benefit of all museums. "Experiencing excitement, interest, and motivation to learn"— in other words, feeling curious about something—could lead to the next several potential experiences, as articulated in strands 2 through 5. The sixth strand, which is about identity development, seems like it would be a culminating outcome that might continue evolving over time.[35]

Like art museums, science and natural history museums benefit from having collections. Generally speaking, one might say that the collections at science centers and children's museums are their exhibitions, while natural history museums have scientific specimens and cultural artifacts. The emergence of science centers prompted the creation of the Association of Science-Technology Centers (ASTC) because the definition of museums, as per the American Alliance of Museums (then called the American Association of Museums), centered around having traditional collections. The primary function of science centers was and continues to be public education rather than preservation and research, and as such, most science centers do not have research scientists on staff. Their focus on public education catapulted them into playing a leadership role in informal learning, evaluation, and accountability.[36] STEM education has gained considerable momentum in American education, and with the help of NSF, science-focused museums, including children's museums, are responding accordingly.

Specimens in natural history museum collections hold evidence of life on Earth over time, and artifacts document human cultural diversity. The messaging that natural history museums have used to present the essence of their interests and work has evolved: thirty years ago, the emphasis was on exemplifying Earth's biological and cultural diversity in the hopes people would appreciate it and want to protect against the reduction of species and the loss of cultures; today, natural history museums focus on showing evidence of evolution and global climate change. In a chapter in *Beyond the Turnstile*, Leonard Krishtalka clarifies the interconnectedness of three biological ideas—biodiversity, evolution, and global climate change:

> natural history museums are at a pivotal point in history. . . . First, their collective mission—understanding the life of the planet for the common good—has never been more important to science and society than it is today. Second, their biocollections—their libraries of life—are critical to meeting one of the grand challenges of the twenty-first century: harnessing knowledge of Earth's biodiversity and how it shapes global environmental systems on which all life depends.[37]

Others have also written about natural history museums in the context of our changing planet. In particular, Emlyn Koster believes the Anthropocene is the ideal reference point for engaging the community in discussions about the most pressing environmental challenge of our time. [38] The Anthropocene accentuates the past, present, and future of "the human journey in an ecological framework with natural systems.[39] In 2012, he and a group of scientists, museum leaders, educators, and evaluators gathered in Washington, DC, for an NSF-funded colloquium titled "Transforming Natural History Museums in the Twenty-first Century."[40] While the intent of the gathering was to generate a learning research agenda, one small working group decided to create a vision statement to provide direction to the research agenda. The group articulated a pointed vision statement called the "Declaration of Interdependence," which hints at the intrinsic value of science museums:

> Humanity is embedded within nature and we are at a critical moment in the continuity of time; Our collections are the direct scientific evidence for evolution and the ecological interdependence of all living things; The human species is actively altering the Earth's natural processes and reducing its biodiversity; As the sentient cause of these impacts, we have the urgent responsibility to give voice to the Earth's immense story and to secure a sustainable future.[41]

John Daniel Rogers, scientist at the National Museum of Natural History in Washington, DC, offered his opinion on the intrinsic benefit of natural history museums and their collections, and in doing so, eloquently summarizes their intrinsic value and benefit to the public:

> Philosophically, all we have is the past; we have a split second of right now, but everything else is the past. If you want to predict the future, you have to turn to the past; if you want to understand the future, you have to apply your current experience with knowledge of the past. Pragmatically, natural history collections are the physical evidence of how the entire planet has evolved, including humanity and once-thriving civilizations. They are the library for understanding the planet—from cultural diversity, to how the Earth's crust formed, to why dung beetles do what they do. Just like you have to know how to read a book to experience the intrinsic benefit of a book, you have to know how to read, study, and ask questions about specimens, artifacts, and material culture to experience and know the intrinsic benefits of the collections, and thereby of museums. But there is one big difference between a library of books and a collection of artifacts: You can read *Walden* any number of times and realize something new with

each read. With an artifact, you can literally discover a new chapter that wasn't there before, that no one else has ever read, because you uncovered it. Books have a first chapter and a last chapter and chapters between; a specimen always has the potential of an unintentionally hiding, a yet-to-be discovered, chapter about our past that scientists are able to access as technology advances.[42]

Natural history museums and their collections bring together current and potential understandings about nature and humankind in one envelope. Their collections hold intrigue and offer endless opportunities to inspire visitors. The intrinsic value of natural history museums' collections to the public lies in the deep knowledge, known and unknown, that collections hold. The onus is on museums to help visitors uncover the story of life on Earth. With the delicate and erratic state of our planet and the precarious position of science (and art and humanities, for that matter) in the policy world, the need to identify the appropriate language to communicate the intrinsic benefit of science and science museums' collections to the public is obvious.

Funding for science museums and associated evaluations has flourished over the last several decades, in part due to the support of NSF and other science-related government agencies such as the National Aeronautics and Space Administration, National Oceanic and Atmospheric Administration, and National Institutes of Health. Such is not the case with history museums, leaving these organizations in a somewhat precarious situation.

The Intrinsic Benefit of History Museums and Historic Sites

Of all the museum types, history museums and historic sites, including historic houses, struggle most to retain their once strong stature in the cultural landscape. Those who work in history museums/sites/houses have observed, anecdotally, declining attendance, which they translate as a declining interest in history. Humanities Indicators, a project of the American Academy of Arts & Sciences, backs up their observations: "In 2012, 24% of Americans age 18 or older had visited a historic site in the previous year. This was 13 percentage points lower than in 1982, with the bulk of the decline occurring from 2002 to 2012."[43] Even more troubling is that the decline is largest among people who are 25 to 44 years and that as people age, "the drop-off in historic site visitation over the life course is at least 25%."[44] Max van Balgooy, president of Engaging Places, a consulting company that works with history-related organizations, blogged about data he reviewed in a NEA longitudinal study, noting that ten million fewer people reported visiting historic sites in 2008 than in 2002 and that participation rates have "steadily fallen since 1982."[45] In another blog post, van Balgooy writes: "many of America's historic sites are experiencing declining attendance, financial instability, and poor stewardship, and they are increasingly viewed by their communities as irrelevant and unresponsive to the societal changes around them."[46]

In 1998, Roy Rosenzweig and David Thelen published *Presence of the Past: Popular Uses of History in American Life*—a seminal and inspiring book about how Americans identify with history. The authors asked probing questions of fifteen hundred Americans, and as it turns out, Americans are not disinterested in history at all; they connect to history through a variety of activities, including attending family reunions, keeping scrapbooks, and building personal narratives about events that they continue to shape and reshape over their lifetimes. While the book only slightly touches on what people think about history museums, the authors note that for some, museums "sparked an associative process of recalling and reminiscing about the past that connected them to their own history."[47] Artifacts, they report, "brought respondents closer to experiences from the past than even eyewitnesses could."[48] Historic sites, in particular, have their own aura, as they "transported visitors straight back to the times when people had used the artifacts . . . or occupied the places where 'history' had been made."[49] In addition to the material and physical elements people find meaningful, they also value the social aspect of museum visiting, noting that museums and sites "allowed them to deepen relationships with people who mattered in their lives."[50]

People experience history as an organic personal enterprise that is deeply meaningful to them. Differences between Rosenzweig and Thelen's data and the Humanities Indicators data can be attributed to the discrepancy between how nonhistorians think about history and how those who work in history organizations think about and present history. History with a capital *H*—the institutional enterprise—seems to present a problem, not the personal history that people remember and experience daily with their families. Another problem the authors identify is the way history is taught in school—it encourages neither personal curiosity about the past nor personal connections to the past.

The work of museum scholar Lois Silverman, who introduced the concept of meaning-making into the vernacular of museums, is noteworthy.[51] Her work on this topic predates Rosenzweig and Thelen's research, and they may have very well taken cues from her, as she and Thelen were at Indiana University at the same time. Silverman notes that people "'make meaning' through a constant process of remembering and connecting" and "memory and past experience shape what one perceives and experiences in the present."[52] She poses several important questions, and the two shared below clarify the essence of the public's challenge with the institutional enterprise of history and historical interpretation: "How might we move beyond the dichotomy that separates 'professionals' from 'laypersons' to more beneficial and inclusive ways of interacting? How can we revitalize the field and its institutions so that they might serve as tools for all people?"[53]

History professionals have made some progress to address the gap that separates professionals' and laypeople's notion of history, such as the International Coalition of Sites of Conscience. The coalition, which includes two hundred members in fifty-five countries, describes itself as "the only global network of historic sites, museums and memory initiatives that connect past struggles to today's movements for human rights."[54] Another sign of progress is History Relevance (HR), established in 2012. The founders of the HR value the role history can play in contemporary life, view it as central to their lives, and passionately believe it should play a greater role in the lives of others. The HR wrote a statement of seven values of history that over two hundred organizations have endorsed (see table 2.3).

Three of the seven value statements describe potential intrinsic benefits of history and history organizations—Identity, Engaged Citizens, and Legacy. Different from the sixth strand for informal science learning, Identity in the case of HR, is about personal identity growth and gaining perspective of one's self in relationship to those who came before. Engaged Citizens is about participating in contemporary American democracy, which parallels what the *Gifts of the Muse* authors note as an intrinsic public benefit of arts participation—that art affords "private benefits with public spillover."[55] Legacy is the foundation on which we all stand, and among all the value statements, it may be the one that distinguishes history museums from other types of museums; legacy might be the intrinsic benefit of history museums.

Elaine Gurian believes history museums are institutions of memory and refers to them as "savings banks for our souls."[56] She writes in another piece that institutions of memory "are the tangible evidence of the spirit of a civilized society . . . and the evidence of history has something central to do with the spirit, will, pride, identity, and civility of people."[57] Below Gurian assembles essential ideas about history museums noted above and ties them to memory:

> if the essence of a museum is not to be found in its objects, then where?
> . . . It is both the physicality of a place and the memories and stories told therein that are important. . . . They [museums], like props in a brilliant play, are necessary but alone are not sufficient. . . . The larger issues revolve

Table 2.3. History Relevance created the Values of History to promote a shared language around the relevance and value of history.

TO OUR OURSELVES

Identity
History nurtures personal and collective identity in a diverse world. People discover their place in time through stories of their families, communities, and nation. These stories of freedom and equality, injustice and struggle, loss and achievement, and courage and triumph shape people's personal values that guide them through life.

Critical Thinking
History teaches us vital skills. Historical thinking requires critical approaches to evidence and argument and develops contextual understanding and historical perspective, encouraging meaningful engagement with concepts like continuity, change, and causation, and the ability to interpret and communicate complex ideas clearly and coherently.

TO OUR COMMUNITIES

Vibrant Communities
History is the foundation for strong, vibrant communities. A place becomes a community when wrapped in human memory as told through family stories, tribal traditions, and civic commemorations as well as discussions about our roles and responsibilities to each other and the places we call home.

Economic Development
History is a catalyst for economic growth. Communities with cultural heritage institutions and a strong sense of historical character attract talent, increase tourism revenues, enhance business development, and fortify local economies.

TO OUR FUTURE

Engaged Citizens
History helps people envision a better future. Democracy thrives when individuals convene to express opinions, listen to others, and take action. Weaving history into discussions about contemporary issues clarifies differing perspectives and misperceptions, reveals complexities, grounds competing views in evidence, and introduces new ideas; all can lead to greater understanding and viable community solutions.

Leadership
History inspires leaders. History provides today's leaders with role models as they navigate through the complexities of modern life. The stories of persons from the past can offer direction to contemporary leaders and help clarify their values and ideals.

Legacy
History, saved and preserved, is the foundation for future generations. Historical knowledge is crucial to protecting democracy. By preserving authentic and meaningful documents, artifacts, images, stories, and places, future generations have a foundation on which to build and know what it means to be a member of the civic community.

Source: Courtesy of History Relevance; for more information visit https://www.historyrelevance.com.

around the stories museums tell and the way they tell them. . . . It is the ownership of the story, rather than the object itself, that the dispute has been all about.[58]

Unintentionally Interrupting the Flow of Museums' Intrinsic Benefits

In art museums, viewing great works of art can inspire awe, as art museum professionals attest, yet when those outside the art museum circle inquire about the benefit of an art museum visit, staff shy away from sharing their beliefs and instead talk about the educational value, in a formal and some-what narrow sense. There is a schism between natural history museums and the public, based on what was presented earlier in this chapter and ac-cumulated knowledge presented through research and evaluation: science collections are awe-inspiring to many, yet most natural history museums neglect to reference the specimens when presenting complicated ideas about Earth's systems—in other words, visitors do not easily see connec-tions between the essential ideas that natural history museums present and the specimens that awe them and inform those ideas. In history museums, there is a disconnect between how history is presented and how the public thinks about and expresses its interest in history, which is personal. These three tensions prevail because external pressures dictate how museums are presenting themselves publicly and politically, essentially as part of the educational establishment, which leaves museums with a narrowly defined version of learning as their raison d'être, even if museum professionals do not believe it is so.

Communicating Science to the Public was published by the CIBA Foun-dation in 1987. Renowned University of California, Berkeley, professor emeritus of botany Watson "Mac" Laetsch contributed to the volume, noting the following about curiosity:

> Curiosity is so obviously a fundamental and powerful characteristic of our species that we fail to take it seriously. . . . Fulfilling curiosity about ob-jects and activities is considered an end in itself for visitors to institutions concerned with informal science education. These institutions know the value of stimulating and fulfilling curiosity by means of active exploration and they increasingly focus their efforts to these ends. They know this is a justifiable end but they hesitate to admit this publicly.[59]

In the same chapter, Laetsch also says, "What a delight it would be to send a proposal for funding to a granting agency for an exhibit that promised to stimulate curiosity and that would be judged on whether it did so."[60] And therein lies another tension. Is stimulating curiosity a virtuous enough goal for those who fund museum programs? When funding agencies—whether government or private—award museums grant money, they often do so because the museum will be teaching visitors; and in return, visitors will be learning. *Learning Science in Informal Environments* broadens the definition of learning considerably, and when museum staff say "learning," there is a general understanding among their colleagues that they mean learning broadly defined. Yet when funders and school administrators *hear* "learning," they think curriculum connection, cognitive gains, and academic gains. While cognitive gains are notable and certainly possible outcomes of any museum experience, wouldn't inciting someone's curiosity need to happen first?[61]

Evolutionary biologist Stephen J. Gould, in recalling his boyhood experience at the American Museum of Natural History, said, "I dreamed of becoming a scientist, in general, and a paleontologist, in particular, ever since the *Tyrannosaurus* skeleton awed and scared me."[62] Those two emotions—awe and fear—lit that first spark of curiosity that would sustain Gould's lifelong interest in fossils and paleontology. Deborah Perry, museum researcher and author of *What Makes Learning Fun?: Principles for the Design of Intrinsically Motivating Museum Exhibits,* writes, "Curiosity is a strong driving force, a prerequisite, one might say, to engaging with exhibits in meaningful ways."[63]

Psychologists have learned that humans are a reward-seeking species, and there are two kinds of rewards: extrinsically motivated and intrinsically motivated.[64] When an action is done to achieve a particular end, such as completing four years of college to obtain an undergraduate degree, the reward is extrinsically motivated. When an action is taken for the pure pleasure of experiencing the action, the reward is intrinsic—coming from within the individual yet spurred by environment. Experiencing a museum's collections—whether a dinosaur fossil, Baroque painting, or the American flag that inspired "The Star-Spangled Banner"—can reward visitors with a feeling of awe, yet often museums interrupt the experience by pursuing instrumental benefits imposed by others, mimicking what might take place in a formal education setting. Similarly, a curiosity-awakening experience can quickly dissipate if the ideas the museum is presenting do not instinctively connect to the inherent qualities of the objects and/or the awe visitors are experiencing as a result of seeing the objects. Squelching awe is akin to squelching curiosity. The intrinsic benefit of museums is the effect the collections have on people; the wonder of nature and humankind can awaken people's curiosity about the natural world, human history and ingenuity, and the innate need humans have to create. These simple realizations can lead to intrinsically motivated learning—learning that happens naturally among humans—if we let it.

Observing Museums

I expect museums to value and celebrate their distinctiveness, as exemplified through their collections of specimens, objects, and exhibits, not take it for granted—yet that is what I was witnessing as early as 2000. Using museums' collections as the platform on which to build the visitor experience may sound antiquated, but what other distinctive quality do museums hold? This section presents three observations—from the perspective of a cultural consumer, museum employee, and consultant. It also describes an epiphany about museum evaluation and research, or as my colleagues might say, "an aha moment," that further clarified the need among museums: a whole-museum approach to impact-driven planning.

The Soul of the Museum

The public ascertains a museum's identity through a host of elements including its physical presence, such as the character and feeling it exudes through its architecture, its location in relationship to other parts of the physical community,[65] and the reputation it has built over time.[66] Its perceptible presence—and whatever it communicates—mixes with the array of exhibitions and programs the museum chooses to create and host to shape a public image and perception of itself. A 2007 *Curator* article expressed my accumulated observations of museums like this:

> Many museums appear to be searching for themselves, presenting a range of public programs to see which ones might bolster attendance and attract new audiences while also retaining existing ones. Although this program proliferation may be an indication that museums are experimenting and taking risks, actions appear haphazard and unfocused rather than deliberate. It also appears that museums are continually searching for the next blockbuster, trying to boost their attendance in every way possible. . . . With so much turmoil inside the museum and so much competition outside, the museum—as institution—appears hesitant, searching for the next trend for short-term gain.[67]

Robert Janes, former director of the Glenbow Museum, and his coauthor, Gerald Conaty, concur and astutely observe that "attendance flows from significance and significance flows from the provision of meaning and value to one's community"—not the other way around.[68] Philippe de Montebello, after stepping down from his directorship at the Metropolitan Museum of Art, wrote that "the trap in which museums are now caught, is that . . . to maintain financial equilibrium, the dizzying momentum in the activity level must be sustained" and further noted that museums have become "hyperactive"—a reaction to a problem that they created.[69] Accompanying art museums on the audience quest are natural history museums and science centers. For example, when world-class natural history museums host the "Dinomania" exhibition it seems disrespectful to those museums' longtime residents—real dinosaur fossils![70]

As discussed in chapter 1, high attendance only means that people walked through the door, and it does not indicate the intrinsic value of the experience or describe qualitative success, personal meaningfulness, or "enlightenment." Michael Kimmelman, columnist for the *New York Times,* wrote a piece about a meeting he attended in Austria with museum curators and directors from thirty-five countries.[71] He noted that while the directors seemed to focus on boosting attendance, "the question that hung in the air was, money aside, to what end?" Museums, he wrote, "do not seem to know whether they are more like universities or Disneyland . . . and their priorities need restating."[72]

At that time, some museums were so focused on boosting attendance that they appeared unrecognizable. This was at a time when "edutainment" had entered museums' vocabulary and museums were thinking that their competition *was* Disneyland. In response, they started hosting exhibitions they did not value (as evidenced by the grumbling heard behind closed doors) and were producing a wide assortment of programs at an alarming rate. While museums may have been searching for the right balance between their traditional work and what they perceived the public wanted, midlevel staff was struggling to keep up while administrators were enjoying short-term financial gains without considering the long-term ramifications. In essence, some museums appeared to be losing their identity and sense of self.

External and financial pressures are real and museums cannot ignore them, but museums shouldn't forget what they are, either, as once they lose sight of their distinctiveness in the American landscape or start trying to be something other than what they are at their core, they may have a hard time repairing the damage and finding their center. Clearly museums should not become stagnant amid all the change that swirls around them every day, but some museums appeared to be at risk of losing their souls if they continued to avoid looking at themselves. They needed to regroup, recall what they are, reclarify their identity and uniqueness, and continually reinforce that reclaimed identity through their work, and while rediscovering what they are, they could also consider what they would like to become in this very fast-changing world.

Historically, museums have been reactionary organizations,[73] often responding to the marketplace, donors' and funders' wishes, and the public—all of which leads to constant change. While such change is inevitable, meaningful and purposeful change is not because it requires hard, intentional work. Deliberate and meaningful change arises from within—from the people who work in the museum. Some museums think visitors have the answer and want to conduct a study to see what the public wants them to do. Visitors may be able to tell a museum what they like and dislike, but they will not be able to clarify an ambiguous identity or offer solutions to communication, cohesiveness, and leadership problems. Before a museum seeks advice from visitors, it might want to first explore its internal challenges. Soul-searching, which takes time, courage, and strength, is always harder than asking others what one should do.

Figure 2.2.   This yin-yang symbol represents two mutually important foci: preserving traditional material and intellectual assets ("Preserve the Core") and achieving public impact ("Stimulate Progress").
Copyright 1994. Reprinted by permission of Curtis Brown, Ltd.

Some may think it strange that an audience advocate would support internal exploration and deliberation. So, to clarify, internal reflection and considering the recipients of a museum's work—the public—is not an either/or proposition. Balancing institutional identity with external needs is key; a museum that is too self-interested is as problematic as one that panders. Imagine museums beginning to refamiliarize themselves with their internal qualities *while* looking outward and considering those qualities in the context of the public's needs and relevance. Consider how business writer Jim Collins thinks about the push and pull of tradition and change; he applies a very positive perspective as illustrated through a yin-yang symbol in figure 2.2 where he places "Preserve the core" and "Stimulate progress" in the equal segments.[74] Though conceived for the for-profit sector, it represents the timeless tension in museums. "Preserve the core" represents the distinctiveness of museums as exemplified by their collections—their traditional assets, and "Stimulate progress" represents external opportunities, including audiences and their changing notions of relevance.

The Size of the Museum

The *Art News Paper* reports that between 2007 and 2014, organizations in the United States spent $5 billion building new museums or adding on to existing ones—at a time when the country was experiencing a significant economic downturn.[75] Building projects always start out hopeful, with museum boards believing that a new facility will increase audience size and revenue (earned and donated income) and reinforce the institution's mission. Board members and other patrons usually support new building projects because they are more sexy and splashy than repairing existing buildings even though doing the latter is often cheaper and greener. Directors lament that it is easier to fund capital campaigns than it is to raise dollars for operations. Experienced museum director John Wentenhall notes in a recent article in *Museum* that "very few new wings lead to sustainable visitation growth anywhere near enough to pay for their operations. . . . I would submit that many expansions may weaken, rather than strengthen, a museum's long-term, mission-fulfilling prospects."[76]

Continuing to build more and more onto existing museums is not a sustainable business model. More times than not, museums cannot afford the operational expenses after opening and need to reduce staff.[77] Sometimes expansions are rationalized by saying the museum needs more space because there are masterpieces in storage—a somewhat weak argument, given that most museums have and will always have masterpieces in storage.

Masterpieces are a means to an end, and an expansion project should address a need among the public—the ultimate recipient of a museum's work. Some new building projects are needed to modernize collection facilities and other parts of the museum, and of course some building projects are successful from a public perspective. For example, art critic and art historian Tyler Green praised the Islamic art galleries built between 2007 and 2014 at the Metropolitan Museum of Art: "When you add galleries to better show people how today happened, that is a good way to fulfill your mission . . . [and] to better inform your public about the world."[78] While some new building projects are successful from a financial perspective, most prove more difficult than predicted, putting undue strain on staff and the institution. Bigger, as it turns out, is sometimes not better, and oftentimes it is simply more expensive than the museum can afford.

So what message does the public hear when museums boast of their size, the number of objects in their collection, or their number of annual visitors? A message that doesn't speak to what museums truly offer. Can a museum balance its desire for numbers with clarity about the qualitative benefits of their collections to people? Similar to a point made earlier, quantitative and qualitative results also are not either/or propositions. The visitor experience is the end point of a museum visit and whatever value and benefits the museum affords it. Harold Skramstad, in his remarks during the Smithsonian's 150th anniversary celebration, said mission statements do not answer the vital "so what?" question and therefore miss an important point.[79] Weil agreed and took Skramstad's remarks a step further, pointing out, "If museums do not have the goal of improving people's lives, on what other basis can we ask for public support?"[80]

Museum Evaluation and Research

When a museum sets out to conduct traditional exhibition and program evaluations, they are often done under the purview of the exhibition or education departments, respectively, and as such, other staff from across the museum are rarely involved in the process. Nevertheless, the hundreds of evaluation reports that have been produced over time collectively provide a wealth of knowledge, and appropriately report the effect of individual projects on people. Museums often carry out audience research in the same way—one department, often either marketing or education, is assigned the project even though such a study could benefit the whole organization. Pointing out that evaluation and research is the responsibility of one or two individual departments is a symptom of a larger problem—

museum staff may not view their work as a whole-museum endeavor. Additionally, museum evaluation's focus on programs and exhibitions inadvertently created a cavernous gap of knowledge about the impact of museums as whole organizations.

As part of the museum evaluation process, staff are asked some basic questions about their project, including: "What did you want your project to achieve?" In other words, "what were your intentions for visitor experience outcomes?" and "Who is your target audience?" Articulating the intent of a project is hard, and often people struggle with the task. Yet doing so is an important factor in staff members' ability to work in unison toward a clearly defined end. When a project team clarifies the intent of a project, the result provides an organically derived structure and direction for project planning and development. What would happen if all staff participated in clarifying the effect they wanted their *museum* to achieve? Would a strong structure and clear planning directives also emerge?

There are other questions, too, that are relevant when considering moving evaluation and research from the programmatic or departmental realm to the organizational realm: are museums prepared to participate in an impact study that would obviously consider the whole organization? Can a museum articulate the impact it wants to achieve on the different populations it serves? Can it prioritize distinct populations it intends to serve? Most museums have a mission statement, which describes what a museum does, but do museums have impact statements, which describe the *result* of what they do on audiences served? Just the way visitor-experience outcomes are necessary for program and exhibition evaluation, an impact statement and associated experiential outcomes would be necessary for impact evaluation. The success of any project (a museum, program, exhibition, or evaluation) depends on the museum having a deep understanding of what it wants the project to achieve on audiences and then preparing a clear statement of intent—if not as a gauge against which to examine results, then as a guidepost for planning, but preferably both.

Taking the Leap to Impact-Driven Planning

Shifting from working in the program realm to the organizational realm would be quite a leap, indeed. The goal: help museums intentionally plan their work to achieve impact on audiences and in their communities. Significant challenges lay ahead, as most museums believed they were already achieving impact because everyone liked the museum. Articulating intentions and impact on audiences and communities requires introspective

work and is part of a continuous process of internal deliberation and clarification, and for a museum to think about such matters requires exploring
and learning about its institutional self.[81]

Gifts of the Muse outlined what the arts community needed to address,
and the authors' suggestions are relevant to all types of museums. Of the
four suggestions they offered, one prompted the framing of the Cycle of
Intentional Practice (presented and deconstructed in the next chapter).
The quotation below is adapted for museums:

> **Develop language for discussing intrinsic benefits.** [Museums] will
> need to develop language to describe the various ways that [they] create
> benefits at both the private and the public level. The greatest challenge will
> be to bring the policy community to explicitly recognize the importance
> of intrinsic benefits. This will require an effort to raise awareness about the
> need to look beyond quantifiable results and examine qualitative issues.[82]

Clear language is required if museums are to make a case for themselves.
With clear, specific, and distinct language about the intrinsic benefits of
museums, advocates will have a way to talk about the qualities that museums afford people. Museums may have to learn a new way of explaining the virtues of their institutions, which may first require a new way of
thinking about, approaching, and doing their work.

The tensions described earlier—between the public and history, natural history, and art museums—are also symptomatic of another problem.
Some museums were losing sight of what is really important: who they
are *and* what is meaningful to the public. They needed to rediscover their
purpose and then learn about and work with their public from this newly
formed vantage point—one that respects their museum as well as their
visitors. There is evidence that museum visitors trust museums and look
to them to provide meaningful experiences,[83] but when a lost institution
attempts to help visitors find their way, visitors may become lost, too. Visitors are astute and pick up what emanates from the museum.

The need for museums to pursue impact-driven thinking and planning
was emerging, as was a vision for the Cycle of Intentional Practice. The
cycle and the work layers beneath it would guide museums in clarifying
their intended impact and support them in working toward their intentions. The work would also include articulating associated outcomes,
evaluating the museum's efforts, reflecting on the museum's work for the
purposes of improving, and realigning work according to the impact it
wants to achieve.

Learning about the Cycle of Intentional Practice

3

Ultimately, human intentionality is the most powerful evolutionary force on this planet.

—GEORGE LEONARD

THIS CHAPTER PRESENTS THREE approaches to museum planning. First, the most commonly used planning tool—the logic model, which is a project-planning tool—is discussed. Second, traditional strategic planning—a mission-driven approach to organizational planning—is debated. Third, intentional practice is presented using the Cycle of Intentional Practice (CIP) as the visualization to guide the presentation (see figure 3.1). The cycle is deconstructed, starting with the centerpiece—impact—and then moving to the plan quadrant, which asks, "What impact do you want to achieve?" Even though the quadrants are presented and discussed in a particular order (clockwise), museums can navigate the cycle in any order, depending on their questions and needs.

While the CIP looks organized and structured with clear boundaries between quadrants, the reality is a messy process for three reasons:

1. Clarifying the museum's impact is iterative.
2. The individual actions assigned to the quadrants are not mutually exclusive.
3. Museums might traverse the cycle in no particular order or direction many, many times.

Figure 3.1.   Cycle of Intentional Practice.

The CIP graphic intends to serve as a reminder that impact on audiences, placed in the center, is the engine that drives all work and decisions and that museums may need to continuously plan, evaluate, reflect, and align their work accordingly. Strategies for doing impact-driven work are presented in chapters 4 and 5, "Intentional-Practice Principles" and "Intentional-Practice Exercises."

Intentional practice is intended as a whole-museum approach to work that supports purposeful decision making with the intent to achieve impact that benefits the public. The Cycle of Intentional Practice depicts the five primary elements that comprise intentional practice: impact, plan, evaluate, reflect, and align. Learning—personal, professional, and organizational—is another primary benefit and result of intentional practice, and as such, my intentional practice progresses with each new experience. My intentional-practice process is ongoing, and your museum's will be, too.

Logic Models

A logic model is a project-specific and visual planning tool that many funders want managers and evaluators to use as they discuss and clarify

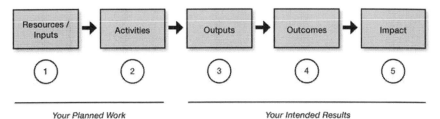

Figure 3.2.   Logic models are used to support planning and evaluation.
Reprinted with permission from the W. K. Kellogg Foundation, copyright 2004.

the elements of a project. A completed logic model shows the relationships among a project's elements and between the elements and the whole project.[1] While logic models may vary in how many elements they contain—such as a purpose statement, resources (or inputs) required, activities, outputs, outcomes, and impact—their intent is consistent: they are meant to help people think through their project from the beginning to the end before they set out to do their project (see figure 3.2).

Logic models first came into use when private foundations and government agencies started recommending outcome-based evaluation (OBE) as an approach to project planning and advocated completing logic models as part of the OBE process. Logic models are enormously helpful project-planning tools, as they support teams in clarifying and organizing their projects while considering the results they aspire to achieve in terms of outputs and outcomes. Outputs are products, such as an exhibition or the number of people who visited the exhibition; outcomes are visitors' experiences including attitudes, knowledge, understanding, skills, and behaviors that might have resulted from visiting the exhibition.

Strategic Planning

"Strategic planning" is an organization's leadership determining which activities it needs to do to live its mission and identity.[2] Traditional strategic planning is a mission-focused process that often includes crafting or tweaking the museum's mission statement;[3] technically, mission statements describe what a museum does, such as inspire, collect, conserve, interpret, and educate. Some museum professionals have criticized mission statements because they focus inward and do not inspire the museum to change what it does or how it carries out its work,[4] while others have challenged museums to write mission statements that answer the vital "so what?"

question.[5] These critics are suggesting museums may need to disband planning traditions in favor of a process that reflects a changing world: It is no longer adequate for museums to think *only* of their traditional work, such as collecting, conserving, interpreting, and educating; they need to think about the purpose of their work.

David La Piana, author of *The Nonprofit Strategy Revolution: Real-Time Strategic Planning in a Rapid-Response World,* questions the usual five- and ten-year strategic planning schedule for a number of reasons: change is accelerating; plans become obsolete before their time; and staff are beginning to recognize they may need to adopt a new way to think about planning and find new tools to support a more flexible and adaptable approach.[6] Some note continuous planning as the new normal.[7] La Piana also points out that

> Traditional strategic plans, once complete, are not fluid and organic but static—and they quickly grow stale. Since variations on the traditional strategic planning theme all share the same basic flaw, it is not surprising that none of them can reliably and efficiently produce the result nonprofit leaders are looking for when they decide to undertake strategic planning: more powerful strategies that will enhance their organization's success. Clearly, nonprofits need a new paradigm of strategy formation.[8]

The Cycle of Intentional Practice

Intentional practice applies a holistic (e.g., museum-wide) impact-based approach to planning. The Cycle of Intentional Practice, as shown earlier, though cyclical (as illustrated with the arrows around "impact"), is not repetitive because as a museum continually pursues impact for the public good, it does so in ever-changing contexts—both inside and outside the museum. Intentional practice comprises four actions—planning, evaluating, reflecting, and aligning—and though not visually explicit in the cycle, it assumes that museum staff are continually working to actualize the museum's intentions. When a museum pursues impact following the Cycle of Intentional Practice, staff are living in a dynamic and changing organization. Intentional practice, as a concept and series of actions, clarifies the link between planning and evaluation, evaluation and learning, reflection and learning, and alignment and planning as well as the relationship between all of the above and intended impact. The four interconnected actions in the CIP are held together by the museum's core purpose, the driver of intentional practice and centerpiece of the Cycle—impact.

The Museum's Core Purpose: Achieving Impact

The word "impact" is a relatively new concept to museums and brings into focus a tension between the products a museum might produce (e.g., programs, exhibitions, and catalogs) and the effect of those products on audiences (e.g., visitor experience). Consider these historical points:

1. In the 1980s and 1990s, public and private granting agencies would ask museums to indicate the "objectives" of their projects. Staff might understand the question as asking about products or output, such as an exhibition or interpretative materials; evaluators might understand it as asking about the visitor experience or outcomes—what visitors would think, know, or do as a result of having experienced the product. This difference in translation well describes a common misunderstanding between museum practitioners and evaluators. New words were needed to distinguish between a museum's products and a visitor's experience, and government granting agencies were the first to offer clarity.

2. In 2000, IMLS introduced and mandated its grantees use OBE and logic models, and in 2008, NSF published a book to help grantees focus on identifying intended results.[9] New concepts and words—outputs, outcomes, and impact—were introduced, which helped distinguish between outputs (e.g., products developed by the museum and number of visitors) and outcomes (e.g., experiential results on audiences), and impact (e.g., making a positive difference in people's lives). Slowly, the idea that the success of a project should be measured based on whether the audience experienced the museum's intended outcomes (rather than on whether the museum created its intended products or that X number of visitors came) started to seep into people's thinking.

3. Most museums have a mission statement to describe what they intend to do (educate, collect, interpret, etc.). If a mission statement describes the work of the museum, what statement might describe the effect of that work on audiences (the "so what" question—impact)? Some museums have a vision statement to indicate what the museum aspires to become. Historically, museums have not articulated the impact they would like to achieve on audiences; if a mission statement describes what a museum does, an impact statement can describe the result of that work on audiences and serve as a companion to a mission statement.[10] If a museum fears

that having too many statements may cause confusion, it could repurpose its vision statement to describe intended results on audiences served.

While intentional practice uses the word "impact" to describe the positive difference a museum can make in the quality of people's lives, there are other words that describe a similar result. Mary Ellen Munley[11] and Carol Ann Scott[12] use the words and concept "public value" in their work. Both are champions of Harvard professor Mark Moore, who wrote *Creating Public Value: Strategic Management in Government.*[13] Impact and public value, at their core, seem interchangeable as they strive for the same end point; public value is about government organizations (in the case of Moore) and museums (in the case of Munley and Scott) contributing to society and benefiting the public in some way—for the common good.[14]

An essential concept behind Moore's thinking is the Strategic Triangle (see figure 3.3). Legitimacy and support (the authorizing environment) is one part of the triangle; operations capacity is another part; and public value makes up the final part.[15] From a museum or nonprofit perspective, legitimacy and support represent the board of directors, and operations capacity is the museum's ability in terms of human resources (skills and adequate staffing) to implement the strategy and deliver public value.

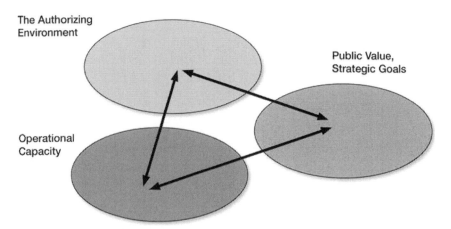

Figure 3.3. Strategic Triangle.

CLARIFYING IMPACT

Intentional practice is dependent on having (1) a clear and concise impact statement that describes what a museum would like to achieve among audiences and (2) supporting outcomes for a finite number of specified audiences. Impact is the positive difference the museum hopes and expects to make in the quality of someone's life. This is the definition that Stephen Weil put forth when he wrote about how United Way changed the course of program planning and evaluation when it adopted OBE. Weil credits United Way with shifting the focus from "mission" or "vision" to answering the question "What do you *ideally* hope to accomplish?" and "*realistically*, what do you expect to accomplish?" (emphasis mine)—two very important questions.[16] The impact statement is more than just a description of a museum's intended results on audiences; the museum uses the statement to drive its actions and decisions—that is, the statement becomes a guidepost for all work the museum undertakes. If the museum is doing work that does not advance it toward achieving its intended impact, the museum is wasting money and the museum's most important and overlooked resources—staff time and intellect. In addition to serving as a guidepost for decisions and actions, the impact statement also serves an evaluative purpose as it becomes the gauge for measuring success.

Sometimes museums conduct a formal impact study prematurely without having an impact statement and outcomes because they believe they are already achieving impact. While this may be true, from an intentional-practice perspective, conducting a study to determine whether a museum has achieved impact is moot if the museum lacks clarity about what success might look and sound like among audiences and in a community. Conducting an impact study without an idea of how the museum defines impact may not provide the museum with meaningful, concrete, and actionable information. Just the way formal program evaluation requires specified outcomes, formal impact evaluation requires an impact statement and associated outcomes. Without these criteria of success, a museum's actions will be haphazard, and the museum will not have the proper context for making sense of the visitor experience because the intended experience was never clarified.

ELEMENTS COMPRISING AN IMPACT STATEMENT

Researcher and business author Jim Collins has written several inspiring books, including *Built to Last*,[17] *Good to Great: Why Some Companies Make the Leap . . . and Some Don't*,[18] and then *Good to Great and the Social Sector*.[19]

In the *Good to Great* books, Collins introduces the Hedgehog Concept, which is very applicable to intentional practice due to the similarities between the components of the Hedgehog Concept and the ideas important to clarifying impact. The Hedgehog Concept,[20] which grew from Collins's research in the for-profit sector, provided an underlying evidence-based structure for developing an impact statement. In "Clarifying Intended Impact," the first workshop in the intentional-practice workshops series, Collins's Hedgehog Concept is presented. It depicts three intersecting circles that state,

- "What you are deeply passionate about"
- "What you can be the best in the world at"
- "What drives your resource engine"

At their intersection, he notes, is a great company. Collins points out that greatness does not emerge from excelling in one or two of the three circles; all three are needed to achieve greatness.[21]

Intentional practice customized the Hedgehog Concept to reflect intentional-practice thinking in a museum context as follows (see figure 3.4):

1. "Impact" replaces "great" at the circles' intersection.
2. Questions replace statements because intentional practice uses inquiry as a primary facilitation strategy.
3. "What are your museum's distinct qualities?" replaces "What you can be the best in the world at." Museums vary in their strengths, and in intentional practice, a museum plays to its strength to achieve impact. Intentional practice is best pursued when a museum knows and celebrates its distinctiveness.
4. The question "What is relevant to your audiences?" replaces "What drives your resource engine." Resources, though important to museums for sustainability, do not determine a museum's core purpose—people do, those who work inside the museum and those who experience the museum. Achieving impact requires that museums participate in three audience-related actions:

   a. Building relationships with its various publics and stakeholders;
   b. Learning what is meaningful to audiences, perhaps through systematic research and evaluation; and
   c. Intentionally applying newly acquired knowledge about audiences to the museum's work.

**What are you deeply
passionate about?**

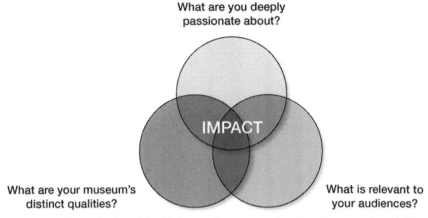

**What are your museum's
distinct qualities?**

IMPACT

**What is relevant to
your audiences?**

Figure 3.4.   Customization of the Hedgehog Concept to reflect intentional-practice thinking
in a museum context.

Intentional-practice thinking prioritizes audiences over resources because
purposeful attention to the museum's various publics can offer visitors
meaningful experiences; and purpose-driven work that provides meaningful experiences may positively affect revenue, build momentum, and
ultimately fuel the resource *and* impact engine.

An impact statement is the melding of the three Hedgehog-related
concepts—personal passion, a museum's distinct qualities, and the museum's relevance to audiences—and staff explore all three concepts as part
of the process of developing an impact statement. The three elements are
discussed below.

1. **Passion is an important ingredient for producing quality
   work**—and fortunately for museums, passion drives the work
   of many museum professionals.[22] Collins notes that "you can't
   manufacture passion or 'motivate' people to feel passionate. You
   can only *discover* what ignites your passion and the passions of those
   around you."[23] One's personal passion for work builds internal
   commitment to the organization,[24] which may eventually radiate out
   to the profession at large, as many individuals continue living their
   passion on a larger stage. Passions are uncovered through a passion
   exercise (see chapter 5), which serves two functions: it reminds
   individuals of why they do what they do; and the exercise provides
   an opportunity for leadership, staff, and stakeholders to learn about
   one another's passions. Sharing personal passions can be uplifting and

invigorating, as invariably new insights about familiar people emerge. All witness that their colleagues share their passion and they come to realize that, collectively, they represent one organization.

2. **Achieving impact requires that a museum play to its strengths.** Whether the museum excels at interpreting a world-class collection, creating innovative programming, forging successful community partnerships, or conducting groundbreaking scientific research, setting aside time to discuss and determine an organization's distinct qualities will help staff make decisions about where and how to expend resources. Discussing distinct qualities can be challenging because sometimes staff believe their museum is strong in many areas, not just a few. The question "What are your distinct qualities?" is intended to help the museum know what it does best and to gently suggest that a museum may not be able to be all things to all people *and* achieve impact.

   The challenge inherent in pondering a museum's distinctiveness is that people sometimes think that by identifying a museum's primary strength, they are inadvertently disregarding or disrespecting other work the museum does. Even though identifying a museum's greatest and most distinctive asset is clarifying, humbling, and empowering all at the same time, intentional practice is about all the parts of the museum working together toward a common end, and if any one segment reduces its effort toward achieving impact, the whole is weakened. As staff begin to see their museum realistically, they realize that accentuating a primary strength is positive and does not automatically negate other areas of the museum's work. The intent behind discussing a museum's distinct qualities is to reclarify the essence of the organization through thoughtful and honest deliberations about what a museum is and can realistically achieve.

3. **Relevance is a crucial ingredient if a museum is to achieve impact**—relevance to people, the issues of our day, and the place/community in which the museum resides. The first two elements presented above—passion and distinct qualities—are about the museum; relevancy is about people and life outside the museum, and how others make sense of their experience inside the museum. Having knowledge about museum audiences and community members is necessary when developing an impact statement. A museum might need to conduct exploratory research to deepen its understanding of how the public frames and thinks about the museum and its value and use. Asking questions of the public

and listening to and hearing the public's responses is inordinately helpful, no matter what work the museum is doing.

Relevance is a powerful, complicated, and dynamic concept. Its meaning fluctuates with people's opinions, perceptions, knowledge, and understandings; societal norms; and individuals' unique circumstances. Relevancy and what is relevant are a moving target that requires a museum's ongoing attention. The Simon Wiesenthal Center project in Jerusalem, soon to open, will provide a community-gathering space for discussing current-day issues. Its founder and dean, Rabbi Marvin Hier, recognizes that "museums must deal with yesterday, . . . today and tomorrow."[25] Elaine Gurian asks in "Museum as Soup Kitchen," "How do we expand our services so that we make these museum assets into relevant programs that reach all levels of community, and are rated by many more as essential to their needs and their aspirations for their children?"[26] In "The Relevant Museum: A Reflection on Sustainability," Emlyn Koster asks: "As news stories unfold and society seeks to understand the nature and significance of events, is the museum field going to adapt to a greater role in exploring the things that profoundly matter in the world?"[27]

What is relevant and to whom cannot be determined without asking those outside the museum. Gail Anderson, a consultant who guest edited an issue of the *Journal of Museum Education* on "Museums and Relevancy," wrote:

Obviously, what is relevant is open to broad interpretation and diverse opinions, but it is clear that determining what is relevant cannot be defined and shaped through internal discussions and decision-making. Museums need to engage their respective communities and publics on an ongoing basis, and to listen and learn about the issues impacting them and the challenges they need help resolving.[28]

IMPACT ON WHOM?

Intentional practice necessitates making difficult decisions. One of the prickliest conversations that staff may have is when they are asked to identify up to three or four audience segments they would like to affect through their work. The conversation about audience segments is purposely intended to introduce realistic thinking about organizational capacity and impact. This conversation is difficult because staff might think that not including an audience segment means that they disrespect those visitors. However, consider these intentional-practice concepts:

1. Intentional practice promotes change, and a museum can choose to focus its resources and work on three audience segments for the next few years and then identify another three audience segments (or switch out one audience for another) on which to focus its resources and work thereafter, and so on.
2. By selecting three audience segments, the museum is not ignoring other audience segments that comprise its visiting population. Staff will still welcome all into the museum. Identifying a finite number of audiences is a resource-management and an impact-driven planning strategy designed to help staff focus their actions and allocate their museum's resources toward achieving impact.
3. Selecting a finite number of audiences is also a strategy to interrupt the habit of thinking that a museum can be all things to all people and achieve impact with everyone.

There are many ways to think about audience segmentation. Historically, museums have thought about audiences according to demographic characteristics such as age and educational background. Demographics can be useful for marketing purposes, but they might not provide insight when thinking about visitors' human qualities (e.g., their museum-visiting personality), the reality of the visitor experience in a museum (e.g., children in tow; on a date), and what knowledge and attitudes visitors might have about the subject matter.[29] From 2003 to 2010, the Dallas Museum of Art (DMA) funded "engagement research" that identified visitors' self-expressed personalities in the context of the DMA. Emerging from that data are useful descriptors such as "Independents," "Enthusiasts," and "Observers."[30] Soon other museums followed suit and conducted engagement studies of their own to better understand visitors' dispositions in the museum environment.[31] John Falk's research, also notable, generated "identities" such as "Experience seekers" and "Facilitators."[32] While conducting original audience research is best, when that is not possible, one can explore existing research conducted in other museums—of a similar size and type and in a similar city or town—to begin learning about visitors' museum personalities.

RELEVANT TO WHOM?
Conversations about what is relevant and meaningful to whom can reveal differences among audience segments, which might create tension inside the museum and potentially outside the museum. Balancing aspirations of both is crucial to achieving impact. Continuing community conversations will help the museum strengthen its relationship with the community,

because as the community learns about the museum and what it has the capacity to do, the museum is also learning about the community—what it values and may need from the museum. After staff have discussed audience options and the museum's viewpoints, the museum's leadership may need to clarify next steps while considering the following:

- Commonalities among audience segments' notions of relevance;
- Potential feelings of disenfranchisement;
- How the museum will demonstrate its distinct qualities, given what is relevant to audiences; and
- How the museum will use its operational capacity to achieve impact while focusing on what the community deems as relevant.

This section has presented the three elements that constitute impact—identifying staff members' passions, clarifying the museum's distinct qualities, and discussing relevance in the context of a finite number of audiences. Impact-related exercises (in chapter 5) and discussions will provide vital information for writing an impact statement. The hope is that the statement, which is always presented as a draft, reflects the museum's aspirations. Given that it is a draft, staff are free to change it as the museum and its work evolves. Impact statements can range from elegant and simple to more complex statements. All are written from a visitor's perspective, often describing what visitors might experience as a result of engaging with the museum and its offerings (see textbox 3.1). Sometimes, when discussing the draft statement, staff ask, "Where is the museum in the statement?" The museum's work can be seen in its mission statement, which should be shown alongside the impact statement. Seeing the two side by side is a reminder that achieving impact is dynamic and interactive and includes two players—what the museum does and what audiences experience.

TENSIONS AROUND IMPACT

Tensions exist in many aspects of museum work, and intentional practice is not immune to them. There are two important tensions associated with achieving impact—what the draft impact statement actually implies, and the organizational requirements for working toward it. While there may be other tensions, these two in particular affect the museum's advancement toward achieving impact.

The draft impact statement is written from the visitor's perspective. Typically, as illustrated in the sample statements in textbox 3.1, impact statements are somewhat aspirational, which of course is expected, given

Textbox 3.1.
Companion Statements: Mission and Impact

MID-AMERICAN SCIENCE MUSEUM, HOT SPRINGS, ARKANSAS

Mission
The mission of Mid-American Science Museum is to stimulate interest in science, to promote public understanding of the sciences, and to encourage lifelong science education through interactive exhibits and programs.

Impact
Inspired by discovery, visitors are encouraged to investigate the world around them and realize science impacts everyone and everything.

THE MORGAN LIBRARY & MUSEUM, NEW YORK, NEW YORK

Mission
The mission of The Morgan Library & Museum is to preserve, build, study, present, and interpret a collection of extraordinary quality, in order to stimulate enjoyment, excite the imagination, advance learning, and nurture creativity.

Impact
Visitors feel intimately engaged with creative expression and the history of ideas.

UNITED STATES CAPITOL VISITOR CENTER (CVC), WASHINGTON, DC

Mission of the Capitol Visitor Center
Working together for Congress to inform, involve, and inspire every visitor to the United States Capitol.

Impact of the Exhibition Hall and Orientation Film in the CVC
Audiences of the Capitol Visitor Center's Exhibition Hall and Orientation Film recognize the significance of Congress to everyday life, the role of citizens in a democratic process, and the evolving understanding of "We the People."

that the statement, by design, reflects staff members' passions. Passion and hopefulness thrive in most museums, and the goal is to honor staff members' ideals while embracing reality. Conversations about audiences and relevance are meant to have a rationalizing effect on the impact statement.

Balancing realism and idealism is a tension throughout the cultural sector, including the philanthropic community, as it grapples with how to best frame measurement. Foundations want to improve measurement and evaluation of *their* work, so they can improve measurement and evaluation of their *grantees'* work, and not unlike intentional practice, they want to build a culture of learning along the way.[33] When CEOs of private and community foundations gathered to discuss assessment, they agreed that the most daunting part of measurement and evaluation is assessing impact. Paul Brest, CEO of the William and Flora Hewlett Foundation, argues for demonstrating "contribution" rather than expecting "attribution," noting that contribution means "increasing the likelihood of success."[34] There is great wisdom in Brest's comment for museums. Museums can achieve impact by *contributing* to public value, but they need not necessarily shoulder the burden of *creating* public value.

Achieving impact is a tall order—even if the impact statement balances realism and idealism. From an intentional-practice perspective, achieving impact requires the strength of the whole museum, which is the focus of the second tension surrounding impact. In 1996, Mary Ellen Munley wrote: "Education is a museum-wide responsibility and endeavor. It takes many forms of expertise, including that of the public, to make a great museum."[35] The same can be said for achieving impact. The tension emerges from the reality that most museums do not function holistically as one organism with staff moving in unison, as often museums do their work following an unspoken hierarchy. The ideal museum looks like a large, interactive network where every person knows the museum's core purpose (e.g., intended impact) and every person's work is connected to the museum's core purpose and every other person's work. The rallying call of an impact statement and the need to achieve impact may not be strong enough to affect how museums do their work, as organizational cultures are often hard to undo, organizational departments have time-bound working traditions, and people struggle to shift their individual work habits.

To address these challenges, intentional practice advocates taking baby steps of change, as any kind of organizational change—no matter the scope—is reason to celebrate. For example, change in how an education department works across the museum could serve as a demonstration to other departments, as they may realize the benefits of working collaboratively across the museum. In that way, even if slowly, an organization might start to function in a new way. Like intentional practice, functioning as a unified staff is a work in progress.

Purpose-Driven Planning
In Stephen Covey's book *The 7 Habits of Highly Effective People,* the second habit is "Begin with the end in mind."[36] Though his book describes

habits of people, the habits are meaningful and transferable to organizations. Achieving impact can happen if the museum takes time to think about what it would like to achieve and then plan its work to achieve those ends. Planning without intention or without purpose-driven discussions and deliberations is planning for the sake of it. For intentional practice, planning work is meaningful only when it focuses on clarifying and accentuating the impact the museum would like to achieve.

A museum can engage in intentional planning activities from two primary vantage points: (1) the whole museum and (2) an individual museum project, such as an exhibition or program.[37] Deliberate planning of any kind provides museums the opportunity to clarify boundaries for themselves and others, enabling staff to say yes to activities that support achieving impact and no to activities that might move the museum away from its center and core purpose. A quotation from *Good to Great* is relevant here: Collins said, "Greatness [achieving impact] is not a function of circumstance. Greatness [achieving impact], it turns out, is largely a matter of conscious choice" (brackets mine).[38] If a museum is expected to deliver what it proposed and planned to do, it will need a disciplined mindset relentlessly focused on intended results.

When a museum uses the Cycle of Intentional Practice for across-the-museum impact planning, the plan quadrant asks, "What impact do you want to achieve?" If the museum uses the CIP to plan an individual project, the question becomes, "Does this project support the impact we want to achieve?" The latter question assumes the museum has already addressed the former question and has a draft impact statement. Intentional practice is an adaptable concept and process applicable to any organization, department, or project, and the museum can change the question in the plan quadrant to accommodate its current need.

If the museum does not have an impact statement that describes the positive difference it intends to make in the quality of people's lives, then it would need to first explore its passions, distinct qualities, and relevance to the public, as discussed earlier in this chapter. The next discussion is about experience *outcomes*; however, note that "impact" is woven into the discussion—first, to distinguish between "impact" and "outcomes," and second, to demonstrate that impact is akin to the hub of a wheel—it holds the cycle together and is relevant and necessary to every quadrant.

DETERMINING OUTCOMES TO SUPPORT IMPACT
Clarity of language—an important part of intentional practice—requires defining terminology, as one word can have different meanings to different

people. Those familiar with planning and evaluation will know the term "outcomes." To clarify the difference between "outcomes" and "impact," "impact" is the *overarching result* of the museum's work on audiences, and "outcomes" are *explicit measurable results* on specified audiences; outcomes are manifestations of results. Staff can craft outcomes that support a museum's impact, and/or it can craft outcomes to support the results of an individual project, which should also support the museum's intended impact. Developing experience outcomes involves envisioning how impact might be actualized in the museum—specifically among the three or four predetermined target audience segments. These actualizations become visitor experience outcomes. Though outcomes are strongly associated with evaluation, creating them is a planning activity, as reflected in Covey's quotation, "Begin [planning] with the end in mind" (brackets mine).[39]

A museum might have one impact statement with several supporting outcomes that add up to achieving impact (see figure 3.5). That is, achieving impact might be envisioned as having a cumulative effect; outcomes also can be organized as if they were on a continuum of achievement. To envision impact, staff discuss their passions, the museum's distinct qualities, and what is relevant to audiences. To envision outcomes, staff consider those same concepts in the context of the museum's work (e.g., exhibitions, programs) and the concrete results staff would like to see from that work on audiences.

Crafting an impact statement and outcomes can be trying; it is a clarifying process that is both an art and a science.[40] The museum field is familiar with having to clarify big concepts, albeit on a smaller scale—for exhibitions. Beverly Serrell's approach to exhibition planning includes crafting a Big Idea, which is a clarification process for determining the focus of an exhibition. For Serrell, "The big idea provides an unambiguous focus for the exhibit team throughout the exhibit development process by clearly

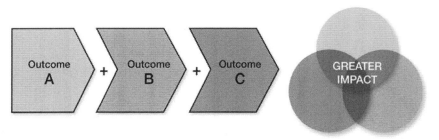

Figure 3.5.   Achieving outcomes can have a cumulative effect—impact.

stating in one noncompound sentence the scope and purpose of the exhibition."[41] Writing an impact statement requires feeling comfortable with sensing what feels right rather than overthinking if it is right. Chapter 5 presents approaches to writing and vetting an impact statement and outcomes.

DETERMINING INDICATORS THAT DEMONSTRATE OUTCOMES AND IMPACT

Indicators are observable and measurable *evidence* that an outcome is achieved. Discussions about outcomes will inform discussions about indicators. Generating indicators continues the ongoing clarification process that is part of intentional practice. In the Impact Pyramid (see figure 3.6), impact is at the top, and it is supported by outcomes, which in turn are supported by indicators located at the base of the pyramid. Indicators might not be a part of every intentional planning project, but they are always part of an evaluation project, as indicators serve two important evaluative purposes: an evaluator uses them to plan the evaluation and design data collection tools, and to guide the analysis of the data.

VALUE AND USES OF AN IMPACT FRAMEWORK

In intentional practice, planning work culminates into an Impact Framework document. Impact Frameworks can vary depending on an organization's needs, but in general, they are concise documents that present the organization's mission, impact statement, distinct qualities, target audiences, outcomes for targeted audiences, and sometimes indicators for tar-

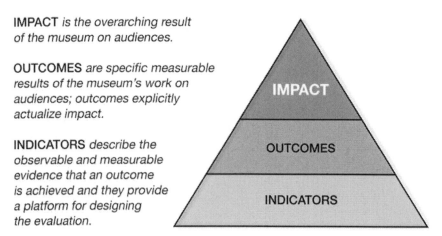

IMPACT *is the overarching result of the museum on audiences.*

OUTCOMES *are specific measurable results of the museum's work on audiences; outcomes explicitly actualize impact.*

INDICATORS *describe the observable and measurable evidence that an outcome is achieved and they provide a platform for designing the evaluation.*

Figure 3.6.   Impact Pyramid.

get audience outcomes (see appendix A for sample Impact Frameworks). Even though staff may view an Impact Framework as a finished product, the document, like the impact statement, is a "draft" or living document. The draft Impact Framework supports intentional practice in three ways:

1. Staff can continue to analyze the contents in the Impact Framework as a check-and-balance strategy to ensure internal consistency of ideas and specificity of language (e.g., are passions represented in the impact statement? Does the impact statement reflect the museum's distinct qualities? Do outcomes support intended impact?).
2. Intentional practice assumes ideas will evolve, and when they do, the Impact Framework will need to reflect the museum's most up-to-date thinking on its intended impact, target audiences, and outcomes.
3. Intentional practice supports continual professional learning, and if staff are always learning from their work, they are changing the contents in the Impact Framework to reflect their new learning.

Adopting the mindset that *all* work is a draft embraces an important reality: the outside world is always changing and evolving, and presumably the museum responds accordingly and evolves, too; therefore, the Impact Framework should also evolve so it can continually serve as the museum's guidepost for its impact-driven work. Additionally, because achieving impact is an ongoing pursuit, all work best be considered a draft.

Impact Frameworks also have many practical purposes that are part of a museum's daily work. For example, they can

- serve as a guidepost for ongoing internal decision making and project planning
- guide interpretive planning
- provide a discussion platform for continued reflection
- provide a discussion platform for community town meetings
- guide discussions during staff annual reviews
- orient new staff and board members
- train volunteers, including docents
- guide evaluation planning
- serve as a gauge for assessing evaluation results

TENSIONS AROUND PLANNING

One tension around planning for impact is that the process is dynamic and ongoing. While nearly all projects have beginning and end points, intentional planning is neither a project nor a product like an exhibition or program; it is a way of thinking, a mindset that if adopted can help museums with their impact-driven work. Intentional planning is not meant to be thought of or experienced as additional work for the museum; planning for and working toward achieving impact is the *only* work of the museum. When a museum participates in intentional planning to develop an Impact Framework, it is embracing new ways of working that fortify its intentional practice, including interdisciplinary collaboration. The challenges are these:

- how to infuse collaborative and interdisciplinary work strategies into the museum's daily work and
- how to spread impact-based thinking and decision making to all areas and functions of the museum—as achieving impact is everyone's responsibility.

Balancing much-valued brainstorming and productivity with impact-driven decision making creates another discernable tension. Intentional practice requires discipline and focus, which is sometimes hard to maintain in the midst of the extraordinary creativity and energy that staff display. Museums that pursue planning through intentional practice will still need to honor creative thinking *while* exercising discipline—by implementing only those programs that move the museum toward achieving impact among the target populations. To that end, the museum can use the impact statement to scrutinize potential programs. Similarly, vetting questions can also address whether the museum has the resources (dollars) and capacity (staff time and expertise) to deliver the program well enough to achieve impact. While these tensions are very difficult to massage, honest and systematic analysis of museum programs is necessary for determining which programs are best suited to achieve impact.

Evaluating Intended Impact

The purpose of this section is to present ideas about evaluation within an intentional-practice context,[42] as historically, evaluation in museums has lived in the program and exhibition realm.[43] Impact evaluation in intentional practice examines the effectiveness of the entire museum's work through the lenses of the impact statement and associated outcomes on three or four specified target audiences, as identified during the planning phase. The evaluate quadrant asks, "In what ways have we achieved our intended impact?" Written into the question is the most important part of intentional practice: *intended* impact. The Stephen Weil quote about intentions presented in chapter 1 bears repeating here: "will any differences do, or is it only intended differences with which we are concerned? In terms of accountability, it must surely be the latter"[44]

Technically, evaluation is "the systematic assessment of the worth or merit of some object" according to a set of criteria.[45] So, in the context of intentional practice, worth or merit is determined by the museum's ability to achieve its intentions, and the criteria are the impact statement and associated outcomes. As noted, adopting the "draft" mindset is very useful, especially in the "evaluate" quadrant. While evaluation is often thought of as something one does at the end of a project (called summative evaluation), evaluation can be implemented for planning purposes to understand audiences in the context of the museum (called front-end evaluation) and as part of testing ideas prior to fully developing them (called formative evaluation). Any evaluation data collected throughout the planning process can be used to inform iterations of the Impact Framework.

TENSIONS AROUND EVALUATION

Certainly, the sharpest tension around evaluation in intentional practice is how the museum community defines success. The objective behind a museum working through exercises that result in an Impact Framework is to explore and clarify the museum's passions (as expressed through its staff), distinct qualities, and relevance to target audiences; this work will illuminate the museum's unique brand of success. There are two underlying tenets of intentional practice that are important when considering a museum's meaning of success:

1. Every museum is distinct from every other museum even though museums have much in common. Distinctiveness emerges from two places: within the organization through its collections, research, exhibitions, programs, and strengths of its staff; and from the place in which the museum resides, which can include what community members afford their place and museum. The work of a museum in a large city is very different from the work of a museum in a small town. A museum that pursues intentional practice means that it is responsible for determining what success looks like and sounds like for itself; if museums choose not to do this hard, deep-thinking work, another entity will do it for them without any particular knowledge about museums and what they can and cannot achieve.

2. In intentional practice, success is not about how big or how much. In the past, numbers—like attendance, how many objects a museum has in its collection, or how many square feet a new wing adds to a museum—were considered markers of success. Numbers are outputs, not outcomes or impact, and as such, they neither implicitly nor explicitly describe how they make a positive difference in the quality of people's lives, and they do not speak to any museum's distinct qualities, intrinsic value, public benefit, and uniqueness in the American cultural landscape.[46]

If numbers do not determine success, then what does? A museum can certainly track numbers for its own edification, but it needs other data to demonstrate intended impact. Intentional practice focuses on describing the *quality* of impact. Even though intentional practice is about articulating the quality of an experience and the public benefit that a museum affords people, museums can define success in other ways, too. Pursuing impact with audiences does not preclude the museum from engaging in other important work, such as raising dollars, increasing membership, and forming community collaborations—all of which can be expressed quantitatively.[47] These kinds of outputs are a means to an end and serve an important purpose. Presumably the Impact Framework guides the use of dollars and suggests which community collaborations, for example, might strengthen the museum's ability to achieve its intended impact.

Another tension around evaluation and intentional-practice thinking, in general, is the expectation to continually increase the number of programs that staff deliver. Some museums tie employees' performance reviews and annual raises to having created more programs and attracted more attendees. The not-so-subtle message is that numbers equal success, and quality might not even enter into the conversation. Continuing to increase program and audience numbers is not sustainable, just like continuing to build additional wings onto museums is not sustainable. Museums in the United Kingdom note a similar tension. "Missions, Models, Money," a British action research program for leaders and funders in the arts and cultural sectors, quotes Adrian Ellis as saying, "The arts sector in the UK is over-extended and undercapitalised, with cultural organisations trying to do more things than they can possibly do well, with both human and financial resources too thinly spread."[48] And according to the Museums Association, "Museums have to work within the resources available to them. The sustainable answer may be to do less, but do it better."[49]

Doing less makes a great deal of sense, but it goes head-to-head with the mindset and culture of producing more and more. As written elsewhere, deliberately doing less disrupts the status quo and can feel scary.[50] What will become of the museum's traditions if some programs are discontinued? What about staff performance reviews—what will be the criteria of success?[51] These questions are important for all staff to discuss as part of their intentional-practice work, as staff can participate in redefining longstanding notions of success and come to a new understanding together. Staff may choose to define success as visitors having meaningful experiences that are personally relevant, significant, and enduring.[52]

HOW IS IMPACT EVALUATION DIFFERENT?

Conducting rigorous, formal, whole-organization impact evaluation is challenging and requires skill and expertise.[53] Rigor usually implies resources, and more important, it implies standards, such as sound sampling techniques and attention to reliability and validity.[54] It also implies a mixed-methods approach (e.g., qualitative methods such as open-ended interviews and ethnographic observations and quantitative methods such as standardized questionnaires and systematic observations) and cross-verification procedures to validate results. Even though evaluation in intentional practice focuses on collecting data that describe the quality of an experience, quality can be measured qualitatively *and* quantitively.

Researchers have taken note of how challenging it is to clarify and then research the impact of a museum's work on audiences and communities.

- In 2006, Douglas Worts and a few other museum professionals published a Critical Assessment Framework. They developed it from a recognized need to reposition museums "within the evolving cultural landscape of our societies."[55] The framework includes three types of indicators—individual, community, and museum—and they urge museum professionals to ask themselves questions about possible outcomes as they think about the programs they create.
- Carol A. Scott conducted research among museum professionals and the public to explore the values museums afford their communities. She identified three types of values—one that benefits individuals, one that benefits the economy of the community in which the museum resides, and one that benefits the society or culture within the community.[56]
- Victor Yocco and his colleagues used Scott's study to create an instrument to measure value perceived by a community toward an art museum.[57]

- Barbara Soren explored elements in a museum or program that might lead to what she calls "transformational museum experiences." Her article presents two case studies—one about teachers' experiences in a summer institute at the Royal Ontario Museum and another about visitors' experiences in a traveling exhibition titled "Bridges that Unite." Soren's work demonstrates that a core requirement for transformational experiences—language she uses to describe impact— is museums' providing opportunities for deep experiences.[58]
- Lynda Kelly explored "how museums contribute to the stock of social capital . . . and what type of social capital can legitimately be claimed as created by the existence of the museum."[59] She carefully chose three Australian museums/communities and studied people's responses to questions that reflected a social capital framework, exploring concepts such as trust and reciprocity. She concluded that museums have opportunities to challenge "how visitors think, inspiring them to take action on big issues and be more informed citizens" and ended with a question, "Visitors want this; are museums ready and willing to provide?"[60]

The work highlighted above provides language and ideas that others can build on as they contemplate the very complicated process of impact evaluation. There are also quite a few literature reviews that explore the collective impact of museums—all of which provide a wealth of information to ponder.[61] The American Zoo and Aquarium Association contracted a fieldwide impact study of its members to benefit stakeholders, including policymakers. While the study reported very positive results about the impact of zoos and aquaria, a published critical review noted "at least six major threats to methodological validity that undermine the authors' conclusions," including the sampling procedure (nonrandom) and the study design (post-only).[62] The critique exemplifies the challenges inherent in conducting an impact evaluation in general and a fieldwide impact evaluation in particular.

From an intentional-practice perspective and from an evaluation perspective, impact evaluation requires

- Clear criteria for success (e.g., an impact statement and outcomes). Based on the critique of the fieldwide impact studies mentioned above, this is where many "impact" studies fall short. Without a clear gauge of success, the data lack context, meaning, power, and relevance.

- A rigorous research plan following acceptable methodological practice, such as random sampling and internal validity.
- Organizational humility to accept all results—those that are positive and those that are not—as important and valuable.
- Organizational desire to continuously learn with the goal of improving practice.

After going through an impact-based planning phase, impact evaluation might seem like the next logical step. However, proceed with caution, as it may take considerable time to align work processes and products according to the Impact Framework, and alignment should prioritize impact evaluation. Smaller interim evaluation studies might be a reasonable way to proceed if only to field-test some of the museum's changes before forging ahead with full-fledged impact evaluation.

Learning to Reflect, Reflecting to Learn

Reflection is about learning and improvement, and increasingly, it has become a vital part of intentional practice. The reflection quadrant asks, "What have we learned? How can we do better?" Reflection is the active process of deliberately stepping back to look closely at an experience, a thought, or a thing with the intent of exploring it in great depth—much like what museum staff hope visitors do with objects.[63] If asked "What do you hope your museum's visitors experience?," responses might include "a transformational experience," "increased knowledge," or "a deep, thoughtful experience." All of these responses relate to learning—not in the formal-education sense but in the personal-learning, self-enriching sense. Susan Glasser, the 2008 winner of the Brooking Paper on Creativity in Museums, wrote about museum staff as "The Forgotten Audience," noting that staff want to learn, too.[64]

Donald A. Schön, author of the book *The Reflective Practitioner,* developed the concept of reflective practice—more specifically, reflection-in-action and reflection-on-action.[65] Reflection-in-action might describe a museum educator's response to a unique situation during a program the moment it occurs; the educator is thinking while doing. The response could be a combination of knowing, talent, and intuition, most of which might be inarticulable at the moment, which Schön fully explains in his book. Reflection-on-action happens when people reflect on something—an experience or something concrete like data or information—after the fact with the intent to analyze, question, explore, evaluate, understand, and think about their thinking.[66] The assumption behind reflection-on-action and reflection in intentional practice is that no matter the experience, there is always something more one can learn from it. Reflection-in-action happens naturally, whereas reflection-on-action requires conscious mental processing (e.g., thinking) of knowledge and emotions that people have already experienced.[67]

The museum field has not conducted reflection research among museum professionals or visitors, but other fields of study have looked at how people approach reflection. Researchers in formal education indicate that learning and reflection are linked. They have identified a continuum of approaches that can support reflection, and in which the learner's perception of the task dictates how the learner will approach reflection.[68] For example, their research shows that a learner can adopt a "deep" approach or a "surface" approach to a reflection task—each of which represents opposite ends of a continuum rather than an either/or scenario. Jenny Moon in England describes the two ends of the spectrum:

> A deep approach is where the intention of the learner is to understand the meaning of the material. She is willing to integrate it into her existing body of previous ideas, and understandings, considering and altering her understandings if necessary. The new ideas are "filed" carefully and integrated. In contrast, a surface approach to learning is where a learner is concerned to memorise the material for what it is, not trying to understand it in relation to previous ideas or other areas of understanding.[69]

Moon also identifies stages of learning, which are very similar to how many museum educators think about stages of learning for museum visitors: noticing, making sense, making meaning, working with meaning, and transformative learning.[70] Reflection in intentional practice is most beneficial when staff have time to first notice results from an evaluation, for example, which might mean reading a report or executive summary or meeting to discuss the results prior to a workshop. In other words, reflection in intentional practice advocates slowing down the learning process. People need time to process new information independently so they can know what they think about the information before participating in and contributing to staff discussions. Sharing their thoughts with colleagues will deepen their personal sense-making and empower them to use the information.

Taking time to reflect may not easily happen, even though the benefits of reflection are obvious. To exemplify a strategy for how to make time for reflection, consider spending the last fifteen minutes of every intentional-practice workshop reflecting on what transpired in the workshop, in part to build a habit of reflection but also to demonstrate that making time for reflection can be as simple as repurposing the last fifteen minutes of a weekly staff meeting!

Many of us probably reflect in our personal lives. Similarly, when reflection happens in the work environment, professional learning is given the space to emerge. In particular, when staff from different departments convene to reflect on their collective work, professional learning is enriched because people in different departments may think about data and experiences in different ways. The skills associated with reflective practice include being, speaking, disclosing, testing, and probing.[71] Among those, "being" is the most vital and most complicated. It implies presence, which assumes honesty, vulnerability, and deep listening with the intention to thoroughly understand.[72] Approaching people and ideas as if experiencing them for the first time further enhances learning, because fresh eyes allow for new ways of seeing and knowing. Even in the absence of data, there is tremendous value in reflection—whether collectively reflecting on an event, an article, or a newly installed exhibition as Serrell suggests in her book *Judging Exhibitions: A Framework for Assessing Excellence*.[73] Listening to your colleagues' ways of thinking offers great insight to them and may suggest new ideas to you.

TENSIONS AROUND REFLECTION

Joseph A. Raelin wrote an article titled, "'I Don't Have Time to Think!' versus the Art of Reflective Practice."[74] The first part of the title clarifies one of the tensions around reflection. People say they do not reflect in the workplace because they don't have time. In response to Raelin's article, Edgar H. Schein says: "I would suggest that if we view time as a cultural [organizational] invention rather than a physical abstraction, we might discover that there are all kinds of time for personal [professional] reflection if we choose to use it" (brackets mine).[75] While many of us are socialized to be people of action, and taking the time to quietly reflect seems counter to the norm,[76] consider that museums employ lifelong learners who are passionate about their work. Consider what might happen if museum directors promoted and modeled museum-wide reflection and rewarded staff for facilitating reflections with their departments. Staff may very well start to feel they have the time to reflect.

Aligning Work to Achieve Impact

Achieving impact may require organizational alignment. Alignment in the context of intentional practice means that all the people in the organization—from leadership to frontline staff and volunteers—know and understand the intended impact of the museum as per the framework; know that target audiences are the beneficiaries of the museum's work; and implement processes and activities to achieve impact on target audiences. Business blogger Sandy Richardson offers a good analogy for alignment: visualize a rowing team where all rowers are working in synchrony, and all are using every ounce of their energy to move closer to their goal— crossing the finish line. When "team alignment and cohesion is off, the boat strays off course, essentially wasting time, energy, and the resources that were invested in trying to achieve the goal of winning the race."[77] For museums, winning is achieving impact, and to do so, staff need to be aligned and unified in their one pursuit.

In the alignment quadrant, staff ask, "How do we align our actions to achieve impact?" Alignment is complicated because aligning a museum's work to achieve impact could mean that the museum will need to change what it does (products) and how it does it (processes), and often, change is hard. When confronted with the task of alignment, it may help to identify the components that comprise alignment; they are interrelated and interactive:

1. The first component is about people:

    a. the leadership (e.g., board and executive director);
    b. the staff who carry out the museum's impact-driven work; and
    c. the recipients of the museums impact-driven work—the public.

2. The second component is about the museum's work:

    a. its processes (how it does its work); and
    b. its products (what it creates and produces).

3. The third component is about resources:

    a. dollars required to support the work; and
    b. staff capacity (e.g., skills and time) to carry out the work.

These components are not independent variables; they interact with and rely on each other. All three components require alignment—among internal elements, such as processes and products; between the components and the impact the museum wants to achieve; and among one another. Similar to the CIP's quadrants where people's work is implicit, people function in all the alignment components even if they are not explicitly

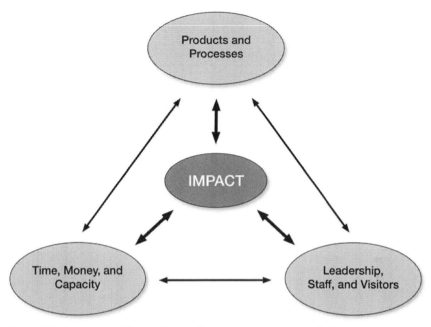

Figure 3.7.   Interrelationships and interactions among components of alignment.

called out (for example, staff are responsible for creating processes and products). Alignment is dynamic in museums, as shown in figure 3.7.

COMPONENT 1: LEADERSHIP, STAFF, AND VISITORS
Intentional practice is meant to be a whole-museum endeavor. Best-case scenario is that intentional work advances from the top down, through the direction and inspiration of the museum's leaders, but sometimes the work progresses from other areas of the organization, such as an individual department or even an individual person. The intentional-planning process often invigorates staff; they enjoy learning about new ideas and appreciate having a chance to discuss ideas important to them and critical to their museum and community. One department's enthusiasm for intentional thinking can sometimes carry the whole museum forward, even without explicit directives from the top of the museum. Intentional practice requires passionate people to champion it, and this is where the Impact Framework can become a useful communication and movement-building tool.

Ideally, most staff will have participated, in some way, in creating the Impact Framework, so they will be familiar with the framework's contents, which would enable them to comfortably talk about the importance of impact-driven thinking to their colleagues across the museum. These champions have another task, too, in terms of alignment: they will need to begin talking with their fellow colleagues about how to best actualize the contents of the framework. Part of this discussion may include analyzing the museum's current strategy for executing work, which may lead to discussing how departments work together. This is where component 1 begins to interact with component 2, products and processes, as explained in the next section.

Finally, the public is the beneficiary of impact-driven work. The Impact Framework identifies the museum's target audiences as well as outcomes for those audiences, and it is intended to serve as a continual guidepost for the museum. The framework is multifunctional, and the museum can use it in myriad ways, including as a platform for discussions in town meetings and community gatherings. Such discussions should happen periodically because they can serve as a feedback loop to staff, whereby staff can continue to update the Impact Framework accordingly.

COMPONENT 2: PROCESSES AND PRODUCTS

Intentional practice includes aligning the museum's processes (how museums do their work) and products (exhibitions and programs) with achieving outcomes and impact on the public. Intentional practice advocates an interdisciplinary collaboration process, in part because achieving intended impact is difficult, and doing so requires all staff to collaborate across departmental lines. As the saying goes, "The whole is greater than the sum of its parts." Chapter 4 presents the seven principles of intentional practice, and interdisciplinary collaboration is one of them.

Working in interdisciplinary teams will be familiar to those who develop exhibitions, and some might recall what happened in the late 1980s and 1990s when exhibition planning was undergoing a significant change. What was once an independent curatorial process was becoming an interdisciplinary- and collaborative-team process.[78] While many complained that exhibition development had become messier and more complicated than before, staff realized that interdisciplinary teams generated rich dialogue as they deliberated how to communicate complex ideas to the public. To achieve impact, the same type of grand change needs to happen across the whole museum—where the executive director, educators, marketing staff, operations, designers, curators, evaluators, and development staff continually convene to actualize the Impact Framework.[79]

The team approach to exhibition development was used as a strategy for creating what the museum field calls the "visitor-centered" museum.[80] Rather than having a museum becoming visitor centered, intentional practice pursues a museum-visitor relationship based on mutual understanding of what the museum has the capacity to deliver and what is relevant to the public. Nonetheless, there is a similarity between the processes museums apply to their visitor-centered work and the processes the whole museum might need to achieve public impact. Realizing that museums have addressed a similar challenge not too far in the distant past may be reassuring to those who want to apply interdisciplinary thinking and processes to their museum's work strategy.

To model this important principle, all intentional practice workshops include exercises for small groups, where participants are predetermined and the groups intentionally comprise people from different departments to sidestep what might happen if staff self-organize (e.g., curators might sit together; educators might sit together). The power of interdisciplinary thinking and work is extraordinary; new ideas and efficiencies are generated, in part because people across the museum are communicating about their work—sometimes for the first time!

COMPONENT 3: DOLLARS AND STAFF TIME AND CAPACITY

Weil wrote, "Once a purpose [impact] has been established, however, the museum is still unable to move forward until either (a) all of the necessary resources can be identified or secured, or (b) the purpose [impact] has been scaled back to match available resources" (brackets mine).[81] Alignment is a crucial element of intentional practice because it clarifies the link between achieving impact and the "what" and "how" of museum work. Achieving impact requires steadfast attention to the impact the museum wants to achieve, the processes and products that comprise museum work, and the resources needed to support those processes and products. These ideas are presented below as discrete questions, which seep into the first and second components, illustrating the complications that surround alignment:

1. Does the museum have the dollars necessary to implement its processes and build its products to achieve the museum's intended impact?
2. Does staff have the time necessary to implement the museum's processes and build its products to achieve the museum's intended impact?
3. Does staff have the skills necessary to deliver the museum's processes and build its products to achieve the museum's intended impact?

Museums that venture onto the alignment quadrant address these questions and others about their work. Alignment analyses prompt staff to explore their processes and products from several vantage points:

- the *elements* that comprise their products (e.g., an exhibition's main messages, an exhibition's design, exhibit types—such as interactive devices or media);
- the *processes* used to create the products (e.g., cross-departmental process, individual department process, advisory committee, contract designer);
- *which processes and products achieve impact;*
- *what can change* to improve the museum's work and achieve greater impact.

Due to the inherent challenges of alignment, museums may want to ease into the alignment process by selecting one innocuous project to explore—one that is neither loved nor hated—to acquaint the museum with the kinds of questions and analyses staff will be asked to explore. As staff become more comfortable and adept with inquiring questions about project elements, processes, and products, they may learn to appreciate the virtues of alignment thinking. (Chapter 5 provides specific exercises with instructions and guiding questions.)

TENSIONS AROUND ALIGNMENT

There is one very deep and wide tension that surrounds alignment, which might be obvious at this point: alignment can lead to change, and change is difficult. Staff may become anxious about long-held traditions, such as holiday programs, or longtime community partners if the alignment analyses do not support continuing these programs and relationships. And what might happen to self-directed workers when interdepartmental processes are introduced? When change is in the air, people begin to feel uncomfortable and threatened, mostly because they do not know what will happen, and the unknown is scary. Shifting work situations are disruptive and may result in people feeling marginalized, wondering what is expected of them. Open, clear communication is vital in such situations.

Prior knowledge and habits are two elements that might block any kind of real change. For example, when faced with a situation that requires some sort of decision, a little bit of knowledge about a past situation (even if the current situation is vastly different) and habit can produce the same decision that was made previously, even though it is inadequate for the current situation. Typically, people move toward what they know when making decisions because that is where they are most comfortable, even though there is a danger in doing so.[82] How to best address this natural human response, of course, is the question. The enormous body of literature on change management is an indication of the challenge and need to find ways to support organizations that want to shift their practices.[83] From an intentional-practice perspective, change is inevitable. Taking small, sensitive steps is imperative.

Intentional-Practice Principles 4

I find that principles have no real force except when one is well fed.

—MARK TWAIN

CHAPTER 3 INTRODUCED the Cycle of Intentional Practice (its center and the four quadrants), provided background information to substantiate its value to intentional practice, and described the tensions in each quadrant that can wreak havoc on the intentional-practice process. This chapter is divided into two sections. The first section presents the seven principles of intentional practice. Labeling the seven ideas described in this chapter as "principles" asserts them as fundamental to intentional practice. A museum that fully participates in impact-driven work through intentional practice will continuously embrace all of these principles—not necessarily simultaneously, but eventually and repeatedly. An underlying goal of intentional practice and the seven principles is to support museums in their effort to achieve impact and to foster professional and organizational learning—the two intended ultimate benefits of intentional practice (see textbox 4.1).

The second section, "Strategies that Support Intentional-Practice Work," shares some guidelines and approaches for upholding the seven principles. Facilitators of the process will be responsible for setting the tone and expectations for participants' engagement, imparting important intentional-practice concepts, and ensuring the process stays focused on achieving impact. First, consider initiating the process by offering the few simple rules of participation presented in this section to ensure the process is beneficial to the museum and all participants. Second, contemplate the

Textbox 4.1.
Seven Principles of Intentional Practice

1. The organization wants to achieve something greater than itself (e.g., impact) among the audiences it serves.
2. Staff know the impact the museum hopes to achieve on specified audiences.
3. Staff regularly evaluate the effect of their work on target audiences to determine what works and what does not work.
4. Staff reflect on evaluation results and their organization's practices to learn from their impact-driven work.
5. Staff align the museum's work to deepen the museum's intended impact.
6. Staff work collaboratively across the organization.
7. Staff use inquiry and active listening to understand and appreciate varying viewpoints.

virtue of the two core beliefs presented at the end of the section, as they play an important role in intentional-practice thinking and execution.

Seven Principles of Intentional Practice

The first five principles of intentional practice echo the Cycle of Intentional Practice, so they will feel familiar to you because of the previous chapter's contents (see principles 1–5 in textbox 4.1). These five ideas are principles because without any one of them, a museum's intentional practice falters and its impact-driven work dissipates; they are the foundation of intentional practice. The remaining two principles (6 and 7) are the primary strategies for working through principles 1 to 5. Collectively, the seven principles create a structure and process for the museum's continual impact-based planning, development, execution, and assessment.

1. The organization wants to achieve something greater than itself (e.g., impact) among the audiences it serves.

This first principle is a prerequisite to intentional practice because wanting to achieve impact on the public is the very purpose of intentional practice. Stephen Weil asked, "If our museums are not being operated with the ultimate goal of improving people's lives, on what alternative basis might [museums] possibly ask for public support?"[1] The ultimate "so what" question for museum staff is, "To what end are you doing your work?" When museums pursue impact through intentional practice, the public is the recipient of their work. An impact-driven museum organizes all aspects of its work to achieve impact, as per an impact statement, which describes what the museum hopes to achieve among specified audiences. A museum that wants to achieve impact through intentional practice looks and sees beyond itself and wholeheartedly wants to attain something greater than itself, and its staff realizes that the museum's primary purpose is to benefit the public. In so many ways, achieving impact through intentional practice will gratify the museum's staff and endear the museum to its community.

A museum working on behalf of the public is not a new idea. What is relatively new is a museum methodically taking steps to clarify the impact it wants to achieve on audiences and organizing its work accordingly. In the past, achieving impact on audiences was seen as the responsibility of museum education departments, and now more and more museums realize that *all* staff as well as their leaders are responsible for working toward a greater good. An impact statement is meant to reflect a museum's innermost desire to do good, and staff can use it as a guidepost to determine new work and revise traditional work; the impact statement can ground staff and serve as a continual reminder of why they do what they do.

2. Staff know the impact the museum hopes to achieve on specified audiences.

An impact statement describes the effect the museum would like to have on its audiences. It is one sentence that expresses staff members' passions, reflects the museum's distinct qualities, and clarifies the aspirations staff have for the visitor experience. George Labovitz and Victor Rosansky, authors of *Rapid Realignment: How to Quickly Integrate People, Processes, and Strategy for Unbeatable Performance,* note, "Every organization needs a Main Thing: a single powerful expression of what it hopes to accomplish."[2] For museums, the Main Thing is reflected in the impact statement. Impact statements, which can vary across museums, should embody realism, idealism, ambition, and passion. Labovitz and Rosansky also note two challenges that organizations face today:

> Keeping . . . people and the organization centered on what matters amid the crosscurrents of change. There are two aspects to that challenge. The first is to get everyone headed in the same direction with a shared purpose. The second is to integrate resources and systems of the organization to achieve that overarching purpose: the Main Thing [impact].[3] (brackets mine)

How do leadership, staff, volunteers, and docents come to know the impact statement? Representatives from all of those groups will have participated in workshops, and others who may not have attended the workshops were invited to submit responses to open-ended questions, received draft Impact Frameworks to review, and attended meetings to discuss the framework. Some attended reflection workshops that helped them explore the many uses of the Impact Framework, such as using it as a tool for onboarding and training new staff and volunteers. From board members to museum leaders and from department heads to frontline staff—all started to think about how to use the framework to guide decision making about programming and resource allocation.

The second word in the principle is "know," meaning that all who work at the museum or on behalf of the museum (e.g., board members, volunteers, docents) have forged a deep personal understanding of the impact statement; they have come to appreciate its meaning in the context of the work they do, connect its content to something in themselves, and internalize it—enabling them to effortlessly deliver on its promise to specified audiences. Everyone who works at the museum or on behalf of the museum knows that the impact statement purposely focuses on three or four target audiences. Yet everyone also knows that regardless of the specified target audiences, they will continue to welcome and treat all visitors equally and respectfully. They understand that the Impact Framework is an organizational and resource-management strategy to support achieving impact on particular audiences while not disenfranchising others. Because change on some level is inevitable, communicating to all, including volunteers, is imperative. Everyone deserves to be kept abreast of the museum's ongoing impact-driven work.

3. Staff regularly evaluate the effect of their work on target audiences to determine what works and what does not work.

Evaluation conducted in museums provides important information about the successes and shortcomings of museum projects based on predetermined criteria. It can also provide basic information and insight about museum audiences. The Impact Framework includes the museum's mission, impact, distinct qualities, and experience outcomes for target audiences, among other elements depending on the project. The Impact Framework embodies the museum's aspirations, and as such, all museum projects and their intended experience outcomes for target audiences should support the impact the museum wants to achieve. Experience outcomes serve a dual function: staff can and should use them to plan their work, and evaluators use them as criteria for evaluation. Evaluators use outcomes and their associated indicators when designing the evaluation, conducting data analysis, and writing the report. The final evaluation report identifies ways in which a project achieved success and where it may have fallen short by examining data in the context of the experience outcomes in the Impact Framework. Though the evaluation is designed to study effectiveness based on predetermined criteria, the analysis also identifies unintended outcomes, which are reported as well.

In the principle stated above, the word "regularly" is meaningful. Evaluation is not meant to be a onetime activity; it is intended to occur regularly. The value of a museum conducting evaluation regularly is to support staff's learning about their work through studying its effects on audiences. Adopting a continuous-improvement mindset and creating a continuous-improvement organizational culture[4] is implicit in intentional practice. Evaluation and reflection are the means for supporting continuous improvement.

Figure 4.1 illustrates how evaluation supports continuous improvement in that there are three evaluation phases—front-end, formative, and summative—and they align with three project-development phases—planning, design/build, and post-presentation. Here is a detailed explanation of figure 4.1, as it requires some interpretation:

- The *left-side column* illustrates two things: (1) Visitors provide input during evaluation—that is, they are the subjects in an evaluation; and (2) there are three phases of evaluation as follows:

  1. **Front-end evaluation,** conducted during content development, explores how people think about and perceive a topic to guide the project's interpretive development, such as for an exhibition. Front-end evaluation can inform a project's conceptual development and refine visitor experience outcomes. As a point of clarification, front-end evaluation is not a marketing study. The museum has already decided to advance the project, and the front-end evaluation will offer insight on how to best communicate the project's ideas, given how people think about and understand the ideas, as indicated in the front-end evaluation.
  2. **Formative evaluation,** conducted during design development, can test themes, interpretive text, interactive exhibits, graphics, and any other elements that comprise a project. Formative evaluation allows the project team to course-correct its work prior to final design.

3. **Summative evaluation,** conducted after installation or implementation (if you are evaluating a live program), examines the overall effectiveness of a project on audiences—based on predetermined visitor-experience outcomes. Even though summative evaluation marks the end of a project, through reflection staff can learn from the project's success and shortcomings and apply summative evaluation results to their thinking about future projects.

- The *middle column* shows three phases of a project's development—planning, design/build, and post-presentation. The arrows in this column show that revisions are made in all phases (based on visitor and staff input—the left and right columns of the figure), resulting in:

  1. experience outcomes,
  2. final design, and
  3. responsive project.

- The *right-side column* shows museum professionals' input throughout project development; museum staff are responsible for content planning, design development, and critical appraisal. Critical appraisal is when a museum invites colleagues from neighboring museums to discuss and analyze the museum's final product, based on their professional opinions and knowledge of best practices.[5]

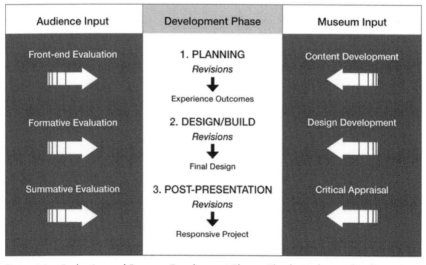

Figure 4.1.   Evaluation and Program-Development Phases. The three phases of audience input and museum input align with the three phases of project development.

Evaluation, like intentional practice, does not magically happen. Evaluation requires deliberate upfront planning, expertise, time, and money as well as the will to follow through. If a museum implements one or two phases of evaluation annually across a range of projects, it will be engaged in ongoing learning about its audiences and impact-driven work; even one evaluation provides insight! Evaluation is an important ongoing activity because of its learning attributes. Often, evaluation is used to judge a project's worth; in intentional practice, evaluation is used to learn about one's practice and work.[6] Learning from evaluation can happen any number of ways. In intentional practice, learning from evaluation may require reflecting on the data and exploring the "why" behind the data to understand it.

4. Staff reflect on evaluation results and their organization's practices to learn from their impact-driven work.

Reflection is part of evaluation practice. After evaluators reflect on the meaning of data from a few vantage points (e.g., the practitioner, the individual visitor, the audience group), they identify and communicate the most essential findings to the museum, and then ask reflective questions to support staff in their processing of the data and results. Chapter 3 mentions reflection-on-action, which requires conscious mental processing or thinking.[7] This kind of deliberate reflection, when focused on evaluation results and a museum's practices, can lead to valuable staff learning that can alter their professional practice.

All audience evaluation data offer insight about how people experience a museum, and the more time one spends reflecting on the data, the deeper the analysis, and the more one can learn. The following is an example of the kinds of questions that can emerge (indicated by the Qs) when one chooses to thoughtfully reflect on audience data (note that an experienced researcher will have conducted a thorough analysis as described below, and the example is presented to make a point about questioning data to understand it):

Four hundred respondents participated in a whole-museum audience study.

- Results say that the average rating of visitors' overall experiences is a 5 on a 7-point scale of "uncomfortable" (1) to "comfortable (7). While 5 is not a terrible average rating, you want to understand what might have precipitated that rating.
  Q "If 5 is the *average* rating, which visitors rated their experience higher than a 5? Which visitors rated their experience lower than a 5?"

- Your question prompts you to explore relationships between ratings and different data points (age, repeat visitation). You discover that first-time visitors, on average, rated their experience 3.5 while repeat visitors, on average, rated their experience a 6.5.

  Q "What might be affecting first-time visitors' experiences?"

- You review more and other data, and in particular you look at responses to the open-ended question that appeared at the end of the survey. It asked about overall experiences, too, and while this question was similar to the standardized-rating question, it invited visitors to write responses.

- You begin to notice a pattern in some of the write-in responses. For example: the museum map was difficult to use, directional signs were inadequate, and the guards were unfriendly.

  Q Did these three deficiencies cause first-time visitors to rate their experience lower on the scale?

- You code all the open-ended responses to determine whether first-time visitors were the ones who were having trouble with the maps, signs, and guards, as it occurs to you that repeat visitors may not need a map or a sign, and they may not have a reason to ask a guard for directions, as they are already familiar with the museum's layout.

Thinking about the "why" behind data in the context of the visitor experience opened the door to exploring an otherwise invisible problem that first-time visitors are experiencing. Reflecting on evaluation data is the first step toward *knowing* the data and your visitors in a deep way. Without a thorough understanding of what the data mean, problems may remain invisible. The above example illustrates the value of maintaining a questioning mindset when reflecting. While curiosity might have initially motivated you to further analyze the data, you might need to harness other personal and emotional qualities, too, as fruitful reflection also requires:

- open-mindedness because reflection may lead to new, unexpected information;
- preparedness to explore ideas beyond what might feel comfortable at the time;
- willingness to accept what the data say and imply; and
- readiness to take responsibility for your thoughts and what you learn from the data.[8]

Though evaluators practice reflection as part of their work, in intentional practice reflection is an essential skill and necessary thought process that can be applied throughout your intentional-practice work; at its best, reflection permeates all quadrants. For example, data are not a prerequisite for reflection; in the absence of data, you can reflect on your museum's organizational practices by thinking critically about what you do and why you do it. This kind of reflection can take place during planning and aligning, for example. Often museums are so busy doing their work that they often forget *why* they are doing their work.[9] There is always value in stepping back and asking the very simple but hard-to-answer question, "To what end?" Reflection across all quadrants can help museums contemplate their purpose and clarify their impact-driven work.

As much as possible, reflection sessions should be neutral and unbiased, devoid of expectations—other than to learn. If you choose to facilitate a reflection session about your museum's practices, such as the processes used to select special exhibitions and/or other initiatives, consider facilitating the conversation with colleagues from a range of museum departments. Collaborative and interdisciplinary conversations result in rich deliberations, which can favorably affect and support personal and professional learning.

Living the next principle, principle 5 (staff align the museum's work to deepen its intended impact), depends on the museum adhering to principles 1–4. For example, consider

- Principles 1 and 2: without an impact statement (#1) and staff deeply knowing the impact the museum hopes to achieve on specified audiences (#2), they will not have the proper context for analyzing their work in alignment (#5).
- Principle 3: "Staff regularly evaluate the effect of their work on target audiences to determine what works and what does not work," serves alignment because evaluation data enhance one's knowledge of museum audiences and sharpen one's understanding of the visitor experience. Evaluation data equal evidence, and evidence is a vital variable in alignment discussions because evidence indicates reality rather than supposition. In sum, evaluators use the impact statement and experience outcomes as the gauge for success *and* staff use them as context for alignment discussions. If your museum does not have data about visitors' experiences, and given that evaluation is a principle of intentional practice, the museum will need to find ways to learn about its audiences.
- Principle 4: Regularly implementing museum-wide reflections will prepare people for the rigor and intensity of alignment discussions.

5. Staff align the museum's work to deepen its intended impact.

Alignment is a principle of intentional practice because impact will remain elusive until the museum realigns its work to support the impact the museum wants to achieve. And though alignment is layered and complicated, the right work environment and organizational culture can support alignment discussions. Kenneth Freeman, dean at Boston University Questrom School of Business, notes the following criteria to support alignment (reframed slightly for a museum context). Below in parentheses are descriptions of how each of Freeman's criteria is exemplified in intentional practice.

- **Everyone knows the heart of the organization.** (The museum's heart is exemplified in its mission statement and impact statement; representatives from different departments have participated in the creation of the impact statement; staff have vetted the Impact Framework; and staff partook in reflection workshops that explored using the Impact Framework.)
- **Leaders continually share what is taking place, believe in transparency, and are always clear about where the organization is headed.** (Facilitators can model and reinforce transparency [e.g., explain what they are doing as they are doing it so participants can take note], share the origins of ideas, review the project goal at every gathering, and ask questions during reflections to improve the process and work. They can explain why the process is workshop-based and inclusive with many staff and board [planning for and achieving impact requires the full force of the museum], and why the workshops have interdisciplinary groups rather than departmental groups [e.g., cross-departmental collaboration strengthens the museum's work and is necessary to achieve impact].)
- **All staff and those who work on behalf of the museum feel their individual role is vital to the museum's success.** (Staff and volunteers, as well as select community members and board members, contribute to the intentional-planning process by participating in workshops where they share their thoughts and experiences.)
- **All staff and those who work on behalf of the museum have the tools and resources to do their job as best they can.**[10] (As staff begin to thoughtfully dissect their work to determine the strength of alignment between a particular program and the museum's impact statement, they might uncover weak alignment and through discussion realize the problem is caused by inadequate staffing, for

example. Their analysis determines that additional resources—whether time or dollars—could strengthen alignment and they can rationally state their case to the museum's administration.)[11]

Sometimes people experience alignment conversations in unanticipated ways, especially if they created the projects under discussion. Prior to an alignment session, consider facilitating conversations around these three points:

a. Alignment requires complete trust, honesty, and a willingness to have open conversations about the work of the museum. Raise awareness of the natural human tendency to hold unconscious biases toward particular people and programs and the possibility that these biases may act as barriers to having productive alignment conversations. If you are the facilitator, you might offer a personal example, such as "Recently I realized that I had negative thoughts about the museum's storytime program even though I had never attended one. Once I realized that I was judging the program without knowing anything about it, I attended a program and then met with the education staff to talk about it."

b. Facilitate a conversation around the learning opportunities that alignment affords the museum. For example, review the discussion questions from the exercise in chapter 5's textbox 5.9 and ask the group which questions might be the most interesting to discuss and which might be the most difficult to discuss. Acknowledging challenges together might relax participants and reduce their stress, thereby enabling them to share their opinions.

c. Allay people's fears about program or staff reduction based on alignment results. Fear inhibits honest conversation and adds resistance to the goal of alignment, which is to discuss and determine which projects and programs achieve impact on audiences and which do not. Let people know no one will be punished as a result of alignment analyses.

Principles 6 and 7 are process principles—that is, they move the collective work forward, through collaboration and respectful inquiry.

6. Staff work collaboratively across the organization.

If intentional practice assumes achieving impact is the responsibility of all museum staff, then it makes sense for staff from different departments to work collaboratively as a strategy for strengthening communication, reducing inefficiencies, and increasing effectiveness. Interdisciplinary collaboration is a principle of intentional practice for a number of reasons:

- Achieving impact is ambitious, and it requires the cooperative effort of people with distinct and diverse ways of thinking and knowing.
- Interdisciplinary collaboration enriches individuals and teams and creates stronger work processes and products.
- Interdisciplinary collaboration builds mutual respect among all colleagues and their work, enabling the staff to work together to create impact among audiences.

"Collaboration is a way of working that attracts and involves people outside one's formal control, organization, and expertise to accomplish common goals."[12] This definition, written by Heidi K. Gardener of Harvard Business School and Herminia Ibarra of London Business School, well describes how intentional practice applies the collaboration concept. If people from different departments are working together on a museum initiative, their collaboration democratizes the work process and creates professional learning experiences for team members. Sometimes work actions are automatic responses, and people act without thinking—that is, until someone asks the "why" question or the "what-does-that-mean" question that challenges them to investigate their actions and thinking. Then we stop and wonder, "Why *do* I do it that way?" When someone unfamiliar with your line of work poses a question that requires clarification on your part, you have an opportunity to reassess your decisions and actions as you explain them to a colleague. Having the chance to think about your work and clarify it to yourself and others encourages meaningful and illuminating dialogue about the work of the museum.

Initiating collaborations with people outside departmental boundaries isn't a natural human behavior, as research shows that when people are "left to their own devices," they will "choose to collaborate with others they know well."[13] In their article "Are You a Collaborative Leader?," Ibarra and Hansen recommend that leaders set the tone by being good collaborators themselves.[14] You can foster collaboration and disrupt people's natural tendency to work only with friends by doing the following:

1. Create a core intentional-practice team composed of three to seven individuals (depending on the size of the museum) representing different aspects of the museum's work (e.g., curatorial, education,

exhibitions). The core team attends all the workshops and planning meetings (or momentum calls) that take place between workshops. Team members can also champion the museum's intentional-practice work to their departments as well as others.

2. Preassign workshop participants to interdisciplinary working groups for all workshops. When staff from up and down and across the organization, as well as board members and community members, have conversations in small groups and then all together as one large group, different sensitivities and ideas have a chance to emerge thereby creating a rich conversational exchange.

Achieving intended impact is challenging, ongoing work that requires ingenuity, cooperative will, and passion for what the museum can offer visitors and its community. The intent behind requesting across-the-museum collaboration is to reconsider standard go-to strategies, create new work habits, and encourage new and better ways of thinking and working together—because that is what's required to achieve intended impact.

7. Staff use inquiry and active listening to understand and appreciate varying viewpoints.

There are two distinct parts of this last principle: inquiry and active listening. They go hand in hand as asking a question without listening to responses makes asking the question moot. Both actions constitute principle 7, and each is dissected below.

USING INQUIRY

Inquiry is the simple act of asking questions in search of information. As museum practitioners will confirm, hearing a visitor inquire about an object, specimen, or experience is exciting, because asking an "I wonder" or a "what if" question is an indicator of active learning.[15] Art museum educators use inquiry to help visitors explore works of art,[16] researchers in science museums study how to deepen visitor inquiry because they have evidence that doing so helps visitors learn,[17] and interpretive writers use questions in exhibition text to promote close looking, meaning-making, prolonged engagement, and metacognition.[18] George Hein writes about the virtues of inquiry and inquiry's well-documented history of use in education:

> The strong empirical evidence that inquiry is essential for learning, based on 100 years of developmental research, is not the only reason

for advocating educational methods that promote its use. Inquiry-based education also has powerful social and moral consequences. Democracies (at least in principle) have long advocated public education that promotes critical thinking for all citizens. Opponents of democracy have also recognized the significance of inquiry in education; the long history of efforts to suppress independent thought and inquiry-based education by totalitarian regimes is well documented.[19]

Inquiry also drives scientists' work and guides evaluators' work: evaluators ask questions of museum staff, then of visitors, and then of themselves—about the data and their analytic framing of the data. Asking the *right* question in the right *way* (e.g., open-ended, neutral tone, and impartial) requires clarity of thought about the goal of the inquiry and sensitivity and openness toward all respondents.

Inquiry also plays an important role throughout intentional-practice work. For example, prior to the first workshop, the project leader or facilitator asks museum staff and leadership questions about the goals of the intentional-planning project. During the first intentional-practice workshop, participants explore ideas by responding to questions about their passions, the museum's distinct qualities, and visitor experience outcomes. The facilitator helps staff clarify their thinking by asking simple probing questions such as "Can you talk about that more?" or "What do you mean by that?" and suggests that participants do the same of each other. Probing for clarity is for everyone's benefit, and the goal is to lead the museum toward someplace, wherever that place may be.

The "content" or "subject" of the inquiry is the museum and you and your colleagues' aspirations for achieving impact on audiences. Learning—yours and your colleagues'—is personal and professional. In general, throughout the intentional-practice process, inquiry

- explores the work and the will of the museum. The ideas embedded in these conversations become the contents of the Impact Framework.
- honors professionals' specialized knowledge and experiences so all can hear about the work of the collective group and museum.
- empowers staff to explore their thinking, come to know their perspectives and the perspectives of others, and reach a collective appreciation for all ways of knowing.
- neutralizes and democratizes the intentional-practice working environment.
- stimulates people's learning—about themselves and their museum.
- furthers learning to support the intentional-practice process.

ACTIVELY LISTENING

Asking questions is a productive strategy, but only if the questioner actively listens to people's responses. "The mere act of listening engages people";[20] and listening connects people to each other and creates common understanding, which is vital to intentional practice. Active listening is a skill that can be self-taught; it requires self-awareness, sensitivity, being fully present, and continual practice.[21] There are three kinds of active listening[22]—all equally important in intentional practice.

1. **Internal listening:** Listening to your voice and thoughts is invaluable to the success of intentional practice. Sometimes people need to overcome barriers in order to listen to themselves—or the voice in their head—including the anticipation of feedback and fear of conflict, which are the two most common barriers to active internal listening.[23]

2. **External listening:** Listening to others' voices and thoughts is as invaluable as listening to your own. Hearing what others are saying, as opposed to assuming you know what others mean by the words they use, sums up the challenge of listening *to understand*. Likewise, hearing what others are saying requires thinking about what you are going to say next. "Your ability to understand the true spirit of a message as it was intended to be communicated, and demonstrate your understanding, is paramount in forming connections."[24] Truly understanding a colleague may be difficult for people who have worked together for a long time. Sometimes preconceptions take hold, and they can inhibit trust—an important ingredient that builds understanding and strengthens connections. In workshops, try to see your colleagues anew, as if for the first time, and ask yourself if you really understand the message the speaker intended. And if there is a shred of doubt, ask a question for further clarification.

3. **Complete listening:** When you listen to yourself and others, you may begin to perceive what unites everyone's ideas and hear the singular purpose behind the museum's work. Complete listening takes place when you trust yourself, allow yourself to trust others, give yourself time to process and understand, ask clarifying questions, and listen without judgment.

Asking questions and listening creates dialogue—a necessity if intentional practice is to thrive. Dialogue takes place throughout the intentional-practice process because the facilitator and others will be asking open-ended questions to ensure understanding. Asking questions allows ideas and aspirations to emerge, which clarifies the heart and mind of the museum. Intentional practice can be a positive, invigorating, museum-strengthening experience for staff and others involved in the process.

Strategies that Support Intentional-Practice Work

Successful interactions may require some general rules of engagement, especially if the museum is unaccustomed to participating in staff workshops. At the start of the first workshop, consider introducing the rules of engagement provided below, and while they might not need to be brought forth at all, they provide good reminders for the interactions that will follow.

1. Participate with Authenticity! Everyone!

This rule will set the tone and expectation for the conversation that will ensue. Essentially, participants need to feel free to share what is inside their minds and honestly and respectfully respond to questions—those that the facilitator asks and those that their colleagues ask. The intentional-practice process provides a dual opportunity for all participants to be heard and to hear what others think, as genuine—or authentic—participation is essential to a successful planning process.

Sometimes museum staff, particularly in large museums, do not often convene—outside of annual or quarterly all-staff meetings or monthly department staff meetings. That is, they do not meet to talk about their museum—other than when a consultant or other guest is there. After workshops, staff have mentioned how much they enjoyed having so many staff together in one room to discuss museum matters. Given the apparent rarity of such gatherings, workshops provide opportunities for all participants—especially junior staff—who might not be invited to many meetings outside their department. Because some might feel intimidated and want to opt out of sharing their viewpoints, workshops should always include opportunities for small-group work, as some may find it easier to speak to a few people than to a roomful of people. Additionally, when creating the small, interdisciplinary groups, consider people's personalities. For example, place a person with a strong personality with someone who can keep that person in check so others have a chance to speak, as the process weakens considerably without input from all.

2: *Listen, First to Understand, Then Respond*

The importance of listening was explained earlier, in the descriptions about focused listening in principle 7: "Staff use inquiry and active listening to understand and appreciate varying viewpoints." Focused listening is about listening to others. This second rule of engagement actually came from a workshop participant who attended an early intentional-practice workshop. This participant observed something about how his colleagues were reacting to one another's comments that caused him to wonder if people were (1) really *listening* to what others were saying and (2) if people were really *understanding* what others were saying. During the reflection exercise at the close of the workshop, he shared his observations with his colleagues and requested that in subsequent workshops, participants listen to their colleagues first to understand, and when understanding was secured (if necessary through additional questions for clarification), then respectfully respond. All agreed that this great idea should be added as the second rule of engagement.

Understanding the intention behind and meaning of someone's words is important. First the speaker has to have clarity of thought, which is a process unto itself; then the listener will need to hear and understand the essence of the speaker's idea. Speaking and listening are independent *and* interdependent processes, and the beauty of conversation is that the speaker and listener can help each other if they accept that clarity and understanding are parts of a complicated communication process and they are on a two-way street. Both have to find the right words to express an idea (the speaker) and ask the right questions (the listener) in order to discover the intended meaning. Sometimes people have an inkling of what they want to communicate, but the fully formed idea is elusive until the conversation unfolds.

Generally, museum professionals are committed to and have passion for their museum, and they also have valuable professional experiences to contribute to the process. To facilitate everyone's understanding and to support positive discussion, consider presenting these two ideas at the outset of intentional-practice workshops:

- **Slow down and take time:** Research shows that when classroom teachers insert "wait time" or "think time" after asking students a question, their behavior and their students' behavior changes. As one might expect, wait time leads to more students raising their hands, longer student responses, and more students providing correct responses. Interestingly, inserting wait time also causes teachers to ask fewer and better questions, and when they ask additional questions based on students' responses, those follow-up questions require "more complex information processing and higher-level thinking on the part of the students."[25] In intentional practice, imposing think time into deliberations is a strategy for supporting authentic and careful communication and continued clarification of ideas. The facilitator can set the pace and continue to reinforce the pace throughout the workshop.

- **Zones of personal engagement:** Literature on leadership and performance management identifies three psychological zones that invariably affect how people relate to each other and to ideas.[26] To illustrate these zones, you can draw the bull's-eye as indicated in figure 4.2, then add the names of the three zones, starting with the center circle, labeled the comfort zone. This is where many spend time, because humans are wired to do what feels good.[27] Yet feeling good asks little of us and protects us from challenges that we might face when stretched beyond what is expected. When we are challenged, we enter the middle zone, labeled the learning zone. Of the three zones, the learning zone is the most advantageous and productive zone because it is where people can grow and change,[28] and it is the most important zone for intentional practice. The outermost zone is the place to avoid—the panic zone. This is where people go when they become nervous or stressed. You can avoid the panic zone by taking a break, breathing deep, or asking a question—all of which can bring you back to the learning zone.

  In addition to introducing the three zones to workshop participants, consider pointing out that the boundaries of these zones vary depending on the person. For example, some people might enter the panic zone several times during a workshop, while others might stay squarely in the learning zone. Because everyone has a different threshold for managing challenges and everyone starts out at a different place, request that participants use sensitivity as they interact with their colleagues. If you or anyone else observes a participant who has entered the panic zone, think about what you can do to bring that person back to the learning zone, and ask all participants to do the same. Likewise, if you notice people have remained in the comfort zone, for the benefit of all participants, you might identify small steps that one can take toward the learning zone.

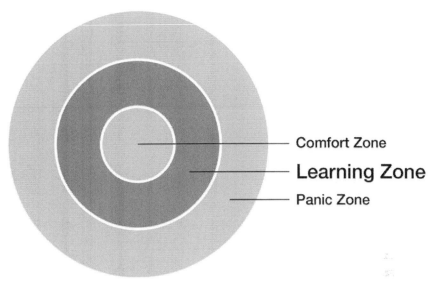

— Comfort Zone

— Learning Zone

— Panic Zone

Figure 4.2.   Psychological zones of personal engagement.

3: Realize Process Work Is an Art and a Science

Intentional practice is iterative and process oriented. Process work can feel messy and chaotic, which can make some people uncomfortable. While the workshops are structured with a defined agenda, refined approach, and theory to support the process, no one ever knows exactly what will unfold during the course of an individual workshop or the collection of workshops that constitute the museum's intentional-practice work. The artfulness of process work emerges from staff as they work together to articulate the contents of the Impact Framework, which could be a new way for the museum to see itself and be seen by others.

The science part of the process can be found in two places in particular:

- **Research supports the characteristics used to create an impact statement:** The underlying structure used to create an impact statement is derived from staff members' collective passions for their work, the museum's distinct qualities (what sets it apart from other museums in its region), and what is relevant to audiences. Two of these concepts are from the Hedgehog Concept—a theory that emerged from rigorous research conducted by Jim Collins and his team for his book *Good to Great*; it identifies three characteristics that move an organization from being a good one to a great one (see chapter 3, note 20, for a full explanation of the Hedgehog Concept). This underlying theory and framing, including the style and tone of the questions (open-ended, neutral tone, nonleading, and unbiased), provides focus during the museum's exploration process.

- **Structured process:** Intentional-practice work is highly structured. The Cycle of Intentional Practice creates the overarching structure for designing a customized, goal-oriented process. For example, workshops include large- and small-group exercises where participants work together to address questions; a core team meets between workshops to move the intentional-practice work forward, supports continued communication, discusses challenges, and addresses people's lingering questions; and all agendas (for workshops and for core team meetings) place a goal atop the page to state expectations for the work.

While the above might seem ordinary and commonplace as well as rigid and unartful, recognize that artfulness emerges through the interactive process, and the tight, consistent, and facilitated structure balances with the messiness and the we-don't-know-where-we-will-land nature of intentional practice. Staff find great comfort and relief in the standardized work processes, as within them they feel able to exercise flexibility and creativity. They are also freed up to focus on the work at hand. Essentially, intentional-practice work is difficult on many levels, and a tight structure reduces distractions and helps museums maintain focus and exercise discipline—requirements for a museum that wants to achieve impact on audiences.

Two Fundamental Beliefs

Two fundamental, interconnected beliefs are woven through intentional-practice work: "Less is more" and "Museums can't be all things to all people *and* achieve impact." "Less is more" originated as a core belief after observing a growing number of museums that were generating a dizzying number of programs, seemingly for the purpose of generating more and more programs. "Less is more" grew into a meaningful and important way of thinking for intentional practice, especially when working in the alignment quadrant. The second belief originated from experiences with exhibition planning and evaluation and the need to exercise pragmatism. "Museums can't be all things to all people *and* achieve impact" reflects two ideas:

1. Museums do not *really* design their exhibitions or programs for all.
2. Audience prioritization can have a positive domino effect—from planning all the way to the evaluation: when audiences are prioritized, planners can allocate resources accordingly, and the evaluator can design data collection instruments to be sensitive and precise, enabling the tools to detect an effect on prioritized audiences.

Less Is More

There are a few dots to connect between "less is more" and intentional practice:

- To achieve the museum's intended impact, the museum implements only those actions that move it toward its intended impact.
- A potential result of doing only impact-driven programming is that the museum eliminates programs and activities that do not move it toward achieving impact.
- When programs are eliminated, staff time and museum resources become available for improving programs and activities that *can* achieve impact.
- Program recipients are the beneficiaries of the museum doing fewer programs (less) because their experiences are deepened (more).

"It's a natural human tendency to want to do more,"[29] so it is not unusual to come across a museum that does too much. Just the way continuing to add more and more space onto existing museum buildings isn't a sustainable business model, adding more and more programs onto people's already overloaded plates isn't a sustainable human resource model. From an intentional-practice perspective, the only work a museum should do is work that moves it closer to the impact it wants to achieve, so it makes sense to "eliminate what doesn't matter to make room for what does."[30] Business author Ron Ashkenas believes "there's a lot to be said for the power of pruning and the importance of maintaining focus," pointing out that "the strategy of 'less is more' has been a powerful driver of success" for some organizations.[31]

The idea of pruning or reducing one's work is not new. Peter Drucker wrote that businesses need to practice "systematic and purposeful abandonment" or they "will be overtaken by events."[32] Collins's research notes that good-to-great companies "made as much use of 'stop doing' lists as 'to do' lists," demonstrating "remarkable discipline to unplug all sorts of extraneous junk."[33] Humans have a hard time doing less and a hard time saying no—two tendencies that can lead to trouble. The ease of saying yes and the challenge of saying no are well known in psychology and the business world.[34] Steve Jobs said, "Focusing is about saying 'no,'" and Warren Buffet said, "The difference between successful people and really successful people is that really successful people say no to almost everything."[35] Intentional practice includes evaluation and alignment, both of which can support decision making when needing to prune the organization's ineffective work, and the Impact Framework is essential as a decision-making tool, too, to help determine what work to continue and what work to stop doing.

Time is a precious commodity and there is never enough of it, so in some ways, learning to say no is a survival skill. Writer Elizabeth Grace Saunders would like to see productive staff commit to less. She sums it up this way:

> It's simple math. Each additional project [and audience] divides your time into smaller and smaller pieces so that you have less of it to devote to anything. Whereas if you reduce your number of responsibilities [and audiences], you have more time to devote to each one. That means on an individual level, you want to strike the ideal balance between the number of projects and the time you need to excel in them. . . . You can actually do more if you take on less.[36] [brackets mine]

Museums Can't Be All Things to All People and *Achieve Impact*

Clarity about the "who" part of a project and museum is necessary for impact-driven work. Are Renaissance art exhibitions designed for elementary school groups? What about a science-heavy exhibition on global climate change? Education departments might use exhibition environments as teaching platforms for their school programs, but the materials (e.g., text, media, graphics) in the aforementioned exhibitions are not usually designed with elementary school–age children in mind. Exhibition teams know who they are designing for, and they need not fear prioritizing audiences aloud. The same holds true for the whole museum. Prioritization is a useful and valuable strategy for resource management and decision making.

Chapter 3 discusses that intentional practice necessitates identifying a finite number of audiences that the museum would like to most affect—the "who" part of intentional-practice work—and notes the various ways one can define and segment audiences (e.g., demographically, personalities). The advantages of identifying a finite number of audiences are far reaching, from exhibition design to evaluation:

- Museums can achieve impact with some, but not all, audiences, at any given time.
- When there are few rather than many audiences to affect, the museum can streamline its implementation strategies and product development.
- When there are few rather than many audiences, resources (time, energy, and dollars) are expended across a smaller field, so targeted audiences are more apt to feel the effect of the museum's effort.
- When there are few rather than many audiences, the evaluator's resources go farther; the instruments are specific to the prioritized audience(s); and the evaluation design, overall, gives precedence to a few rather than many audiences, thereby increasing the chance of detecting an affect.

Prioritizing audiences is akin to prioritizing exhibition ideas. Creating exhibitions is hard work, and that work can become infinitely easier when curators and designers identify and focus on a "big idea" throughout their process.[37] Similarly, detecting the effect of exhibitions on audiences (e.g., evaluation) is also hard, and it becomes infinitely easier when exhibitions are designed with particular audiences in mind because staff can apply their resources accordingly and avoid wasting resources on materials and audiences that are not their primary ones. And finally, detecting the effect of a whole museum is hard, too, and it is best for the museum to zero in on affecting a few audiences at a time. When audience prioritization frees up staff time and museum dollars, the result could lead to enhanced programmatic quality and a deepened visitor experience.

Identifying target audiences and reducing the number of annual programs and exhibitions are two less-is-more strategies for deepening visitors' experiences. Both actions are difficult to practice, especially at the same time, so approach pruning methodologically, slowly, and with sensitivity toward your colleagues. The Impact Framework can guide some of the decision making, but you may also need to conduct evaluation to learn what is relevant to audiences and to determine the relative effectiveness of different programs.

Intentional-Practice Exercises 5

> *The art and science of asking questions is the source of all knowledge.*
>
> —THOMAS BERGER

INTENTIONAL-PRACTICE WORK is mostly workshop-based with periodic working sessions with the core team, both of which are punctuated with momentum meetings or calls between workshops to maintain focus and keep the process forward moving. This chapter is designed to guide practitioners who want to facilitate the intentional-practice process in their museum. Workshop exercises explore the general questions posed in the Cycle of Intentional Practice, which are intended to help museums articulate, continually consider, and organize their work around the impact they want to achieve. The exercises will help staff explore their museum, their own thinking, and their colleagues' thinking, and they will also generate data meant to be used to create the contents for an Impact Framework.

For staff who are curious about how long it takes to complete intentional practice work, see table B.1, Proposed Schedule for Intentional-Practice Work, in appendix B. Keep in mind that intentional-practice work is ongoing and that museums should review their impact statement and other associated work periodically for several reasons: staff change, communities grow, notions of relevancy shift, and expectations of museums evolve accordingly. The fast-changing external world requires all organizations to keep up, as what may have felt right two years ago might seem outdated today.

Even though all intentional-practice projects are heavily facilitated and use the Cycle of Intentional Practice to guide the work, the uniqueness and distinctions of museums always emerge. No two intentional-practice projects are alike because no two museums are alike: museums have varying contexts and needs, and intentional-practice work responds accordingly. The intentional-practice and facilitation strategies herein apply evaluation practices and skills, most notably, asking questions in pursuit of clarification and articulation, collecting data (e.g., documentation of conversations and group work) from workshop interactions, and analyzing the data in search of trends, meaning, and understanding.

The exercises in this chapter are unembellished without museum-specific customizations. Customization takes place once the project goal becomes clear. If you are interested in facilitating these exercises at your museum and are new to facilitation, consider exploring the many available guidebooks for ideas on different facilitation approaches, including exercises for "warmup" and "brainstorming" activities and ideas for ensuring group participation.[1] I am somewhat of a purist when it comes to facilitation and stay close to the problem at hand. Weigh what feels comfortable to you and shy away from strategies that feel gimmicky, as maintaining focus on impact-driven work is vital. Above all else, you will need to feel comfortable in your role and confident to address whatever might come your way.

Exercises for Creating an Impact Statement (Workshop)

This workshop is usually the springboard workshop for intentional-practice work, as it focuses on creating an impact statement and associated experience outcomes. Staff, board, community members, and other stakeholders participate in three exercises to generate "data" for creating an impact statement:

1. exploring passions
2. identifying distinct qualities
3. envisioning outcomes

All three exercises take place in one workshop in the order presented above. The facilitator provides the instructions for each exercise, prepares worksheets, and so on, and usually conducts the analysis of participants' responses. The analysis process results in a draft Impact Framework, which the core team reviews before sharing more broadly. Typically, team members will debate the meaning of individual words and ideas in the framework to make sure they represent participants' intentions. In essence, they are thinking about their own thinking and engaged in metacognition—a very important part of intentional practice.

Exercise: Exploring Passions

The passion exercise, in all of its simplicity, is surprisingly personal, powerful, and invigorating for staff to experience with their colleagues (see textbox 5.1 for steps to the passion exercise). You can implement this exercise using an approach called "The Five Whys." Japanese industrialist and founder of Toyota, Sakichi Toyoda, originated the Five Whys, and business researcher and author Jim Collins popularized it in the United States.[2] The Five Whys exercise was designed as a tool to find the root of

---

Textbox 5.1.
Passion Exercise: The Five Whys

- Assign participants to interdisciplinary groups of five people, comprising staff, board members, and community members.
- Ask groups to appoint a scribe who records people's responses as they go around the table, answering the initial question and three or more of the follow-up questions shown below.
- After the first person answers the initial and follow-up questions, a second person answers all the questions, and so on. Most important is that all respondents answer the "why" follow-up questions and go as deep as they can until they reach the root passion for their work.
- Once all have had a chance to respond to the questions, the groups synthesize their results and report to the larger group, sharing where people started and where they ended up.
- All notes are collected before moving on to the next exercise.

THE FIVE WHY QUESTIONS:

Initial Question: What about your work with X museum is most important to you?
   Follow-up question: Why is that important?
      Follow-up question: Why is *that* important?
         Follow-up question: Why is *that* important?
            Follow-up question: Why is *that* important?
               Follow-up question: Why is *that* important?

a problem, and while the passion exercise does not use the strategy exactly as intended, it works beautifully to find the root of people's passion for their work. Note that some people may become overcome with emotion—sometimes because they never really explored why they do what they do and are stirred by the meaning they have found; and sometimes people who are isolated at the office feel happy to be asked such a simple yet deep question about their work.

As a problem-solving questioning strategy, five levels of "why" questions may be necessary; however, when museum staff use the strategy to explore what about their work is most important, only three follow-up questions may be necessary. Facilitators can alter the details of the initial question to accommodate the mix of workshop participants. For example, if the majority of workshop participants are from outside the museum, the initial question could be "What about your work or association with X museum is most important to you?" When nonmuseum workshop participants respond to the question, staff begin to realize how others perceive and experience the museum—an important perspective for them to know.

Exercise: Identifying Distinct Qualities

Chapter 3 introduces Jim Collins's Hedgehog Concept (see chapter 3, note 20), noting the parts that have been customized for intentional-practice purposes, specifically as reflected in this second exercise. This is a large-group discussion derived from the part of the Hedgehog Concept where Collins states, "What you can be the best in the world at." For intentional practice, the question becomes, "What does your museum do better than any other organization of its kind?" adding a clause if necessary, for example: "in your area/region/city?" Depending on the type of project, you might ask a follow-up question and generate a second list—this time asking about the future of the museum. If the intentional-practice project is meant to support strategic planning, a second question could be "What *could* the museum do better than any other organization of its kind (in your area/region/city?)" Staff enjoy answering these kinds of questions because they have a chance to think about all the excellent work their museum does and all the great work they aspire to do.

After creating one or two lists on large pieces of paper, prompt the group to step back to think about whether the museum really does *all* the things on the list "better" than any other organization of its kind. Sometimes a staff member raises the question first; other times you may need to initiate that part of the conversation. It is important for staff to feel good about their work *and* also think critically about it. So, to address the second point, lead staff through a discussion using one or more of these points and then ask a question:

- Most museums are very busy doing many things.
- Most museums are very busy doing many things and lack the resources to do *that* many things *really well—well enough to achieve impact.*
- Most museums are very busy doing many things and have resources to do *a few* of those things *really well—well enough to achieve impact.*

    Q So what does your museum do *really well*? What is *truly distinct* about your museum?

Distinctiveness is an important element for cultural institutions to nurture because it can contribute to a museum's identity. A museum's strength comes from its inherent assets (e.g., collections, staff intellect and abilities) and how staff use those assets in their daily and strategic work. If staff objectively and critically address the question of what their museum does better than any other organization, the list of distinct qualities should be relatively short and reflect the museum's inherent assets. Refer to the Impact Frameworks in appendix A for examples of how museums identify their distinct qualities.

The first two exercises are about the museum—its staff and the work the museum does. The third exercise focuses on the recipients of the museum's work—audiences.

Exercise: Envisioning Outcomes

The goal of envisioning outcomes is to begin articulating what the museum hopes target audiences experience from their museum visit, given staff's passions and the museum's distinct qualities. Outcomes are *explicit measurable results* on specified audiences. The reason envisioning outcomes follows the passion and distinct qualities exercises is because passion and distinct qualities are important considerations when articulating outcomes: if staff do not exude their passion and display their museum's distinct qualities in their work, visitors will have dreary and unremarkable experiences. In addition to passion and distinct qualities, outcomes also need to reflect what is relevant to the museum's audiences, as when a museum is relevant to audiences, visitors will have personally meaningful experiences. The ideas and input that community members and other stakeholders offer during this part of the workshop are vital, especially in the absence of evaluation or audience data.

Before assigning the exercise, you may need to provide a tutorial on outcomes, as developing outcomes can be difficult for those who have never had to write them (see textbox 5.2. Outcomes: Key Ideas). Refer to the Impact Frameworks in appendix A to see examples of outcomes.

The envisioning outcomes exercise is simple because it focuses on one question that small, interdisciplinary breakout groups answer: "What positive difference do you intend to make in the quality of [your target audiences'] lives?" All groups answer the same question, and the number of target audiences the museum identifies determines the number of times the groups envision outcomes. If there are three audiences, groups spend ten minutes envisioning outcomes for audience 1, then move on to audience 2, spending ten minutes envisioning outcomes for that audience, and so on. While the groups are brainstorming, visit them to answer questions and ask about the outcomes they generated to ensure they are clear and communicate their intention. Groups write their outcomes on large sheets of paper that you will collect at the end of the exercise for analysis.

After completing the exercises, you or a skilled analyst on your team will thoroughly scrutinize the results and continue to review, discuss, and further clarify the outcomes with the core team. All conversations about outcomes are valuable because discussing and articulating what you hope your museum achieves begins to build a collective understanding about intended results

Textbox 5.2.
Outcomes: Key Ideas

Outcomes describe a result (short-term and/or long-term).
Outcomes are concrete statements.
Outcomes are specific to the context in which they occur.
Outcomes describe what visitors can realistically *and* hopefully achieve.
Outcomes benefit visitors.
Outcomes are written from the visitor point of view (e.g., "Visitors will think, feel, be able to. . .").

Outcomes can describe:
Understanding (e.g., knowledge, awareness)
Attitudes (perceptions, beliefs, values)
Engagement/interest (feelings, appreciation)
Skills (thinking, abilities)
Behaviors
Other results

Greater impact is reached when multiple outcomes are achieved.

across the museum. This process is useful and powerful because it exemplifies the value of slowing down to clarify ideas with utmost precision and demonstrates how hard it is to find the right words to express an intention.

The outcomes exercise is important for intentional practice because outcomes serve as planning guideposts for staff decision making. Whether you are an exhibition developer, interpretive writer, exhibition curator, or a gallery teacher, outcomes can guide your actions—what to do and how to do it. If museums are serious about the outcomes their audiences experience, they may need to change what they do so their work more strongly aligns with the outcomes and impact they want to achieve among target audiences.

Chapter 3 discussed and illustrated the relationship between achieving outcomes and impact; essentially, achievement of multiple outcomes adds up to greater impact. Does achievement of one outcome indicate achieving impact? It might depend on the outcome, and it most certainly depends on how staff choose to measure their museum's success. Because there is no existing protocol for what might determine a museum's impact, consider creating your own. Collectively determine where you want to set the impact bar and realize it will fluctuate because the museum may change its outcomes, target audiences, and the impact statement at any given time. Intentional practice is about achieving impact *and* learning from your work, so fluidity is important to embrace. In intentional-practice work, if you learn from your work, changing how you do your work is inevitable.

Two things take place after outcomes are "envisioned": (1) writing a draft impact statement, and (2) continuing to develop and tweak outcomes in a second workshop where staff have an opportunity to review, critique, clarify, and revise them.

DRAFTING AN IMPACT STATEMENT (POST WORKSHOP: CORE TEAM)

Drafting an impact statement requires reflecting on and considering staff passions, the museum's distinct qualities, and the outcomes that were generated during the first workshop. The ideas that these three elements embody become the inspiration for the impact statement—a one-sentence statement that describes the museum's intended impact on target audiences. There is not a specific strategy or recipe for writing an impact statement other than to consider the results from the three exercises and begin to craft a succinct sentence that reflects the contents from the exercises. Often there are many, many drafts of the impact statement over the course of several months before staff settle in on one that feels right. After the core team reviews and alters the draft, invite a larger staff group to vet it in a follow-up workshop.

Vetting Outcomes (Workshop)

During this second workshop, staff have an opportunity to review detailed results from the first workshop, including staff passions, the museum's distinct qualities, and audience outcomes. Edits to staff passions and the museum's distinct qualities are made in real time, and then staff spend their remaining time critiquing the outcomes using the questions in textbox 5.3, Critiquing Outcomes/Questions to Consider.

Textbox 5.3.
Exercise: Critiquing Outcomes/Questions to Consider

Does the outcome represent one idea? Sometimes outcomes are written as compound statements—meaning that a visitor would have to do or explain more than one thing to achieve the outcome. An outcome should present one result.

Is the outcome concrete? Sometimes outcomes are vague and do not suggest what success might look like or sound like. If you can't visualize the outcome, clarify the outcome so it is concrete.

Does the outcome describe a *result*? Sometimes outcomes describe an *action* that the museum will take, such as offering minds-on tours, rather than the *result* of a minds-on tour on audiences. If the outcome doesn't start with "visitors will" or "participants will," the statement is probably a museum action and not a visitor-experience outcome.

Is the outcome grounded in reality with a bit of aspiration? The passion staff have for their work sometimes affects what they think is possible for visitors to achieve in a museum. You may want to consider these three factors to avoid overestimating what is possible for visitors to achieve:

1. developmental readiness (e.g., are school-age children, for example, developmentally able to achieve the outcome?)
2. prior interest in and knowledge of the subject (which might be determined through front-end evaluation)
3. time spent in or intensity of the museum experience

Are any of the outcomes similar? Sometimes two outcomes seem different at the time they are written, but upon review their distinctiveness is less clear. Scrutinize outcomes to ensure they are distinct.

After staff have agreed on the list of outcomes for all target audiences, the prioritization process begins, as sometimes there are too many outcomes. How many is too many? While there isn't a magic number, there are practical considerations: if the same outcome is listed under more than one target audience, then having more outcomes may be fine; if there are different outcomes for all the target audiences, then having fewer outcomes is wise. For example, if there are three target audiences and five outcomes for each, that is fifteen outcomes overall! While all individual outcomes listed may be realistic to achieve, when there are fifteen distinct outcomes, the museum may not have the resources (staff time and dollars) to expend toward achieving all of them. When there are too many outcomes, staff and their resources are spread thin, reducing the chances of achieving the museum's intended impact, thereby defying the purpose of intentional practice. (Remember the core belief, "less is more" from chapter 3?)

Reducing the number of outcomes per audience is a two-step prioritization process, as shown in textbox 5.4, Prioritizing Outcomes in Two Steps.

In summary, outcome-based thinking has several layers.

Textbox: 5.4.
Exercise: Prioritizing Outcomes in Two Steps

Step 1: Write outcomes on a large sheet of paper and ask all participants to consider these questions and then vote independently by marking their top-three outcomes:

- Which outcomes are most important to achieve *(for you, for target audiences, for funders, for stakeholders)*?
- Which outcomes are most realistic to achieve, given what you know about your target audiences?
- Which outcomes most strongly align with and support the draft impact statement?
- Which outcomes are most realistic to achieve, given the museum's offerings?
- Which outcome(s) might be a prerequisite to achieving others, suggesting a continuum of achievement?
- Which outcomes might be more realistic to achieve in the future (giving the museum time to plan and implement new programs)?

Step 2: Review voting results together and select the top-three outcomes. If three feels like too few, add the fourth-most-selected outcome to the final list.

LAYERS TO OUTCOME-BASED THINKING

Identifying intended outcomes
Clarifying intended outcomes
Critiquing outcomes
Prioritizing outcomes
Determining whether the outcomes are on a continuum of
    achievement
Identifying indicators as evidence for achievement of outcomes

The layers in outcome-based thinking lead up to identifying indicators. Indicators, which are evidence for achievement of outcomes, are discussed in the next section—about evaluation—because indicators are necessary for evaluation projects.

Exercises for Planning Basic Audience Research and Impact Evaluation (Core Team)

Conducting basic audience research is usually the first step a museum takes to understand its audiences. If a subsequent audience study is done several years *after* completing the intentional-planning process, and the museum has instituted changes in how it carries out its work—based on the Impact Framework—the study can be framed as an impact evaluation. Both study types—basic audience research and impact evaluation—require careful preparation and planning; each are discussed below.

Planning for Basic Audience Research

Museums new to studying audiences may want to start by conducting basic audience research. There are no hard-and-fast rules about the best time to conduct it, other than realizing that having some audience information is better than having no information. The timing of the study will determine what and how questions are asked. Regardless of when a study is conducted, the data within a study will be tremendously valuable, and like evaluation, conducting audience research should occur at regular intervals.

With the advent of online survey platforms, administering a study has become remarkably easy. The ease of *administering* a survey, however, shouldn't be confused with *the challenge of designing a study that produces useful information*. The most important part of an audience research process is the planning stage, as without a sound plan, strong rationale, well-designed instrument, and thorough plan for analysis, results might not be reliable and actionable, leaving staff in the same place they were at before the study.[3] The first question to address is the study's purpose, which will emerge from discussing responses to a series of probing questions about the museum's need for a study, including what the museum hopes the study will provide and how it might use the information (see textbox 5.5, Determining the Purpose of Audience Research: Questions to Discuss).

The conversation that emerges from discussing the questions in textbox 5.5 will clarify the study's purpose, which then becomes the platform for making other research-related decisions. The task of writing the questions, which is often the first thing that people want to do, takes place later in the planning process, after thinking through other planning considerations applicable to conducting an audience study. Once the purpose of the study is established, you are ready to begin planning the study using the questions in textbox 5.6, Planning Audience Research: Questions to Discuss.

Textbox 5.5.
Determining the Purpose of Audience Research: Questions to Discuss

First consider these questions:
1. What are your expectations for this audience study? Specifically, what information do you want it to provide?
2. What do you *want* to know about your visitors? What is *essential* to know about your visitors?

Then ensure that what you want to know is what you need to know:
3. What are the *top-three* essential issues/questions that *must* be explored in this study?
4. What are the three *secondary* issues/questions that also must be explored in this study?

Then visualize applying information that the study would gather:
5. How do you intend to use the information that the study generates?
6. How will this information help you make decisions regarding your work?
7. What specific actions might you do differently once you have this information?
8. What is the plan of action for changing how you do your work, based on the information the study might generate?

Then step back and reclarify the purpose and objectives of the study:
9. Given the scope and depth of what has been discussed, how would you describe the specific purpose of this study (your response will explain *why* you must do this study)?
10. What are the specific objectives of the study?

Textbox 5.6.
Planning Audience Research: Questions to Discuss

1. **Who is the target study population?** Strongly consider studying the target populations identified in the Impact Framework.

2. **What is the most appropriate data collection method(s)/instrument type(s)?** This is determined by the type of information the museum needs to know. See questions in textbox 5.5, Determining the Purpose of Audience Research: Questions to Discuss.

3. **What is the sample size?** This depends on whether the museum will be using a qualitative approach, quantitative approach, or both; if the study will be quantitative, sample size depends on the museum's annual visitation, details regarding what the museum needs to know, the number of subsamples you will create from the larger sample (e.g., how many age groupings), the depth of the statistical analysis, and the sampling strategy.

4. **What is the plan for systematically collecting data?**

5. **What is the analysis strategy?** This depends on whether the data will be qualitative, quantitative, or both.

6. **What is the reporting strategy? Do you need more than one report to accommodate different stakeholders?**

7. **What is your plan for pretesting the instrument(s)?** Results from the pretest might require changing the instrument design and some of the individual questions.

8. **How will you execute the study?** Who will collect the data? Who will process the data? Who will analyze the data? Who will prepare the report?

9. **What is the data collection schedule?**

10. **How much will the study cost?** Do we have the resources or do we have to raise funds?

When planning and executing research and evaluation, there are questions you ask yourself, and there are questions you ask visitors. The two textboxes (5.5 Determining the Purpose of Audience Research: Questions to Discuss, and 5.6 Planning Audience Research: Questions to Discuss) identify the questions you will ask yourself. Writing questions in the right way for visitors—especially if they are standardized—is different and requires know-how, as sometimes gathering useful and actionable information can be challenging. You will want to carefully construct your questions so they are unbiased and reliable, meaning, respondents consistently understand precisely what the museum is asking. A pretest will reveal which questions you may need to rework. Your goal: plan and design a study that yields valid and actionable information. Clarifying what you need to know by discussing questions about the study's purpose and making sure the information is worth knowing—before writing a single question—will help produce relevant and useful information (refer to note no. 3 for resources).

Planning for a Museum Impact Study

An impact study is a serious endeavor and requires deep commitment to explore the museum's successes and shortcomings—all in the spirit of professional learning and organizational improvement. From an intentional-practice perspective, a museum that is ready to conduct an impact study is a museum that has an Impact Framework and carries out its daily and strategic work using it as a guidepost. Some museums may have to change some actions because their previous work was not aligned to the impact statement and envisioned outcomes. The planning questions posed in the previous section are also relevant for planning an impact study. Like any evaluation or basic audience research study, without a solid, well-conceptualized, airtight plan, the study has little chance of delivering reliable information. The onus is on the museum and researchers to ensure that every step has been taken to produce a high-quality study that informs and guides the museum in its impact-driven work.

Developing Indicators (Workshop)

The Impact Framework can serve as a platform for planning an impact study *and* analyzing its results. The challenges of planning and conducting an impact study were noted in chapter 3. To clarify, an impact study looks for evidence that the intended impact, as stated in the framework, has been achieved. The envisioned outcomes describe the hoped-for impact, and the indicators represent desired evidence that target audiences displayed those behaviors and had those experiences. Indicators describe what impact success looks and sounds like. They have specific characteristics and criteria (shown below) that staff can consider as they write them. Studying some examples will help as well (some Impact Frameworks in appendix A include indicators). See the exercise in textbox 5.7, Developing Indicators, when you are ready.

CHARACTERISTICS OF INDICATORS

- They are demonstrated by people, preferably those in the target populations.
- They describe the evidence that an outcome has been achieved.
- They are detectable, observable, and measurable (you know it when you see it, hear it, or read it in someone's written response).

- They are specific to the audience and context in which they occurred.
- They may manifest immediately, shortly after, or long after an experience.

Textbox 5.7.
Exercise: Developing Indicators

For all prioritized outcomes per target audiences, discuss these two questions and identify three to six indicators through rapid brainstorming.

1. What would someone from the target audience need to do, say, or write to demonstrate achievement of the outcome? In other words, what is the evidence that would confirm outcome achievement?
2. Will the indicators manifest immediately, shortly after the experience, or long after the experience?

After facilitating the workshop for developing indicators, it makes sense to review the impact statement and outcomes because clarifying what the museum wants to achieve is ongoing, affected by the changing internal and external environments and circumstances. Continuing to ask questions of yourself and others is paramount and necessary in intentional practice. When reflection becomes a regular activity, staff will begin to feel comfortable asking questions about past work and moving between having faith in past work and wondering if there is more clarity to be found. Learning is the goal for museum professionals, and continuous reflection is one way to get there. Reflection will lead to periodic updating of work, including the Impact Framework; changing the Impact Framework is a demonstration of the organization's learning and advancement.

Exercises for Reflection (Workshop)

Reflection in intentional practice is designed to prompt learning from evaluation and research data as well as from one's practice. The context of any reflection and the individuals who will be reflecting determine the reflection experience. For example, when people are asked the same questions twice, a month apart, hopefully what they hear the second time will be different from what they heard the first time because they are in a different place. In this way, learning spirals upward and leads to a higher level of planning on the Cycle of Intentional Practice. That description of experiential learning echoes David Kolb's Experiential Learning Cycle (see figure 5.1). Kolb, who wrote about experiential learning and learning styles, identified four stages of experiential learning; reflection is among them.

KOLB'S FOUR STAGES OF EXPERIENTIAL LEARNING

1. **Concrete experience** is when the person, team, or organization is given a task to do; Kolb believes that one must do something to learn effectively.

2. **Reflective observation** is about stepping back and answering questions about what was done to support thinking about what was done.

3. **Abstract conceptualization** is about interpreting the events and making sense of them. People, teams, or organizations can compare and contrast experiences and information as well as contemplate previous knowledge—whether from previous experiences or materials they have read.

4. **Active experimentation** is about determining how new learning will be put into practice by identifying what will be done first, second, third, and so on. The act of creating a concrete plan is part of learning, as decision making allows staff to process and imagine applying new ideas.[4]

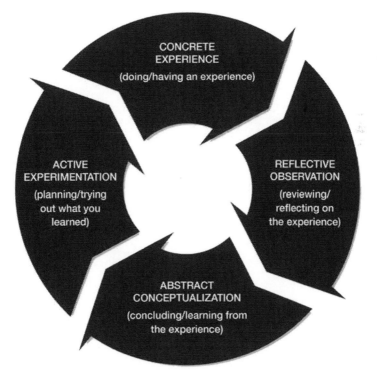

Figure 5.1. Experiential Learning Cycle.
Adapted from David Kolb's Experiential Learning Cycle.

In intentional practice, all planning projects allocate time for reflection, and so do all evaluation and research projects. Reflections are designed to help museum staff process the information generated from a study or discuss a current challenge or lingering question. Like all exercises in intentional practice, reflection exercises use inquiry, and they strive to touch on Kolb's four stages listed above. When reflecting on evaluation data, obviously the first step is to present results from the study (this represents the action that was taken—Kolb's first stage). Intentionally, staff are presented with layered questions, moving from easy-to-answer questions to more complex questions (in layers 1 to 3)—similar to how one might organize questions in a visitor interview guide. The questions are designed to incite interest and encourage participation in the reflection process. The exercise in textbox 5.8, Reflecting on Data: Four Layers, includes sample reflection questions presented in four layers. The first three layers are explored in one or more workshops usually after a presentation of evaluation or audience study results, and the fourth layer, the project's final reflection, is conducted in a meeting with the core team.[5]

Reflection, if done regularly and collaboratively, should come to be known as a safe time for exploring past actions and their consequences without judgment. Reflection can also invite staff to practice and hone their question-asking skills, as asking the right question at the right time and in the right way will promote productive rather than destructive conversations.[6] Unfortunately, some questions can come across as offputting to some because they are heard as accusatory or critical rather than exploratory or curious. Questions can be crafted to collect new information, support dialogue, promote analytical thinking, and provide a strategy for processing information and past experiences. Applying humility and warmth when asking a question will generate positive results during reflection and when addressing the next quadrant in the cycle—alignment.

Textbox 5.8.
Exercise: Reflecting on Data: Four Layers

Layer 1
- What data were most surprising?
- Which results did not meet your intentions and aspirations?
- What data felt most rewarding?
- What is the one result or takeaway that will stay with you as you work on future projects?

Layer 2
- Which results *most resonate* with you and your work?
- Which results *support your assumptions* about visitors?
- Which results *challenge your assumptions* about visitors?
- Which results are *most actionable* (e.g., suggest a change you can make)?
- Which results are *most perplexing* (e.g., may require further discussion to interpret)?

Layer 3 has three clusters of questions for small groups to discuss using the Impact Framework and a summary of relevant results distributed during the workshop.

1. **Cluster A** focuses on outcomes that *were **not** achieved* by target audiences in the Impact Framework
2. **Cluster B** focuses on *low-achieving outcomes*
3. **Cluster C** focuses on the *impact statement*

Cluster A Questions:
- Which exhibition or program elements can be changed to improve the chances of achieving the museum's intended outcomes and impact on target audiences?
- How, if at all, might staff from across the institution collaborate to strengthen work and improve the chances of achieving intended outcomes and impact on target audiences?

Cluster B Question:
- What is the work plan for improving results of low-achieving outcomes?

Cluster C Questions:
- What aspects of the impact statement fall short, given the evaluation results? Why?
- What might you change in the impact statement (and outcomes) so the museum and its potential are better aligned with what is realistic to achieve without belittling your aspirations?
- What actions and practices might you change so the museum and its potential are better aligned with what is realistic to achieve without belittling your aspirations?

Layer 4 includes questions for the project's final reflection, which usually takes place with the core team. Questions ask team members to think about the project as a whole:
- What elements of the intentional-planning project/evaluation process might you duplicate for future use?
- What elements of the intentional-planning project/evaluation process might you change for future use?
- How, if at all, has this project affected you? How you work? The organization?

Exercises for Alignment (Workshop)

Alignment conversations involve deep reflection and honest dialogue. If the museum regularly reflects on its work, it will be prepared to discuss complicated and sometimes sensitive topics such as the relationship between the museum's public dimension (e.g., programs, initiatives, exhibitions, etc.) and the Impact Framework (mission, impact, distinct qualities, and outcomes on target audiences), as well as the challenges of pruning back existing programs and vetting potential programs. Questions in the exercises below are intended to promote thoughtful, unbiased conversation about the museum's work (e.g., programs, events, exhibitions, and initiatives) without fear of judgment.

There are many operational facets to an organization that also can be aligned, and they require a different alignment strategy—one that focuses on efficiency and operational effectiveness, for example. While impact, efficiency, and operational effectiveness are interrelated,[7] the alignment exercises presented here are designed to serve three purposes:

1. help the museum explore whether and how its public-dimension activities align with the Impact Framework
2. help the museum prune or change activities
3. help the museum vet new program ideas or requests from outside the museum

Aligning Museum Activities with the Impact Framework

Alignment in intentional practice helps a museum think about how it applies its processes, creates products, and uses its resources to achieve impact. It examines whether the products and processes the museum creates are impact-driven, accentuate the museum's distinct qualities, are the result of across-the-museum collaboration, and effectively use the museum's resources to achieve outcomes and intended impact on specified target audiences. Alignment from an intentional-practice perspective examines exhibitions, programs, and so on in the context of the Impact Framework. The exercise for aligning work with the Impact Framework can be found in textbox 5.9. Note that figure 5.2, Impact/Resource Grid, is part of the exercise.

Alignment conversations can be uncomfortable. Intentional practice assumes a museum's work and decisions are impact-driven, and if neither the work nor the decisions explicitly support achieving impact on target audiences, the museum is wasting its resources. Yes, impact-driven thinking is stringent, and yes, alignment conversations are complicated. As staff

Textbox 5.9
Exercise: Aligning Work with the Impact Framework

Instructions: Select exhibitions, programs, and so forth for small interdisciplinary groups to discuss and analyze using the categorized questions, shown below. Distribute the Impact Framework to ensure that staff discussions are appropriately focused. (An impact statement and target audiences are provided below, courtesy of the North Carolina Museum of Natural Sciences. See appendix A for the museum's complete Impact Framework.)

Impact Statement: Audiences appreciate the process that scientists use to study our world—past, present, and future—and contemplate the countless ways they can engage with others in the scientific enterprise.

Audiences: (1) adult learners; (2) middle-school-age children, and (3) academic community

Discussion Questions about Distinct Qualities:
- Does program X (or exhibition, initiative, etc.) accentuate two or more of the museum's distinct qualities? Which ones and in what ways?
- What will you change about program X to further accentuate the museum's distinct qualities?
- Are there other distinct qualities in the Impact Framework that program X could accentuate?

Discussion Questions about Impact and Outcomes:
- In the presence of data, what evidence is there that program X achieves impact on target audiences, as per the Impact Framework?
- In the absence of data, in what ways, if at all, do you believe program X achieves impact on target audiences, as per the Impact Framework? How do you know?
- Which program elements (e.g., interpretation, voice, interactive), if any, help audiences *appreciate the process that scientists use to study our world?* (Consider outcomes, too.)
- Which program elements, if any, help audiences *contemplate the countless ways they can engage with others in the scientific enterprise?* (Consider outcomes, too.)
- Which elements will you strengthen, and in what ways, to support achieving outcomes and greater impact on target audiences?

Discussion Questions about Staff Collaboration:
- Does program X encourage interdisciplinary collaboration across the museum? With whom and in what ways?
- How will you increase interdisciplinary collaboration across the museum to enrich program X and the experiences of target audiences?

(continued)

Textbox 5.9 *(continued)*

Discussion Questions about Resources:
- How much staff time and money does the museum expend to deliver program X?
- Where does program X belong on the Impact/Resource Grid? Place a mark on the Grid (refer to figure 5.2).

Summary Decision Questions:
- Based on your discussion, what actions will you take to strengthen alignment between program X and all elements that comprise the Impact Framework?
- Based on your discussion and where program X is plotted on the Impact/Resource Grid, is it necessary or prudent to reduce resource expenditures? If so, what actions will you take?

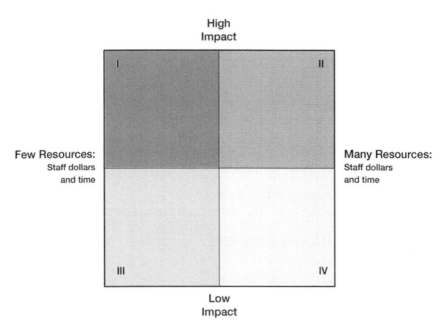

Figure 5.2.   Impact/Resource Grid for plotting program assessments for alignment exercises.

have these challenging conversations, maintain focus on your and your colleagues' passions, the museum's distinct qualities, and what is relevant to your target audiences. The Impact Framework and achieving impact are both works in progress. The framework will change over time, as it should, to reflect the museum's growth as an organization. Today's target audiences may be different from tomorrow's target audiences because the museum decides to prioritize one audience segment over another, which means that outcomes will also change. The objective of periodic alignment is to ensure staff are applying resources toward achieving impact with target audiences—whomever they may be at the time.

Pruning Museum Activities

The previous chapter noted the virtue of purposeful pruning. There may be a strong correlation between work that is most valuable and work that is most difficult to do! Pruning is certainly a valuable action with many benefits, and it is certainly hard to do. To support the pruning process, consider facilitating interdisciplinary discussions among staff using carefully worded, open-ended questions, as shown in textbox 5.10, Pruning or Changing Museum Activities.

The purpose behind pruning is to free up time so you can focus on programs that support the impact your museum wants to achieve. What might happen if staff had some freed-up time? Knowing the museum's intended impact, you might

- analyze other programs according to the museum's intended impact
- develop novel approaches to deepen and align visitors' experiences with the museum's intended impact
- follow your curiosity and experiment with a range of offerings as you consider the museum's intended impact

Both alignment exercises (textboxes 5.9 and 5.10) will help museums identify and strengthen work that supports the Impact Framework. Intentional practice means that all the activities a museum selects are ones that help it achieve its intended impact, and it also means that the museum will stop doing other activities because they do not help it achieve its intentions. Each exercise is challenging in its own way. A third challenge, discussed next, is learning to say no to opportunities that move the museum away from its central purpose—achieving intended impact among the target audiences it serves.

Textbox 5.10.
Exercise: Pruning or Changing Museum Activities

Instructions: Before getting started, select which programs, exhibitions, or other museum activities to analyze and assign one or two to each breakout group. Consider holding alignment sessions over several months for two reasons: the work is tiring, and you want to build an alignment routine as part of your intentional practice.

Discussion Questions about Audience:
- Is the primary audience for program X (or exhibition, initiative, etc.) one of the target audiences on the Impact Framework? If not, discuss ways to change the program so it is relevant to one of the target audiences.

Discussion Questions about Distinct Qualities:
- In what ways, if at all, does program X accentuate two or more of the museum's distinct qualities? If it does not accentuate two or more of the museum's distinct qualities, discuss ways to change the program so it does.

Discussion Questions about Impact and Outcomes:
- What evidence is there that program X achieves impact on target audiences, as per the Impact Framework?

Discussion Questions about Resources
- How much staff time and money does the museum expend to deliver program X?
- How many people receive the program?
- What is the dollar cost per person served?
- What depth of impact on target audiences does program X deliver?
- Discuss where to place program X on the Impact/Resource Grid. Place a mark on the grid (refer back to figure 5.2: Impact/Resource Grid).

Summary Decision: Based on your discussion and where you plotted program X on the Impact/Resource Grid, what will you do:
- Keep the program as is because it aligns with all parts of the Impact Framework?
- Change program X so it is for one or more of the target audiences in the Impact Framework?
- Change program X so it more strongly aligns with the museum's distinct qualities?
- Change the content and execution of program X so it achieves results as articulated in the Impact Framework?
- Change program X so it uses fewer resources (staff time and dollars)?
- Put program X on hiatus so you can overhaul it?
- Stop doing program X?

Vetting Potential Museum Activities

Learning to say no is a valuable life skill—one that is essential for survival. Maintaining focus on the impact the museum wants to achieve is also necessary if the museum is to move forward with its impact-driven work. Sometimes people want to say no to an opportunity but don't know quite how to do so. As such, another way to apply alignment thinking is to use the Impact Framework as a vetting tool—to *help* you say no (see textbox 5.11, Vetting Potential Opportunities).

The individual exercises in this suite of intentional-practice exercises can be adapted, altered, and revised to accommodate any museum's unique situation or particular problem that might arise. Posing questions is the primary strategy, and you can rewrite them to suit your needs. The platform for the exercises is the Cycle of Intentional Practice, which places impact at its center. Thus, if you alter the exercises and questions, they should maintain focus on the museum's primary purpose—achieving impact. Impact-driven work depends on the museum's leaders creating and

Textbox 5.11.
Exercise: Vetting Potential Opportunities

Instructions: Provide applicable context about potential opportunities to the small interdisciplinary groups, including whether the opportunities are from inside or outside the museum. Distribute any pertinent information and the Impact Framework to ensure that discussions are informed and focused.

Alignment Discussion Questions:
- Who are the primary audiences for this opportunity? Are any of them one of the target audiences in the Impact Framework?
- Does the opportunity accentuate any of the museum's distinct qualities?
- Is there any indication that this opportunity will result in experiences that support outcomes for target audiences and the museum's intended impact?
- Does the museum have adequate resources (staff time and dollars) to support this opportunity?

Summary Decision: Based on your discussion, what will you do?
- Say yes to the opportunity.
- Graciously decline, noting that the opportunity, while wonderful, doesn't quite align with the museum's current impact-driven work.

fostering a culture where all staff feel comfortable asking questions about their museum and their museum's decisions.

In 1990, Peter Senge wrote *The Fifth Discipline: The Art & Practice of The Learning Organization,* where he said: "Learning organizations [are] organizations where people continually expand their capacity to create the results they truly desire, where new and expansive patterns of thinking are nurtured, where collective aspiration is set free, and where people are continually learning to see the whole together."[8] On a micro level, an underlying goal of all of these exercises is to achieve clarity of thought and precision of action to help the museum spiral upward on the Cycle of Intentional Practice as the museum continues its impact-driven work. On a macro level, an underlying goal is to encourage new habits of thinking and working that pull disparate parts of the museum together into a unified whole that continually learns from its work. My hope is that your intentional-practice work inches you closer to Senge's idea of a learning organization.

Case Studies **6**

An identity would seem to be arrived at by the way in which the person faces and uses his experience.

—JAMES BALDWIN

INTENTIONAL PRACTICE AFFECTS museums and their staff in different ways, depending on needs, project goals, personal perspectives, and organizational cultures. And as such, people's intentional-practice experiences vary. The ten case studies that follow collectively illustrate the variety of paths that are possible in intentional practice. Even though every project has goals—end points we strive to meet—no one knows where we will land; no one knows what will transpire; and no one knows how people and projects will be affected. As a holistic approach to impact-based thinking and working, the purpose of intentional practice is to help museums find their soul, move staff members closer to it and the impact they hope to achieve on audiences, and continually apply what they have learned along the way.

These ten stories represent a diverse collection of experiences. Reading these stories, as told from the perspectives of those who experienced the process, lends a personal voice to intentional practice. The contributing organizations (and their authors) were invited to share their stories because of one particular unique quality and, in some cases, innovative quality that their project actualized in the context of intentional practice. Below I provide a preamble for the case studies, as I wanted to share what prompted me to invite the authors to chronicle their intentional-practice experience.

Why These Intentional Practice Stories?

Creative Discovery Museum, Chattanooga, Tennessee

The Creative Discovery Museum has a researcher on staff who, in collaboration with the firm RK&A, used the impact statement and outcomes to develop data collection instruments for an impact evaluation the museum will be implementing. Prior to working with RK&A on an intentional-planning project, the museum had already completed a Learning Framework—a document that expresses its core beliefs and values. Having an Impact Framework, with a clear statement of impact and supporting experience outcomes to guide evaluation planning, brings the museum closer to conducting an impact evaluation.

Exploration Place, Wichita, Kansas

Exploration Place applied intentional-planning processes to an exhibition and associated educational programming about flight. This case study accentuates the evaluation quadrant, including evaluation capacity building. Based on the impact-planning process that led to the development of an Impact Framework, the museum was starting to see the relationship between evaluation and planning for impact and outcomes. When the time came for RK&A to evaluate the educational programs, the staff wanted to participate in the process, given that they had determined the programs' outcomes and overall impact. RK&A and Exploration Place collaborated in two ways: they codeveloped a tool for formative program evaluation using the Impact Framework as a guide, and the museum would learn to conduct formative evaluation under RK&A's mentorship.

History Relevance, www.historyrelevance.com

History Relevance comprises history professionals interested in increasing the visibility, importance, and value of history and history-focused organizations, such as museums and historic houses. The team had productive planning sessions several years ago, with all agreeing they could achieve the ambitious intentions outlined in their Impact Framework. Eventually, the core group came to realize that it had taken on more than it could realistically achieve. Adjusting the Impact Framework to reflect reality was its only option. History Relevance's story shows respect for the "draft" nature of intentional practice and demonstrates the courage needed to reduce the actions in the Impact Framework two years after it was developed. Rarely does an organization make the deliberate decision to do less.

Mead Art Museum, Amherst College, Amherst, Massachusetts

The Mead, an art museum on a college campus, applied intentional planning to support developing a strategic plan that would guide the museum for the next five years. The intentional-planning sessions were inclusive, taking place with all museum staff, some advisory board members, and select college faculty and staff. This case study demonstrates what happens when a museum adopts another organization's ways of knowing so it could be a more effective collaborative partner for the benefit of students. The authors realized their collaborative efforts within the museum needed attention and will take the lessons they learned from this external collaboration back to the museum. They have identified the goal of moving from a model of partnership and cooperation to a model of substantial collaboration.

Museum of the City of New York, New York

The Frederick A. O. Schwarz Education Center at the Museum of the City of New York (MCNY) uses all the quadrants in the Cycle of Intentional Practice to improve its programs so it can maximize impact on students, teachers, and families. MCNY staff has learned that planning and evaluation are linked, and they value the clarification process associated with developing and honing outcomes—whether during planning or, again, during evaluation. As the museum educators examined observation results—that provided clues about how educators delivered programs—and students' written assessments as evidence of student learning and experiences, they saw how they could course-correct their work. Alignment is challenging, yet MCNY staff embraced the opportunity to advance their work and moved onto brainstorming ideas to improve what they do, which in turn, will affect students' experiences.

National Museum of Natural History, Washington, DC

A few years ago, the National Museum of Natural History opened Q?rius (pronounced "curious"), a learning lab with science tools and specimens. The Q?rius team and RK&A applied intentional-practice strategies to the summative evaluation of Q?rius. While this evaluation occurred at the end of the project's first iteration, you will read in the museum's case study that the Q?rius team developed the space by conducting mini-evaluations and reflecting on results. Team members carried this practice forward with data from the summative evaluation, and they continue to regularly collect data and reflect on and ask questions about their work. The *Q?rius* team's dedication to using evaluation and reflection to achieve the lab's goals and visitor experience outcomes continues to advance their education practice *and* intentional practice.

North Carolina Museum of Natural Sciences, Raleigh, North Carolina

The North Carolina Museum of Natural Sciences' Nature Research Center features laboratories where scientists work in public view and interactive exhibits in the adjacent public space. Staff participated in an intentional-planning process that involved developing an Impact Framework and fine-tuning outcomes in preparation for a formative evaluation and an alignment exercise. Using data from the evaluation, staff convened to work through a series of questions to determine whether their work was having the effect they intended to have among audiences and, if not, what might they change prior to the next formative evaluation. This honest commentary shares the struggles that a museum staff might have when asked to review their own and their colleagues' work without bias.

Philadelphia Museum of Art, Philadelphia, Pennsylvania

The education department at the Philadelphia Museum of Art took Sherlock, a successful curriculum for first-year medical students, and revised it for fifth and sixth graders. This case study demonstrates the iterative and "draft" nature of intentional practice and what happens when evaluation is used as a learning tool. An outcomes framework is always in draft form, and so is a curriculum, as it turns out. As museum educators reflected on evaluation results in the context of the outcomes framework, they discussed which activities were not aligned with the outcomes they had identified. In the spirit of advancing Sherlock's effectiveness and processing what they had learned through evaluation, they removed unproductive activities from the curriculum.

Whitney Museum of American Art, New York, New York

This case study describes the personal journey of a museum educator who was appointed chair of education at a crucial point in the museum's history. Her story, told with great humility, recounts her development as a leader and the education department's evolution into one of the nation's most respected museum education programs, supported by ten years of intentional planning, and transformed by a dramatic move to a new building and location. As her leadership skills continue to mature, the chair of education discovers she has a new platform and new opportunities to continually test and challenge her enormous capacity to lead.

The Wild Center, Tupper Lake, New York

The Wild Center opened its doors in 2006. With exhibits in place, staff spent the first decade creating and field-testing public programs. Among the many programs they created, perhaps the best known, is the Youth Climate Summit—now more than a decade old, recognized by the White House and represented at the Paris Climate Summit. The executive director wanted her staff to reflect on the successes and shortcomings of all their programs and apply what they learned to their exhibits to reenergize, strengthen, and align them to what the Wild Center had become over time. This top-down approach to exhibit development represented a new, impact-driven way of working. In addition to developing a plan for exhibit revitalization, the process also prompted staff to modify the mission statement so it, too, could reflect an evolved Wild Center.

A Practical Approach to Building Internal Evaluation Capacity

Creative Discovery Museum, Chattanooga, Tennessee
Shannon Johnson, Director of Exhibit Development and Evaluation, and
    Henry Schulson, Executive Director

For many years key staff at Creative Discovery Museum (CDM) wanted to evaluate our exhibits and programs in more meaningful ways. However, capacity was always a huge obstacle. In 2016, we were awarded an Institute of Museum and Library Services (IMLS) Museums for America grant that allowed us to strategically build our internal evaluation capacity and hire an evaluation coordinator for the three-year grant project. We wanted to create a consistent and sustainable evaluation process for assessing our educational impact with the goal of improving our exhibits and programs by making data-driven decisions. We also wanted to use the data to support our fundraising efforts.

When we launched our evaluation program, we discovered that we already had many of the building blocks in place, including mission, values, and vision statements and a learning framework. (A learning framework varies by museum, but it is "defined as the educational standards and/ or outcomes by which museums guide the development of exhibits and programs."[1]) These building blocks define who we are, whom we serve, and how we serve them. However, we also needed to define the desired impacts and outcomes that we wanted to have on our audiences for our in-house evaluator, which would enable her to design instruments and conduct meaningful and useable evaluations of our exhibits and programs.

We contracted with RK&A to help us achieve this goal. Working with RK&A, we developed the following impact statement: "Children and families engage in playful experiences that spark new passions, expand their curiosity, and deepen connections to their community and world." This statement was a critical component in developing a pragmatic evaluation program.

As a next step, we identified four exhibits and programs to evaluate. We selected projects that are critical to our strategic goals, address key audiences, could be executed in a timely manner with existing resources, and would help us build our evaluation capacity. They are (1) our teen volunteer program, which we think has a high impact on the teens involved, but we have never evaluated it; (2) the simple machines exhibit on our rooftop, which will change as part of an upcoming renovation; (3) the early childhood exhibit gallery, which we would like to expand in the upcoming renovation; and (4) school outreach programs for which donors are requesting additional evaluation results. These four projects also enabled us to develop and test a variety of evaluation tools, and we hope to use the evaluation results to generate additional financial support for these exhibits and programs.

For the four projects, CDM and RK&A developed audience outcomes and indicators and an evaluation plan based on the Impact Framework. As part of the evaluation plan we also determined the purpose of the study and how we would use the data. Our evaluation coordinator is developing evaluation instruments for all of these projects, and at the time of writing this case study has begun collecting data for two of them and will complete all the projects in 2019.

Developing the impact statement and having an evaluator on staff served as a catalyst for other evaluation projects. We have become more nimble in how we develop and actuate our evaluation projects and make sure that evaluation projects align with our impact statement and with each other. For example, we have aligned our school program evaluation surveys to reflect the outcomes outlined in the Impact Framework for our guided school group audience. Instead of having different evaluations for each school program (for example, outreach lessons that occur in school classrooms, tours of the museum exhibits, and science workshops in museum classrooms), we now ask attendees to all school programs the same questions—ones that reflect our intended impact. For example, "To what extent did you see your class engage in trial-and-error problem solving?" Aligning goals for this intentional audience moves us closer to our museum-wide goals. One unexpected outcome is that museum employees that give tours report that they have changed the way they introduce exhibits in order to better achieve the museum's intended impact.

In another example, our events geared for young adults, Drink and Discover, also illustrate how evaluation is helping us in unexpected ways. Many of these young adults visited the museum as children. While they do not yet have children of their own, they are excited to return because it brings back wonderful memories. Also, they want to support and stay connected to the museum. We are beginning to develop evaluation tools to gain a better understanding of how we can strengthen our relationship with this group for fundraising purposes. Also, we believe that this group may provide us with the opportunity to explore the impact that the museum had on the lives of children who are now adults.

As we had hoped, the application of museum-wide evaluation capacity building can be seen in most departments, including marketing, grant writing, exhibit renovations, and capital campaign fundraising. In a third example, CDM staff recently went through a branding process with a local advertising and marketing firm. Our learning framework and Impact Framework were key in informing the process and developing the brand-positioning statement. Going into this process, we had not considered how much the firm would use these documents. In regard to grant writing, we are starting to include our evaluator in conversations about proposals. She works closely with our grant writers to develop evaluation plans that many funding agencies require. Although a goal for our capacity building was using the data we collected to make a case for support, we had not fully realized the role that the evaluation coordinator could play in our grant-writing process. Additionally, evaluation data will influence our decision making during the exhibit development phase of our renovation project. Finally, the impact statement and evaluation results will help inform our case for support during the capital campaign launching in fall 2018.

Our pragmatic approach to how we use our Impact Framework has deepened our intentional practice in expected and unexpected ways. As hoped, we are expanding CDM's internal capacity to improve our exhibits and programs through data-driven decisions, which in turn has strengthened our fundraising potential.

Strengthening Intentional Practices through Collaboration
Exploration Place, Wichita, Kansas
Cathy Sigmond, Research Associate, RK&A; and Laurel Zhang, Director of Special Projects, Exploration Place

In 2016, after four years of planning and fundraising, Exploration Place (EP) received a substantial grant from the National Aeronautics and Space Administration (NASA) that enabled the museum to bring *Design Build Fly*—a future-focused aviation exhibition and education project—to life. Wichita, Kansas—the home of Exploration Place—is widely considered the Air Capital of the World. As such, the museum hoped that the *Design Build Fly* exhibition and associated education programs would not only showcase the science of aviation but also reinvigorate community pride in Wichita's aviation industry and inspire the next generation of youth to consider careers in aviation.

RK&A and EP collaborated on planning and evaluating *Design Build Fly*'s exhibition and education programs. The process started with a series of workshops designed to help Exploration Place articulate the impact it hoped the project would have on four target audiences. A variety of stakeholders were invited to participate, including professionals from aviation, formal education, and museums to collectively answer the questions "To what end are we doing this project?" and "What result are we hoping to achieve among audiences with the *Design Build Fly* project?" The workshops resulted in a comprehensive Impact Framework that guided our collaboration through all aspects of *Design Build Fly*, including exhibition development and design, program development, and evaluation.

Embracing Evaluation
The original plan called for RK&A to conduct formative evaluations of exhibit components and contract with a local consultant to evaluate the education programs. After RK&A evaluated the exhibit components, circumstances changed, as often happens in long-term projects, serendipitously presenting us with an opportunity to rethink our origi-

nal approach to program evaluation. We had planned to have a local contractor evaluate the education programs, which made sense logistically, but now that RK&A was fully involved in the project, this idea no longer felt comfortable to us, and Exploration Place did not want to be distanced from the evaluation. Instead, we decided to collaborate to develop a tool for formative program evaluation based on the Impact Framework and that Exploration Place would learn how to use the tool and conduct formative evaluation under RK&A's mentorship. We immediately saw value in and were excited about this shift in approach as it would allow EP staff to deepen its understanding of evaluation methods, practice collecting data, learn to apply evaluation results to their program development work, and most important, better understand how outcomes, as described in the Impact Framework, support evaluation planning and design.

Designing an Impact-Driven Evaluation Strategy

Over the course of a few weeks, RK&A worked closely with a small team of EP staff to create a formative evaluation tool based on the Impact Framework. The tool needed to accomplish a few goals:

1. It had to be general enough so it could be used to evaluate any of the fifteen *Design Build Fly* programs.
2. It needed to allow staff to capture unique aspects of individual *Design Build Fly* programs that might require adjustment.
3. It needed to pair data collection methods with explicit opportunities for reflection. That is, the tool needed to allow staff to practice data collection strategies, like observation, and have built-in, explicit prompts to remind staff to think critically about how the data tied to the larger vision for *Design Build Fly* as articulated in the Impact Framework.

To that end, RK&A designed a two-sided guide that paired observation with reflection. One side focused on program logistics (e.g., were there enough materials for attendees?) and the other on how the observed program aligned with the audience outcomes from the Impact Framework. In accordance with the two-sided aspect of the tool, there was space for EP staff to take notes on their observations (i.e., record data) and reflect on the meaning of that data for program improvement (see table 6.1).

Table 6.1. Program Observation/Reflection Tool.

EXPLORATION PLACE PROGRAM OBSERVATION/REFLECTION GUIDE	Data Collector: _____

1. PROGRAM CHARACTERISTICS

Program name	Date & Time
Name of facilitators	# of Program Attendees
Description of attendees (e.g., age, group size, etc.)	

2. PROGRAM OPERATIONS

CHARACTERISTIC	RATING	OBSERVATIONS (During/Immediately after)	RECOMMENDATIONS (After program)
	Weak　　　　　Strong 1　2　3　4　5　6　7		
Preparation/Materials ■ Could attendees use materials as instructed? ■ Did attendees use materials as instructed? ■ Was facilitator prepared? ■ Did facilitator present on time? ■ Were the supplies organized? ■ Were there enough materials for attendees?			

Facilitation/Activity ■ Were instructions clear and concise? ■ Was facilitator enthusiastic, friendly, and open? ■ Did students display positive participation through body language or verbal expression? ■ Was facilitator attentive to questions/perceptive of confusion among attendees?	Weak Strong 1 2 3 4 5 6 7	
Closing/Wrap-up ■ Did facilitator provide closing comments? ■ Did attendees have time to complete the activity as intended before closing? ■ Did facilitator thank attendees for coming/actively participating?	Weak Strong 1 2 3 4 5 6 7	

3. OUTCOMES

OUTCOME ***See impact framework for description of achievement**	RATING	OBSERVATION	RECOMMENDATIONS (After program)
Facilitators/activities help attendees **broaden their understanding of the aviation industry.**	Weak Strong 1 2 3 4 5 6 7		

(continued)

Table 6.1. *(continued)*

OUTCOME *See impact framework for description of achievement	RATING	OBSERVATION	RECOMMENDATIONS (After program)
Facilitators/activities help attendees **broaden their understanding of how engineering and manufacturing processes are integrated to create a functioning aircraft.**	Weak Strong 1 2 3 4 5 6 7		
Facilitators/activities help attendees **experience wonder and delight at the scope and scale of aviation objects, concepts, and activities presented.**	Weak Strong 1 2 3 4 5 6 7		
Facilitators/activities help attendees **broaden knowledge, awareness, and understanding of the diverse STEM skills needed in the aviation industry.**	Weak Strong 1 2 3 4 5 6 7		
Facilitators/activities help attendees **recognize the importance of the aviation industry to the Wichita community.**	Weak Strong 1 2 3 4 5 6 7		

Once the tool was drafted and tested, RK&A led a professional-development webinar for a larger team of Exploration Place staff to provide an overview of basic evaluation methods and to train them to use the tool. After the workshops, Exploration Place staff members from a variety of museum departments including education, visitor services, and marketing and communications conducted dozens of observations of all *Design Build Fly* programs. To ensure staff would reflect on the data through the lens of the Impact Framework, RK&A staff facilitated periodic 30-minute mentoring phone calls with EP staff members who had conducted observations. The calls provided museum staff with an opportunity to ask questions about the data collection process and discuss how their observations over time supported or did not support the outcomes outlined in the Impact Framework.

Throughout the mentoring process, RK&A reiterated that evaluation was about the relationship between the visitor and the program and that the overall goal of the observations was program improvement. During mentoring phone calls, RK&A maintained focus on the process as well as the depth and quality of written observations so that EP staff could begin to understand what the data were saying about visitors' program experiences. Individual museum staff felt comfortable asking questions about the tool in ways that were meaningful and useful to the individual, a boon to any organization with staff that have a range of experiences. As a result of the mentoring calls, EP staff honed their program evaluation skills.

Our Concluding Thoughts

Combining formative evaluation with a mentoring experience was invaluable for both collaborators. From EP's perspective, staff professional development maximized the value of evaluation dollars from the NASA grant while increasing EP's ability to evaluate other elements of its work. Staff are better able to observe the relationships between the visitor and program content and communicate findings from observations with colleagues to ensure clear and consistent delivery program delivery. The museum hopes to continue its evaluation and reflection practices and is excited to adapt the tool for use in program evaluations outside of *Design Build Fly*.

From RK&A's perspective, working with Exploration Place to develop the observation/reflection tool and mentor staff as they used it demonstrated the virtue of slowing down the evaluation process and isolating procedures in order to teach them. There is tremendous value for all when there are opportunities to reflect on the connection between evaluation results and the intended outcomes that were created during the planning phase because sometimes the impact articulated during planning feels like a faraway memory when work shifts to evaluation. This experience reminded RK&A of the importance of transparency throughout the entire evaluation process. Moving forward, RK&A will explicitly share how evaluation is intertwined with the contents of the Impact Framework and find ways to actively involve museum partners in both evaluation and reflection. This way, the vision of impact is continuously evolving from a place of deep, shared understanding of planning, evaluation, and intentional practice.

Crafting an Impact Statement to Reflect Relevance and the Value of History

Tim Grove, author, museum consultant, and founding member
    of History Relevance, www.historyrelevance.com

The story of the History Relevance (HR) initiative begins with a group of history practitioners who grew increasingly bothered by the continual emphasis of STEM (and then STEAM) in so many conversations at the expense of history. They recognized that people care about their family histories, support movies like *Lincoln*, and buy enough history books to put them on the bestseller lists. Yet their interest in the past is not reflected in society's priorities—evidenced by the disproportionate funds available for history education, historic preservation, and history museums. Those who study the past know the value of applying its lessons and of critical thinking and other skills that are part of the historical research process. They know that these skills are vital to a healthy democratic society.

Ultimately HR group members recognized that history does not enjoy the strong brand that STEM does and wondered, "How can we raise awareness of history's value in American society?" Without an official organization backing us and acknowledging that an effective national branding campaign would require a big budget, we began to look within our ranks to consider what the history field across the spectrum was doing to articulate its value to the outside. If the brand was weak, what could we do to change this? We started by exploring perceptions of history and turned to an American study from the 1990s showing that Americans thought of "history" as dates and names and rote memorization. It also confirmed that people value learning about the past, suggesting the problem wasn't the discipline but rather the way it is often taught. We decided early on that promoting the teaching of historical thinking skills is vital to changing perceptions of history.

We also looked at messages to see what the history field was failing to convey about history. As we continued thinking and exploring, the group quickly connected two core concepts—value and relevance. Something that is valuable is also relevant. The more relevant something is to a person's life, the more valuable it becomes. We realized that the history field was not doing enough to make a case for the relevance of history. What happened in the past affects where we are in the present. History is not only "nice" but necessary to a solid understanding of where we are as individuals and as a nation.

We addressed this void by producing a "Values of History" statement, crafted with help from practitioners across the history spectrum. We consulted with everyone from scholars to history students and teachers, hoping the process would result in a feeling of ownership by all. The resulting value statement of seven ways history is essential offers a unified language that articulates a strong message and can be adapted and used with many types of audiences (see table 2.3 [page 33] for the most recent Values of History statement). We decided to ask organizations to endorse the statement, with hopes that an endorsement would signify intended uses of the values. Organizations of all shapes and sizes have signed on, and the number continues to grow, with over two hundred to date.

While we initially wanted to change the world, we realized the enormity of that task, and we also struggled with a few basics, such as, who is HR's audience? and what did we ultimately want to achieve? To help us address these basic questions, we participated in an intentional-planning workshop in which Randi encouraged us to select three audience groups to which we would focus our work. We eventually settled on history organizations, K–20 education, and funders. The general public was missing from our list mainly because we changed our focus from trying to reach the public to empowering target audiences to work together to affect *their* collective audiences.

As we were working through audience selection, we never lost sight of the importance of relevance, the Values of History statements, and the importance of teaching historical thinking skills, as they are vital to changing perceptions of history. Therefore, all the intentional-planning exercises generated these top-of-mind ideas, and as such, any impact statement would embody these ideas, too, particularly historical thinking. The impact statement is "History organizations encourage the public to use historical thinking skills to actively engage with and address contemporary issues and to value history for its relevance to modern life."

Focusing our work with history organizations seemed like an obvious place to begin because all of us work with history organizations. Yet from the beginning, we attempted to include the entire history field, including scholars and academics, archivists, preservationists, and everyone along the spectrum. We acknowledged the wide gulf that exists between public historians and academic historians and knew that engaging the wider field could pose a challenge and would require a different strategy than if we narrowed our focus to history organizations.

Over time, as we reflected on and discussed the Impact Framework, we continued to hone it as well as reduce what we were trying to do. First, we had decided to focus mostly on history organizations, with some efforts on the K–20 audience. Funders would have to wait. Then we eventually realized that even those reduced goals were unrealistic. The deeper we worked with history organizations, the more work our interactions generated. We decided to put the K–20 efforts on hold, also, and to combine colleges and universities with the history organization audience.

Earlier, when we were focused on creating the values statement, we began to look for examples in the field where history organizations were measuring their impact on local communities and could support these efforts with strong data. We were surprised at the limited number we found and realized that the STEM brand is strong in part because funders require science organizations to carry out rigorous evaluation to demonstrate impact. Neither history organizations nor their funders place the same emphasis on collecting data to demonstrate impact. Thus, we are trying to find a way to correct this by creating tools so history organizations can develop metrics and begin to measure their impact. Our goal is to begin to build a national map that shows the history field's impact on society.

As HR's band of intrepid and passionate history practitioners (who are all volunteering their time to work on behalf of HR) moves forward, it continues to reshape, modify, and assess the scope of its large vision. What began as a desire to change the world's perception of history and create a strong history brand has shifted to a movement to rally the history field from within to be more intentional about its messages and to work to demonstrate relevance to a society that has begun to struggle even more with the need for critical thinking and an understanding of how past impacts present.

It Takes Two (or More) to Make a Thing Go Right: Collaboration as a Strategy for Impact

Mead Art Museum at Amherst College, Amherst, Massachusetts
Danielle Amodeo, Public Programs and Marketing Coordinator;
  Jocelyn Edens, Interim Assistant Museum Educator; and Eileen
  Smith, Financial and Administrative Assistant

Nestled at the center of Amherst College's campus, the Mead Art Museum houses an encyclopedic collection of more than 19,000 artworks and cultural artifacts and serves Amherst's academic community as well as the wider public of the Pioneer Valley. The Mead has ten full-time employees, each working overtime to meet core demands. Amherst College opened in 1821 to educate "indigent young men of piety and talents." In 1975 the college became coed. Within the last twenty years, the college has funded admissions policies prioritizing socioeconomic equity and more recently institutionalized support systems for students from underrepresented backgrounds while they are on campus. As the museum becomes more integrated into this diverse college community, we are faced with a new problem: without increasing budget and staff, how can our small team responsibly meet the needs of our audiences and prioritize inclusivity?

To help address this growing challenge, we invited museum and non-museum staff to participate in a collaborative intentional strategic-planning process. The objective: work with partners to identify what we do best, clarify our intended impact, and streamline our efforts to create the greatest impact for our audiences.

We see collaboration as the strongest pillar of the Mead's practice. We aim to nurture strong partnerships across campus, most meaningfully with the five newly founded Amherst College Resource Centers devoted to inclusivity and anti-oppression work on behalf of the college's new student body. With a commitment to learning from one another and sharing resources, the Mead and staff and students at the Resource Centers co-conceptualize projects that build mutual trust. Before we could collaborate, though, we had to show up for them: attend their programs, get to know their audiences, and become patrons of their spaces. The collaborative programs that emerged applied a model already at work in their sites (informal lunches that give students learning opportunities in nonintimidating formats). Our desire to adopt their priorities and ways of knowing made students and the centers comfortable enough to tell us what they need from the museum. The result: the Mead and the Resource Centers found common ground that makes collaboration possible.

The Mead invites featured artists into the physical spaces of the Resource Centers to engage with students who otherwise do not visit the Mead. At the suggestion of the Queer Resource Center (QRC), a center that affirms, celebrates, and supports the queer and transgender community at Amherst College, the Mead invited its first transgender guests to campus. Multimedia artist, photographer, and producer Zackary Drucker and gallery owner Tarrah von Lintel participated in a formal panel discussion with Mead director David E. Little and Resource Center education specialist Babyface Card. (The program coincided with the exhibition of a photographic series by Drucker and Rhys Ernst that depicts everyday trans life.) The QRC's mission and staff guided our conversations, kept the panel inclusive, and highlighted questions that mattered most to our audience.

The following day, instead of speaking in a museum lecture hall, Drucker and von Lintel sat in a circle with students, faculty, and staff within the bright purple walls of the QRC. The two ate sandwiches and spoke candidly about their current projects, what it was like to come out as trans, and how the art world responded. They answered questions and lingered at the QRC for more than two hours after the program's scheduled end time. The connections that emerged between guests and members of the Amherst community were genuine and affirming to all who participated.

This type of interaction between students and artists was possible only because we sought out and listened to experts in the field of queer identity, built a relationship of trust with campus partners, and worked behind the scenes to make it happen. The program was especially inspiring to us as museum staff because it created a space for an important dialogue about tough topics that we don't usually talk about as part of our art historical practice. We continued our strategic planning process with this program in mind. Our impact framework—the document that will become the platform for the strategic plan—now prioritizes integrating art and programming across campus in order to harness our assets in support of the everyday work of our collaborators.

We learned a lot from this one collaboration and wondered what we could apply to our work inside the museum. Looking forward, we will implement a working model across the entire museum based on trust and shared resources in the form of time, dollars, and expertise. This means moving from a model of partnership and cooperation to a model of substantial—and therefore difficult—collaboration. That is, we realized we need to create new patterns of working in the museum that are iterative and long-term, driven by common commitments toward sharing resources and rewards.[2] Our new objective: develop collaborative systems that foster two-way communication, build an atmosphere of respect for everyone's knowledge and lived experiences, and embrace change, iterative ideation, and risk as integral aspects of our creative process. We hope these systemic changes will enable collaboration across museum departments and institutional divides and facilitate our ability to best impact our audiences.

New York at Its Core: Intentional Development and Refinement of School Field Trips

Museum of the City of New York, New York
Franny Kent, Vice President of Education, MCNY; and Stephanie
    Downey, Director, RK&A

What makes New York, New York? This very question is at the heart of what the Museum of the City of New York (MCNY) does. MCNY connects the past, present, and future of the city through its work while presenting differing perspectives on issues related to New York. From 2007 to 2017, the museum implemented a modernization and expansion project that concluded with *New York at Its Core*, an exhibition that explores over four hundred years of the city's history and examines present-day conditions and future challenges of the city. With the opening of this new exhibition, the museum's Frederick A. O. Schwarz Education Center made plans to offer a new menu of field trips, educator programs, online lesson plans, and out-of-school-time programs. With generous funding from many private and public sources, including the Thompson Family Foundation and the Institute of Museum and Library Services, the museum was able to pilot our programs, including new 60-minute field trips for each of the three galleries that constitute the exhibition.

Applying Intentional-Practice Thinking

MCNY's museum educators have long recognized the importance of thinking deeply about program goals for students, teachers, and families as well as the importance of third-party evaluation. In 2007, after securing funding, Education Center staff had an opportunity to contract RK&A to evaluate three new field trips. That evaluation experience underscored the importance of being intentional from start to finish, although "intentional" was not part of our vocabulary at the time. We learned the importance of clarifying desired results for audiences, evaluating whether those results were achieved (and reflecting on why or why not), and realigning the work to better achieve those results. It became clear to staff that evaluation was of colossal importance to our growth and ability to be responsive to students' learning needs and styles.

In the decade since, MCNY educators have internalized the Cycle of Intentional Practice, using many techniques to reflect on and enhance existing and new field trips, including those affiliated with *New York at Its Core*. Thus, with the generous funding noted previously, MCNY and RK&A evaluated multiple facets of *New York at Its Core* programming: K–12 field trips, teacher experiences, and free online lesson plans. Although intentional practice informed all aspects of educational programming, this case study focuses on two specific elements of the field trips in the three *New York at Its Core* galleries—Port City, 1609–1898; World City, 1898–2012; and the Future City Lab.

For this work, MCNY focused on the evaluation quadrant in the Cycle of Intentional Practice; all full-time education staff participated in a planning workshop that explored the question "What impact do we want our field trips to have on students and teachers?" The workshop resulted in well-articulated outcomes, which we vetted and prioritized. In the end, we identified outcomes for students and teachers (this case study focuses on students only). We honed and refined the student outcomes to ensure they were measurable and observable.

For the Port City and World City field trips, student outcomes included these:

- Develop interpretive skills to read objects to understand the city's history
- Understand that New York City is shaped by a variety of perspectives

For the Future City Lab field trip, student outcomes included these:

- Understand that a city is shaped by choices and compromises
- Develop skills to use data to understand and solve problems
- Students think critically about their agency in shaping the future of New York City

RK&A used a mixed-methods approach that included observations of field trips (to see how well the program design supported outcomes) and rubric-scored student assessment (to determine whether students demonstrated these outcomes). Though MCNY offers the programs to all grade levels, RK&A targeted second to eighth grade for observations and fourth to eighth grade for student assessments to reduce the variables under consideration. Evaluation results revealed areas of strength and areas needing improvement (and for the purpose of this case study, we present select results only). For example, evaluation results for the Port City and World City field trips found that while the educators' use of open-ended questions was strong and consistent, other aspects of the program limited students' participation to cursory responses.

RK&A recommended that MCNY explore ways to increase student participation and elaboration of their responses and to identify strategies to nurture students' skills for reading objects in the object-rich galleries. Evaluation of the Future City Lab field trip found that the program was strong in drawing students' attention to the challenges of the city and trade-offs inherent in solutions; however, some educators' use of close-ended questions limited students' ability for active participation. Recommendations suggested MCNY focus less on data points, as students struggled to understand them, and add an activity to help students describe trade-offs inherent in solutions to the city's challenges.

Alignment

MCNY staff responded to the evaluation by strengthening alignment between the field trips' design and student outcomes. For example, the museum added a hands-on activity to Future City Lab to better support the two outcomes: "understand that a city is shaped by choices and compromises" and "think critically about their agency in shaping the future of New York City." This activity is meant to concretize student learning about trade-offs when designing solutions for problems around affordable housing, transportation infrastructure, and parks and open spaces. It provides tactile and visual aids to teach the pros and cons of possible solutions to the city's various challenges; promotes discussion and enhances students' abilities to debate the best and worst solutions to these problems; and prepares students to play the virtual games in the lab, which reinforce questions posed in the hands-on activity. The hands-on activity and virtual games work together to better equip students to discuss the questions that professionals ask themselves when making design decisions: Is the budget on target? How do the building materials and design affect the environment? How many people does the new design accommodate?

MCNY also significantly revised its staff training for the Port City and World City field trips to strengthen alignment between program design and the outcome to "develop interpretive skills to read objects to understand the city's history." To properly honor that, field trips offer object-based experiences, and museum educators meet every two to three months for an object-focused workshop and are required to research an object and briefly present beyond what is showcased in the exhibition. The presentations follow best pedagogical practices and are rich with discussion and Q&A that help staff consider different perspectives of a single object as well as how the objects relate to others displayed nearby. Curators are invited to participate and further enhance the content by adding information about the "journey of the object." These workshops, with concentrated analysis and discussion, help educators and curators develop a deeper understanding of the objects and collaborate with their colleagues while learning—an important part of intentional practice. These in-depth conversations prepare educators to have meaningful experiences with students in the galleries so they can address every school group's interests.

Conclusion

MCNY educators' intent is that programmatic changes and enhanced staff training will produce meaningful experiences for school audiences and achieve stated outcomes. With intentional planning and evaluation, and creating opportunities to reflect and align, the museum maximizes program improvement and its organizational evolution. Providing time and resources for these important steps sustains the museum's programs because staff builds in opportunities to continually consider audience impact, which changes over time. The Cycle of Intentional Practice instigates and celebrates periodic changes to programs to obtain optimal results for the museum and provides deeply satisfying experiences for school audiences.

Q?rius, The Coralyn W. Whitney Science Education Center: Where Intentional Practice Thrives

National Museum of Natural History, Washington, DC
Shari Rosenstein Werb, Director of Education and Outreach

The Smithsonian National Museum of Natural History (NMNH) is a dynamic scientific research institute with hundreds of scientists asking big questions about earth through the disciplines of anthropology, botany, entomology, vertebrate and invertebrate zoology, mineral sciences, and paleobiology. With this incredibly knowledgeable community and a 10,000-square-foot space set aside for education, the education department had a unique opportunity to create a new science learning center. We wanted to connect the museum's public audiences, especially ten- to eighteen-year-olds, to the museum's behind-the-scenes research by offering access to the scientific equipment that museum scientists and curators use to study the thousands of specimens and cultural objects that inspire their work and prompt their questions. We realized that a new learning center for the public could also function as a learning laboratory for staff; we were eager to experiment with new presentation and interpretation approaches, and we wanted to model scientific processes and practices and observe their effects. In the spirit of the museum's scientific research, we named the space Q?rius to embody a key attribute of our scientists, educators, and volunteers while evoking a quality we hoped to nurture among the public.

Early on, we established two audacious goals for Q?rius:

1. to inspire responsible citizens who are aware of current issues related to the natural and cultural world, understand their role in addressing those issues, and participate in experiences that inspire stewardship, conservation, and protection of natural and cultural diversity; and
2. to build new youth audiences and increase youth participation in a continuum of opportunities that inspire, nurture, and diversify the next generation of STEM professionals.

Adaptability—Our Design Principle

The success of Q?rius depended on strengthening our relationship with the science community and building a relationship with the teen community. We viewed both groups as stakeholders, co-owners, and, ultimately, active users. As such, we created a teen advisory committee and worked with nearly two hundred experts from across the museum to help us develop Q?rius. We often discussed the changing forces that surround us: seasonal shifts in visitation, rapid cultural changes, advances in understanding informal science learning, and the active and evolving scientific enterprise. We questioned the virtue of a fixed-design space amid a world of change and as a result, we introduced a core principle—adaptability. Pragmatically, this meant putting everything on wheels—tables, chairs, collection storage units, and activity elements. And if spaces and equipment would become adaptable, our professional practice needed to become flexible, too! We also created an access principle: we wanted to ensure that visitors would have physical and digital access to the museum's six-thousand-object collection and a smorgasbord of interactive, participatory, and engaging programs—some self-guided and others led by scientists, educators, and adult and teen volunteers. We also imagined a flexible "black box" theater space that could accommodate a range of needs—our own as well as those of interested scientific and cultural groups.

Reflection and Evaluation

Throughout the four years of developing Q?rius, we actively engaged in reflective practice by conducting research, experimenting, prototyping ideas, and collecting audience feedback. After opening, we were ready to conduct a formal evaluation. With so many new approaches and features, we wanted to understand the outcomes they produced—expected and un-expected—as well as identify areas to improve so we could continue learn-ing from our work. Our team wanted the evaluation to become part of the innovative culture of Q?rius by "balancing a systematic and defensible approach to data collection and analysis with demonstrating innovation in evaluation of audience engagement and impact," which was part of our initial request when we sought an evaluator. To this end, the evaluators facilitated a workshop with staff and stakeholders to clarify and define out-comes and notions of engagement. Their intent was to create engagement metrics, unique to Q?rius, to explore and measure science engagement among the target audience.

Even though we have a strong culture of reflection, we were taken aback by how challenging it was to clarify and define actual notions of en-gagement. Whom exactly was our target audience for the evaluation? And what were the intended results we wanted to see? Through considerable dialogue and reflection, ultimately, we agreed on a framework with two au-diences—youth (ten- to eighteen-year-olds not in school groups) and adults (visiting with youth)—and four outcomes. We wanted our audiences to

1. strengthen their personal connection to natural history research and the natural world through experiences with experts, researchers, and facilitators;
2. explore questions and curiosities by practicing the skills of natural history research;
3. value the opportunity to engage with authentic processes and tools and use objects of natural history research; and
4. increase their interest in the connection between natural history research and current environmental/social issues.

The evaluators used four evaluation strategies—timing and tracking observations, learning environment ethnographies, questionnaires, and in-terviews—and through their work we began to learn how our visitors were experiencing *Q?rius*. The final report showed that we were reaching our target audience (70 percent of visitors were ages ten to eighteen), and they were spending between 15 minutes and 2.3 hours engaged in a variety of experiences. We learned that this audience spent much of its time in Basecamp, the first space one encounters entering the space, and the most time in the Collections Zone, whose specimens captured visitors' attention.

Two of our four intended outcomes scored well on the matrix (see figure 6.1). Youth and adults were exploring questions by practicing skills of natural history research; in fact, 93 percent engaged with objects/specimens, tools, and scientific processes, and 61 percent recognized the importance of natural history research. Youth and adults demonstrated that they valued the opportunity to engage with natural history specimens using authentic processes and tools. They reported that their experience was memorable and enjoyable. The evaluation also identified two key areas that needed our focused attention: strengthening visitors' personal connection to natural history research and increasing their interest in the connections between natural history research and current environmental and social issues. These findings informed our future conversations and emerging practices.

Achievement of Two Outcomes Scored on 4-level Rubrics

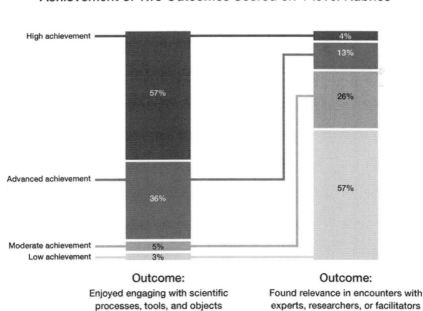

Figure 6.1.   Results showing four levels of achievement on two outcomes.

Galvanizing Our Intentional Practice

With Q*?rius* operating on a daily schedule and the results of the evaluation in hand, our team regrouped and enthusiastically returned to the Cycle of Intentional Practice, reflecting and planning out next steps. With so many visitors stopping in Basecamp, we realized that we needed to explicitly connect current science issues and research to people's lives. We needed to accentuate the relevance of natural history research, which meant we needed to invest in volunteer training to support our floor staff in facilitating conversations with visitors. We wanted visitors to connect to and find personal meaning in natural science and cultural research (without our lecturing, leading, or pressuring them to do so).

The evaluation prompted us to create an experience and engagement design "response" team that continues to lead departmental conversations and workshops about learning research and design thinking. We call our effort the "Q? method" approach to experience design. When developing experiences, staff and volunteers focus on collecting data about what visitors are doing, how they engage in the experiences, what is working, and what isn't. When something is not working, we study and revise it through the Q? method. For example, though we had tested an early microscope activity in Basecamp, after opening we observed visitors ignoring the activities and, instead, putting their hand under the microscope. We revised the activity to teach microscopy skills by studying one's own hand!

One of the most transformative experiences took place during the summer of 2017. In partnership with the New Zealand Embassy, we hosted a nine-day "Maori cultural immersion" in conjunction with a miniversion of its *Tuku Iho* exhibition. The adaptability of the space allowed Maori men and women to make the space their own; they demonstrated boat building, tattooing, and dancing, and led engaging conversations with thousands of visitors each day. When we decided to host this experience, we wanted to ensure that we would learn from the event and be able to use it as a model for future ones. We took notes, conducted observations, administered surveys, and wrote a report noting what we learned with recommendations for hosting such events in the future.

As a museum committed to science and the scientific method, it is fitting for our education team to adopt a scientific approach—or our own intentional practice—for designing innovative visitor learning experiences. In this way, we are learning with and from our visitors, and we, along with our programs and experience offerings, are continuing to evolve.

Coming to Terms with Alignment

North Carolina Museum of Natural Sciences, Raleigh, North Carolina
Wendy Lovelady, Senior Exhibit Developer

The founding director of the North Carolina Museum of Natural Sciences (NCMNS), H. H. Brimley, once said, "The building of a museum is a never-ending work. A finished museum is a dead museum, and such a one must deteriorate and begin to lose usefulness from the time its growth stops." True to that vision, NCMNS has continually expanded and improved its offerings over its long evolution as a museum—the newest of which is the Nature Research Center (NRC), an 80,000-square-foot "public laboratory" that offers participatory informal science experiences for visitors of all ages (see figure 6.2).

Thanks to a generous grant from the IMLS, the museum was able to undertake a multitiered evaluation study of the impact of the NRC's integrated science engagement experiences on visitors. We wanted to know the "unique values" that the NRC offered visitors. Emlyn Koster, the museum's current director, and John Falk wrote in "Maximizing the External Value of Museums" in 2007's *Curator: The Museum Journal,* "Historically, most museums have taken a 'one size fits all' approach that defines 'good' as 'serving the public' or attempting to meet the needs of

Figure 6.2.   Exterior of the Nature Research Center, North Carolina Museum of Natural Sciences, Raleigh, NC.
Courtesy of NCMNS.

all the individuals served by the institution,"[3] but that old paradigm was falling away. Koster and Falk recommended that museums first "define and measure the intended impact on the audience segment" and then "measure the net changes in institutional assets needed to serve the audience segment."[4] Museum staff hoped intentional planning would provide a unified vision for staff that would help us focus the work of the NRC toward a specific result. Our intent was that all staff would work together to address the problems inherent in operationalizing the bold idea of placing working research labs in an informal learning environment such as a museum.

Museum staff and stakeholders from all departments and stations participated in four workshops that addressed each of the following in turn:

- clarifying our intended impact
- developing outcomes and indicators for the evaluation that would follow
- assessing alignment between what we were doing (developing new video programs, interactives, carts, and two-way microphone programs with researchers—rather than educators or docents) and our intended impact
- developing a plan to strengthen alignment

Our work resulted in an Impact Framework, which became a foundation document for all subsequent discussions (for the complete Impact Framework, see table A.5 in appendix A). It included an impact statement ("Audiences appreciate the process that scientists use to study our world—past, present, and future—and contemplate the countless ways they can engage with others in the scientific enterprise") and specified three target audiences (adult lifelong learners, middle-school-age children, and the academic community). For each of the three audiences, we developed three to five outcomes and, for each outcome, several indicators—specific words or actions by visitors that would serve as evidence that the exhibit or program had achieved that outcome. The associated evaluation would allow us to find out whether reality was matching our intentions so we could clarify our way forward as "one museum."

Everyone felt great after the first two workshops. We had discussed our strengths and purpose, identified the qualities that made our organization unique, and brainstormed outcomes that we believed the public would experience from our programs and exhibits. Clearly it is easier to be upbeat when talking about how you excel and what you think you have done right. We also embraced discussions surrounding evaluation planning (where we would assess how well our programs and exhibits had achieved those lofty outcomes). We were all curious about what visitors would say. We planned prototypes and programs to test; we identified questions we wanted to explore; and we matched our intended outcomes to each element we wanted to evaluate.

As we entered the homestretch, we had reason to be optimistic, if cautiously so. But alignment is where any difficulty would reasonably begin because successful alignment might mean that some programs could be diminished or even cut, while others grew. In that situation, there would be winners and losers. The previous workshops had been analogous to studying and taking our final exam. These final workshops would be like getting our report card. How did we do? Did everything we tested get an A? In a room full of academics and professionals, no one was expecting *less* than a passing grade.

Indeed, nerves were jittery during the alignment workshop. We first heard a presentation on evaluation results, which were visualized on a heat map with dark colors indicating high-achieving outcomes and light colors indicating lower-achieving outcomes. It was the proverbial "report card" we were anticipating—and not every program was equally high achieving. Then we broke into small groups to discuss which outcomes supported our assumptions and which challenged them.

Following that discussion, we were then tasked with rating each program on an impact-resource grid with four quadrants that assessed resource use (dollars and time) and demonstrated impact. We wondered how to account for resources required to start a new initiative as opposed to the amount needed to do the work every day. Would a program that used many resources but offered little impact be inferior to one that offered high impact using few resources? Would new, resource-heavy initiatives not do as well on the impact-resource grid? One colleague asked for clarification, and we agreed to compare only the money and staff time used daily to perform the tasks, not new equipment and development costs associated with a component or program, as those dollars were already spent.

After the four working groups plotted their programs on the graph, we saw that almost everyone had placed their program or exhibit in the "high impact/few resources" quadrant of the grid and only one exhibit appeared in the "low impact/few resources" quadrant. Even though we knew no one was going to lose a job or a pet project as a result of this specific exercise, it was hard to be honest with ourselves. All were worried what it might say about us if we admitted to creating something that cost a lot and discovered that it delivered little in terms of impact. We left the workshop committed to further discussion, maybe refining the wording of some of those difficult-to-reach outcomes. Had we been too ambitious? Were we trying to do too much with available resources?

It was during the weeks and months following that final workshop that the strength of intentional practice became clear. The impact-planning workshops helped us to articulate what longtime and new staff from every section of the museum agreed was the desired and intended impact of the new Nature Research Center. Being able to clearly define visitor experience outcomes reminded us that *visitors* are our centering focus, not our individual initiatives or objectives.

A few months after the final workshop, Director Koster wanted to build consensus around the outcomes and key recommendations and to that end created a set of enhanced visitor experience task forces. These task forces, composed of cross-functional groups, focused on potential improvements in the museum's mission and its meaning, the standard of visitor hospitality and extent of interpretive services, and the value propositions for the three-aforementioned audiences. Through meetings and discussions, the task forces created a list of initiatives that would advance all aspects of the visitor experience, from improving wayfinding and seating to refining events, exhibitions, and programs. The Impact Framework provided the foundation for these discussions due to its clarifying and galvanizing message: start with the impact and outcomes you envision for visitors, then pursue actions that produce those outcomes. The six-month-long endeavor resulted in a list of specific improvements in museum facilities, visitor interactions, and programs.

Often change in museums is slow. What is a museum at its core but a group of people who want to conserve a collection, preserving it for future generations—as represented in our museum's nearly two-and-a-half-million specimens housed across multiple facilities, containing everything from fossils to freshwater mollusks? We like holding on to things. But a finished museum is a dead museum. Our visitors are an ever-changing landscape of real, complex individuals, living with us in a quickly changing world. Putting them at the center of our conversation means that change will always be a part of our framework; we have no choice.

Developing Curriculum with Intention

Philadelphia Museum of Art, Philadelphia, Pennsylvania
Barbara Bassett, The Constance Williams Curator of Education, School
& Teacher Program, and Amanda Krantz, Managing Director, RK&A

In spring 2017, the Division of Education at the Philadelphia Museum of Art (PMA) began to develop, pilot, and evaluate a new eight-part multiple-visit program for fifth and sixth graders called Sherlock. Named after the master of observation himself, the Sherlock program arose from an earlier collaborative research project of the PMA and the Perelman School of Medicine at the University of Pennsylvania. The project sought to discover whether looking at art through a laddered curriculum of looking and thinking routines could enhance first-year medical students' abilities in observation, creative and critical thinking, and communication and collaboration. When the results of the study showed statistically significant gains among students in the treatment group compared with the control group, PMA educators wondered if they could adapt the program's strategies to achieve similar results with middle-school students.

Though a curriculum model existed for the medical program, PMA educators knew they should adapt and refine it for fifth- and sixth-grade students. To develop the new curriculum, PMA educators identified two sets of partners they needed: (1) a core group of fifth- and sixth-grade classroom teachers, their students, and the art teacher from each school to help refine and pilot the curriculum and (2) a research team to serve as a thought partner through every step of Sherlock's development to support identifying clear and actionable outcomes for the program and continually assessing, reflecting, and refining the curriculum so it aligns with those outcomes. In this case study, the coauthors describe the collaborative planning and evaluation process around Sherlock through their respective lenses as an educator and evaluator.

Planning for Impact: Outcomes Workshop

In summer 2017, RK&A staff convened with PMA education staff to clarify student outcomes for the Sherlock program—outcomes describe the intended results of the program on students. Since the general framework for Sherlock existed (i.e., program for medical students), PMA educators had already identified a loose set of student outcomes and developed the curriculum around them. However, work together around the outcomes was twofold: (1) to modify the outcomes to fit fifth- and sixth-grade students and (2) then clarify precisely what these outcomes mean so all PMA educators and RK&A staff were operating from a shared understanding of Sherlock's intent. In the outcomes-development workshop, we started brainstorming outcomes as well as indicators (i.e., specific evidence of an outcome) in an open-ended way in response to these two questions: (1) What difference do you intend to make in the quality of life among students who participate in Sherlock? (2) How will students be different after the program? In addition to recording all that was shared by PMA educators in this brainstorming session, RK&A began identifying connections among ideas and then synthesizing the outcomes and indicators.

In the second half of the workshop and subsequently, RK&A staff and PMA educators worked together to prioritize, clarify, and hone the language of the outcomes and indicators that were developed. Precision is important in crafting outcomes and indicators as they can guide PMA's planning and RK&A's evaluation. After a few postworkshop exchanges, we had a draft outcomes framework—one that could guide the development of the pilot curriculum, yet everyone understood that it may be further refined after the formative evaluation. Shortly after development, we shared this draft framework with teachers participating in the pilot study because we wanted their feedback, and we wanted them to know the intentions of Sherlock. Figure 6.3 shows the outcomes framework from the summer; outcomes are identified in bold text in the gray boxes, while indicators or evidence of the outcomes are listed in bullets below the outcomes.

Piloting Sherlock: First Step in Aligning the Curriculum with Intended Outcomes

In fall 2017, the PMA piloted Sherlock with three classrooms—all of whose teachers and students had a relationship with the PMA, setting up a best-case scenario, which is not uncommon for formative evaluation (see figure 6.4). During the pilot, PMA educators followed a predetermined curriculum but remediated Sherlock along the way based on weekly reflections on their teaching experiences. Simultaneously, RK&A conducted a formative evaluation that included observations of the six museum visits that comprise the program. For RK&A, the outcomes framework served as the lens through which to evaluate the program to help PMA educators strengthen alignment between the curriculum with Sherlock's intended outcomes. RK&A shared evaluation results after every two program observations to encourage use of the findings. Evaluation results were shared at a PMA museum educators' weekly meeting devoted to reflecting on Sherlock and in written reports.

Reflecting on Sherlock: Second Step in Aligning the Curriculum with Intended Outcomes

In December 2017, after concluding the pilot study, RK&A facilitated a reflection workshop to help PMA educators apply the results of the formative evaluation to the Sherlock curriculum. Using the outcomes framework

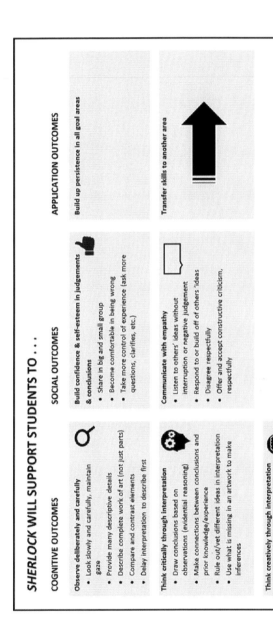

Figure 6.3.   First Outcomes Framework (before Reflection Workshop).

Figure 6.4.   Sherlock School Visit—St. Francis Xavier.
Photo by Tim Tiebout, courtesy Philadelphia Museum of Art.

as the lens for the work, RK&A staff and PMA educators discussed how the current program activities were supporting the outcomes (see table 6.2, which shows how RK&A perceived connections between activities and intended outcomes based on results from the formative evaluation). On their own, PMA educators had concluded that some of the activities were not meeting their needs and had started thinking about how to refine or replace curricular activities. Discussions during the workshop furthered this work to ensure that the remaining program activities supported the results intended for students. For example, based on PMA educators' conclusions and RK&A's recommendations, certain activities, such as Shapes, Lines and Colors and the Personal Response Tour, were removed from the curriculum because they did not adequately support the outcomes.

In addition to serving as a forum for discussing alignment between activities and outcomes, the reflection workshop provided an opportunity to revisit and edit the draft outcomes framework. With lessons learned from piloting Sherlock, PMA educators were able to further prioritize and clarify the outcomes. In comparing an early draft of the outcomes framework (refer to figure 6.3) to the version amended during the outcomes framework (see figure 6.5), you will notice that the outcomes themselves

Table 6.2. Matrix showing connections between program activities and visitor experience outcomes.

		OUTCOMES			
Visit #	Activity	Observe deliberately & carefully	Think critically through interpretation	Think creatively through interpretation	Build confidence & self-esteem in judgments & conclusions	Communicate with empathy
1	Compare & contrast	✓	✓		✓	
	Elaboration Game	✓	✓		✓	
2	Shapes, Lines & Colors	✓			✓	
	Back to Back Describe and Draw	✓				✓
3	See, Wonder, Connect	✓	✓	✓	✓	✓
	Before/After	✓	✓	✓	✓	
4	Observation/Interpretation	✓	✓		✓	
	Generating Questions	✓	✓	✓	✓	
5	Step Inside	✓	✓	✓	✓	
	Circle of Viewpoints	✓		✓	✓	✓
6	Creative Connections	✓	✓	✓	✓	✓
	Personal Response Tour	✓				✓

SHERLOCK WILL SUPPORT STUDENTS TO . . .

COGNITIVE OUTCOMES

Observe deliberately and carefully, maintain gaze
- Look slowly and carefully, maintain gaze
- Provide many descriptive details

Think critically through interpretation
- Use observations to support interpretation/inferences (evidential reasoning)
- Use prior knowledge/experience to support interpretations/inferences

Think creatively through interpretation
- Ask multiple questions relevant to observations
- Imagine a perspective other than own
- Imagine possibilities

SOCIAL OUTCOMES

Build confidence & self-esteem in judgements & conclusions
- Share in big and small group
- Become comfortable expressing opinions (even those opinions different from others)
- Take more control of experience (ask more questions, clarifies, etc.)

Communicate with empathy
- Listen to and respond respectfully to others' ideas
- Build on others' ideas
- Come to collaborative interpretation or solution

APPLICATION OUTCOMES

Build up persistence in all goal areas

Transfer skills to another area

Practice metacognition

Figure 6.5.   Second Outcomes Framework (after Reflection Workshop).

remained except for adding metacognition to acknowledge its presence as a recurring practice within Sherlock. We also reduced and edited the indicators listed in bullets below each outcome (e.g., "look slowly and carefully, maintain gaze" under the outcome "observe deliberately and carefully").

Summative Evaluation: Not the End but Next Step in a Continuous Feedback Loop

At the time of this writing, RK&A staff and PMA educators are preparing for a summative evaluation of the program, which will include interviewing participating teachers and assessing two student groups—a control group and a treatment group. The student assessment will mimic the Sherlock curriculum—that is, RK&A will analyze written responses to prompts about a work of art as well as an excerpt of text (to explore transfer of critical thinking skills from discussions about art to English Language Arts). While a summative evaluation is sometimes considered a final evaluation phase, PMA educators envision it as a next step in a constant feedback loop about Sherlock. PMA educators will use the framework and evaluation to help them maintain focus and exercise discipline as they make decisions about Sherlock, with the intent of improving it as it evolves.

You Can't Move Forward without Knowing Yourself: Reflecting on My Personal Journey

Kathryn A. Potts, Helena Rubinstein Chair of Education, Whitney Museum of American Art, New York, New York

When I was appointed Helena Rubinstein Chair of Education at the Whitney in 2008, I became the fifth director to take the reins of the department in ten years. As anyone who has worked in a cultural organization with senior management in a constant state of flux can attest, these leadership changes can create a chaotic, confusing, and erratic environment for both staff and audiences. In the case of the Whitney, each education director had come in with his or her own agenda. One director was an expert in distance learning, so she focused on web projects and partnerships with organizations in other states. Another director had curatorial interests and initiated public programs to introduce emerging artists to Whitney audiences. All the while, the department continued to offer a suite of legacy programs developed by a director who had left more than a decade earlier. Our overall program had grown to represent the combined vision of all those leaders, but it did not have a coherent strategy. Over the years, the education staff added new programs on top of old programs and now it was an unruly mess.

I was an internal hire, which presented some benefits and also considerable drawbacks. Having been at the Whitney for over a decade, I had deep knowledge of the museum and its collections and had built strong relationships with everyone on the education team. I also had been an understudy for the chair of education, serving twice as acting chair of the department and also working closely as the number two to the last of the string of directors. However, changing roles was more of a challenge than I'd anticipated. For the first time in my Whitney tenure, I had to represent the department as a member of the senior staff, communicate our work to external stakeholders, collaborate with colleagues across the museum, and lead my own team. Another challenge was my own background, which was strong in curatorial, public programs, and interpretation but significantly lacking in experience with school, youth, and family programs. What kind of education chair doesn't know how to give a school tour? That was me!

In the early days of my new leadership role, I was asked to describe our programs to a group of prospective foundation and government funders. I prepared a lengthy overview that detailed all of our many programs. About halfway through my presentation I realized that I was essentially reciting a long laundry list. I had fallen into the very trap my director Adam Weinberg loved to tease me about, saying that he "never met an educator who didn't like a program." We had programs galore, but I couldn't articulate the thinking and goals behind our work. I didn't have the language to speak intelligently about what we were doing or why we were doing it. Without that understanding, how could I map out a vision for the department? If I couldn't find the words, then how could I speak to my colleagues across the museum, our board, funders, external audiences, and even my own staff? If we didn't have a clear picture of what we were trying to achieve with our programs, how could we determine if they were successful?

Further complicating matters, there was another fast-evolving situation that demanded my immediate attention. The Whitney was in conversation with architect Renzo Piano to build a museum downtown in the Meatpacking District. My team and I would have a chance to become deeply involved in the planning of a new building—which was both tremendously exciting and totally terrifying. The internal weaknesses that had plagued my fundraising efforts would also hinder discussions about the new building. It's impossible to plan and design spaces if you don't have a good idea of what you want to accomplish and how you want to work in the future. I felt ill-equipped to answer any queries from the newly formed design team about our program requirements for the new education spaces.

With this building project on the horizon, I realized I needed help. The project was going to be a historic moment for the Whitney and for the department. There was already an exciting discussion under way about creating the Whitney's first-ever Education Center. The new project would be the perfect opportunity to refine and relaunch our education program. However, it was clear to me then that the department had to do some serious soul-searching and planning before jumping into conversations about square footage and building materials. One of my colleagues in the department put it this way: "You can't move forward without knowing yourself." And so began Whitney education's multiyear intentional planning process and the start of a personal and professional journey of self-discovery and leadership development.

The highlight of our first intentional planning workshop was an activity featured in the previous chapter, the "passion exercise." Randi and her colleague Ann-Clayton Everett (ACE) asked us to break into pairs to uncover the personal motivations behind our work as Whitney educators. The exercise starts with one partner asking the other, "What about your work is most important to you?" After an initial response, the follow-up question is always, "And why is that important?" and after that response, "And why is that important?" This line of questioning continues until the responses inevitably become quite personal and heartfelt. Through this deceptively simple exercise we collectively mined our reasons for working at the Whitney, in the field of museum education, with art, with artists, with audiences of all ages, and with underserved communities.

For many of us what emerged is that our personal motivations were based on strongly held principles about equity and social justice and a belief in the power of art to change and enrich people's lives. In the course of the group discussion that followed, partners shared what they learned about each other with the larger group. In this fashion, the exercise was an effective team-building tool for a department, but even more important, we learned that we collectively shared a set of underlying values. These values cut across all the department's different program areas: schools, families, public programs, community, and so on.

Our discovery that values were the underpinning of all our work was a significant breakthrough for my colleagues and me. Focusing on values rather than tactics or even outcomes brought authenticity to subsequent conversations. Instead of endlessly discussing "engagement" strategies, programming goals, or numbers of people served, we spent the next year working together to articulate a set of shared values and developing precise language to describe those values. Interestingly, we've seen our list of core values change as our own practice evolved and as the Whitney went through its own radical transformation and move downtown. Even now, more than ten years after we began our planning work, I find myself still tweaking the values.

While they are the conceptual structure on which all our work is based, the values aren't set in stone. By allowing them to be somewhat organic and flexible, the department can continue to respond to changing circumstances and conditions. Over time, these values enabled us to know ourselves better and speak with clarity to internal and external stakeholders. They have also helped us keep our programming on target and prevent the mission drift that we had experienced previously. We use them as a litmus test to critically examine everything we do and choose not to do. They have also been an effective way of onboarding new staff by being transparent about who we are and revealing our big-picture thinking and ideas behind the programs.

The next phase of our planning work was externally focused. Our discussion shifted to the larger context of our work within the Whitney. After revising our departmental mission statement to better reflect the work we had done with the values, we thought carefully about how we could better align our departmental work with the Whitney's overall institutional mission. For many years the department had defensively guarded its programmatic independence by working somewhat under the radar. This was one of the habits we had to break, and the only way to break it was to bring our colleagues across the institution into our planning conversations. This need for a collaborative approach was planted early in our intentional practice work when Randi and ACE urged us to engage departments and individuals we had deliberately avoided. There were some very difficult conversations, and yet they were necessary in order to more fully align our work with theirs and for them in turn to better understand our thinking. In the coming years, as our department grew strong and became a thought leader in the Whitney, we were reminded again not to get too far ahead without bringing our colleagues along; sometimes old habits are hard to break.

Over the ten years that I have been pursuing intentional practice, I learned how to be a leader. No one begins a new job knowing exactly how to perform it. Like so many people, I received on-the-job training, making plenty of mistakes along the way, but in the process discovering I loved being a director of education. In May 2015, the Whitney opened its doors downtown in a spectacular new building with a breathtaking display of American art. At the same time, Whitney education opened the Laurie M. Tisch Education Center and launched our artist-driven programming. I couldn't have been prouder. The intentional planning process was not easy, but we embraced the difficulty with enthusiasm. I know that the Whitney education department would not be where it is today without those efforts.

Acknowledgments

I would like to thank Adam D. Weinberg (Alice Pratt Brown Director of the Whitney) for his longtime support and friendship. Thank you to Connie Wolf, who hired me at the Whitney and was the former director of education who most inspired me. Finally, I want to acknowledge the Whitney colleagues who share the credit for all that we accomplished together: Anne Byrd, Eileen Farrell, Dina Helal, Megan Heuer, Dani Lencioni, Danielle Linzer, Heather Maxson, Hannah Swihart, Margie Weinstein, and Sasha Wortzel.

Using Impact-Driven Thinking to Strengthen Our Exhibits

The Wild Center, Tupper Lake, New York
Stephanie Ratcliffe, Executive Director

The Wild Center (TWC) is a natural history museum located in the Adirondacks of upstate New York. In addition to the Youth Climate Summit, TWC has three other signature programs: Visual Thinking Strategies for kindergarten to sixth graders; the Community Maple Project; and Building a Greener Adirondacks (BAGA). As a new organization it did not have protocols for developing programs; that is, nothing was weighing us down. Our culture encouraged staff to push beyond traditional program formats, which was wonderfully fruitful and dependent on an informal, iterative development process. We were comfortable trying out an idea, failing, and trying again.

We also have several indoor exhibition spaces, including live animals, and many of those spaces were determined long before the current staff arrived. We have never formally evaluated our exhibitions except for some iterative testing to improve individual components. Since opening day, the exhibit storyline and components have been essentially frozen in time. On the other hand, our programs have always moved us forward, so the question became, how can we modify the exhibits so they provide a cohesive visitor experience that lives the mission? TWC's ten-year anniversary prompted me to reflect on our collective work—programs and exhibits—and consider a different way to push our thinking about what we do.

TWC opened with a mission statement, but it did not have an impact statement. Even though we had evaluated a few of the grant-funded programs, we had never formally articulated outcomes for them. Intuitively I knew that the process of articulating an impact statement would help us clarify how we think about our programs. An impact statement would also guide us in future evaluations that would ultimately provide insight as to whether we were really succeeding in living our mission. Our commitment, enthusiasm, and risk-taking ethos had served our programs well, and we were ready to use some of that energy and ingenuity to reinvigorate our exhibits.

Looking Back to Create a Path Forward

Like many museums, we are immersed in the present. Once I chose to reflect on our work, I realized how much we had evolved over the last ten years and wondered if I could articulate what we had become. Were there synergies between our mission and evolved self? We had developed our programs based on pressing contemporary issues and our ability to connect with certain local groups in our rural community. Our programs and exhibits are *the* elements that comprise TWC experience, yet the two parts are distinctly different—in focus and content. It was time to unite them around our intent to achieve impact. I wanted staff to step back with me and reflect deeply on what we were accomplishing and then look across all programs to find any commonalities. Then I wanted us to explore programs and exhibits as a cohesive unit.

The process involved developing outcomes for individual programs and a draft impact statement for the whole organization (see table A.4. in appendix A for the complete Impact Framework). Finding the essence of each program and the language to articulate outcomes was difficult at times but in the end a gift. The impact statement grew from the outcomes as well as our passions and distinct qualities. The most surprising result of the process, though unexpected, was an eventual suggested revision to our mission statement. In hindsight, thinking about impact and mission as interactive makes a great deal of sense; our mission statement describes what we want to do, and our impact statement describes what we want to achieve from our work, as illustrated in textbox 6.1, TWC Mission and Impact Statements.

Textbox 6.1.
The Wild Center Mission and Impact Statements

Differences between the mission statements may appear subtle, but the tone, implicit assumptions, and scope expressed in the original statement were starting to feel like an ill-fitting shoe.

Original Mission Statement: Ignite an enduring passion for the Adirondacks where people and nature can thrive together and set an example for the world.

Revised Mission Statement: Ignite an enduring passion for nature, the Adirondacks, and its story—where people are working to thrive with nature and offer an example for the world.

Impact Statement: People deepen their connection to nature and consider their role in sustaining their natural world for future generations.

We used program outcomes, the impact statement, and discussion questions to explore how we typically implement our programs and whether we believed our actions and strategies supported the outcomes and impact statement. We had some evaluation data about a few programs to draw from, but mostly we had to rely on our insights and observations. I think all staff would say they were deeply uncomfortable at times, given the brutal honesty required to do this work. After a thorough debate, each small group was asked to plot on the resource-impact grid the programs under discussion and the floor exhibits. This exercise, humbling to all, prepared staff for the next exercise—an honest discussion about TWC's exhibits, using the impact statement as the lens. See figure 6.6 for where programs and exhibits fell on the grid.

Then we explored the indoor exhibit areas. In many ways, staff found it easier to think critically about the exhibits because most people were not at TWC when the exhibits were developed. Small groups of staff were assigned to explore a few exhibit areas using the two parts of the statement—(1) *People deepen their connection to nature* and (2) *consider their role in sustaining their natural world for future generations*. Groups had leeway: they could vote to remove an exhibit (if it did not support either part of the impact statement); they could recommend an immediate low-cost fix; and they could suggest a higher-cost fix. If staff saw alignment between an exhibit and the impact statement, they attached a red dot (for the first part

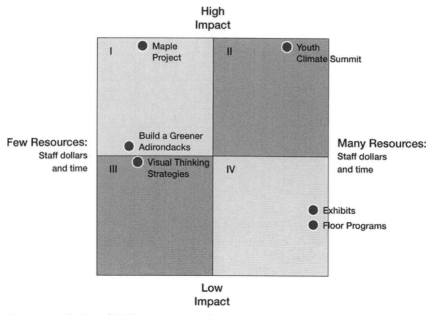

Figure 6.6.   Plotting of TWC's programs on the Impact/Resource Grid.

of the statement) or green dot (for the second part of the statement) near the exhibit. The process provided us with a clear road map for exhibit revisions that will take several years to implement. The framework provides a focused interpretative outline and will narrow our choices when we delve into planning.

Our Next Task

When the new museum opened with completed exhibits, we felt complete freedom to innovate public programs, and we did! This alignment process helped me realize that the programs represented the kind of museum I wanted to create, and I was now ready to rework the exhibits to reflect the same caliber as the programs. While the exhibits represent the organization's aspirations when TWC was conceived, the world and our place in it have changed. As we revise our exhibits, I hope our current team finds the same kind of inspired freedom staff had when we created our programs. At the very least we have a programmatic model to emulate and an impact statement to guide us.

Learning, the Continuous Journey   7

It does not matter how slowly you go as long as you do not stop.

—CONFUCIUS

LEARNING, AS AN IDEA, appears in nearly every chapter, noting that a benefit of intentional practice is to further personal, professional, and organizational learning, as supported by the Cycle of Intentional Practice and the exercises that constitute intentional-practice work. Without ongoing professional learning and the application of that learning to your intentional-practice work, achieving impact on audiences might not happen. In intentional practice, learning and achieving impact are unending, interactive, and responsive processes that are ultimately beneficial to museum staff, the museum, and the public. When all museum staff work together to continually clarify and pursue the impact the museum wants to achieve, they are operating with holistic intentionality, and staff and the museum are on an upward spiral of learning that creates value for the public.

Staff's personal and professional learning and the organization's learning are neither mutually exclusive nor independent. The connection between personal and professional learning may be more obvious and fluid than the connections between the former and latter and organizational learning. Obviously, you are responsible for your personal learning, and you and the museum are mutually responsible for your professional learning. Museum directors are responsible for your learning, too, as they can model openness, inclusiveness, humility, collaboration, and curiosity, all of which can become infectious, thereby creating an organizational culture that values learning. Continued learning, whether prompted by the individual or by the leader of the organization, is essential for impact-driven work. The beneficiaries of learning are you, your organization, and the public.

Personal Learning

Museum staff spend a great deal of time supporting visitors' personal learning. Intentional practice, while focused on achieving public impact, offers museum staff a range of opportunities to learn—about themselves, their colleagues, their organization, and their visitors. Because personal learning is private, it has never been an explicit focus of intentional-practice work. While discussed, it is neither pushed nor explored as part of the work. Nevertheless, sometimes people's personal learning is obvious, as evidenced by any kind of change (e.g., attitudes, skills, behavior, etc.). If change is the gauge, learning is observable in intentional-practice situations. For example, a person who is quiet during the first few workshops might slowly start to share ideas with the large group; another who has a negative attitude about a colleague apologizes after a misunderstanding; and yet another shares an observation knowing it is risky to do so. Change, as in overcoming fear or shifting an attitude, is learning, and it is also a personal triumph. Sometimes it takes only one in a group to demonstrate personal courage, and as others observe, they respond by following suit.

Professional Learning

Professional learning happens daily in museums—with or without intentional-practice work—because staff continue to learn about their chosen field, whether art history, natural sciences, education, design, or marketing. Professional learning also results from intentional practice. Professional learning, no matter where or how it happens, is necessary if a museum wishes to achieve impact on its target audiences. Whether learning about visitors through audience research or impact evaluation or reflecting on your museum's operational systems, your professional learning is a powerful force that will advance your museum's impact-driven work.

Professional learning is augmented when someone shares an individual learning experience during a departmental staff meeting, for example. Professional learning is further amplified across the museum when staff from different departments share their learning or convene to reflect on a newly opened exhibition or data from an evaluation. Different jobs afford people unique experiences and perspectives. Discussing anything across departmental boundaries enriches staff discussions and reflections and increases the chance for professional learning to take hold and broaden and deepen across the museum.

Professional learning is brought on by other factors, too. For example, when a new person is hired, others will have the chance to experience someone who may have different skills and knowledge. Changes in staffing and leadership invariably affect the organization's inner and outer workings and relationships. Similarly, the outside world is always in flux—from quickly shifting social norms to endless innovations in technology to changing notions of relevance. Change—regardless of where it originated—is often met with a response, sometimes initiated by staff and other times by the museum's leaders. The depth and quality of professional learning might depend on how these changes are facilitated. Are all staff invited to discuss the changing situation? Does the museum's leadership reflect openness and curiosity when listening to others' comments and thoughts? Are staff inspired to continue learning about their work and the public? If the museum exudes a culture of thoughtful deliberation and honest discussion about the work of the museum, personal learning will have a chance to flourish and affect the whole organization.

Learning Organization and Organizational Learning

There are two terms that people talk about when discussing learning at the organizational level: learning organization and organizational learning. The meanings of these two terms are worth clarifying. Peter Senge wrote *The Fifth Discipline* in 1990 where he introduced the term and concept of a learning organization. He defines a learning organization as a place "where people continually expand their capacity to create the results they truly desire, where new and expansive patterns of thinking are nurtured, where collective aspiration is set free, and where people are continually learning how to learn together."[1] The *Business Dictionary* defines organizational learning as an "organization-wide continuous process that enhances its collective ability to accept, make sense of, and respond to internal and external change. . . . It requires integration and collective interpretation of new knowledge that leads to collective action and involves risk taking and experimentation."[2] Both terms are relevant to intentional practice. A learning organization would be the result of an organization that has created and operationalized organizational learning systems and strategies.

While most museums learn, due to staff members' continuous professional learning, intentional practice emphasizes and values *why* the organization learns (to achieve impact on target audiences), *what* it learns (how to improve practice so it can advance its impact-driven work), and *how* it learns (through systematic impact-driven planning, evaluation, reflection, alignment, planning, and so on).[3] The "why" aspect of organizational learning is addressed when a museum decides to participate in intentional practice, as the work and process revolve around its desire to articulate its intended impact and organize its work accordingly. "What" the organization learns is suggested through evaluation and reflection. The intent behind those two processes is to help the museum understand evaluation data so it can make decisions about what to change and how to change it, thereby improving its professional practice. In the absence of evidence, the museum can convene to discuss its assumptions about its work and consider ways to advance it. Alignment, as demonstrated in earlier chapters, involves a deep analysis of the museum's work that may help staff identify what work they should continue doing and what they should stop doing because it does not help achieve the museum's intended impact. The ideal result of intentional practice is twofold: the museum continually learns about and improves its impact-driven work, and visitors begin to experience the museum's intended impact while gaining respect for and learning to value the museum for its passion, pursuit of excellence, humility, and continual focus on achieving impact for the public good.

Intentional practice offers many personal and professional rewards—the greatest of which is learning. Will you be taking one step forward and two steps back occasionally? Yes, but celebrate congruous times and realize there will be incongruous times; ask questions to understand so you can move beyond them. Intentional practice is flexible within a tight structure; asks simple yet provocative questions; can address big-picture issues and daily challenges—and all this will require your focused attention. It promises to be very invigorating, continuously stimulating, and *always* surprising.

Appendix A
Impact Frameworks

Table A.1. The Contemporary Austin, Austin, Texas

IMPACT-PLANNING FRAMEWORK
The Contemporary Austin (TCA) Teen Program

Mission	The Contemporary Austin reflects the spectrum of contemporary art through exhibitions, commissions, education, and the collection.
Vision	The Contemporary Austin aspires to be the contemporary art museum for Austin and an essential part of city life. Through its unique combination of urban and outdoor sites, The Contemporary will embody an eclectic and collaborative spirit.
Impact	Teens build a community that strengthens and inspires their creative expression, propensity for risk taking, and critical engagement with art and contemporary ideas.
Audiences	1. Creative teen leaders 2. Teens who create art 3. Walk-in teen visitors
Staff Passions	■ Sharing our love of contemporary art and expanding teens' definitions of art ■ Providing access to art resources that are not available to teens in school ■ Creating an inclusive and supportive environment that fosters a sense of community among teens ■ Cultivating leadership skills among teens ■ Embracing teens' unique perspectives
Distinct Qualities	■ Teens are exposed to different perspectives ■ Programs focus on contemporary art ■ All programs and supplies are free for teen participants ■ Programs foster relationships between teens and adults working in the arts ■ Teens are responsible for in-gallery museum initiatives

1. CREATIVE TEEN LEADERS

Outcomes
Intended results

Indicators
Evidence of achievement of outcomes

Teens increase their awareness of the social importance of contemporary art

- Articulates connections between contemporary art and a (non-art) contemporary social issue
- Integrates new contextual knowledge that deepens their understandings of a work of art
- Demonstrates an understanding of connections between contemporary art and current events

Teens strengthen their leadership skills (i.e., collaboration, creative inquiry, creative thinking, problem-solving)

- Describes a specific instance where s/he blended ideas with other program participants
- Identifies a problem encountered and a concrete step taken to address the issue
- Asks questions of their peers in meetings and at events
- Communicates about art with confidence

Teens feel ownership of The Contemporary Austin

- Describes relationship with TCA using the possessive, "my museum, our museum, etc."
- Provides a concrete example of when s/he felt trusted by museum staff to take a leadership role at the museum
- Maintains a relationship with museum staff after leaving the program
- Brings friends and family to the museum

2. TEENS WHO CREATE ART

Outcomes
Intended results

Indicators
Evidence of achievement of outcomes

Teens broaden their understanding of art/the creative process

- Gives an example of how the program shaped their understanding of what art is
- Describes concrete examples of how his/her art-making process evolved
- Provides an example from his/her personal life that the creative process applies to more than art-making
- Describes how the art-making process is as (or more) important than the final product

(continued)

Table A.1. *(continued)*

Outcomes *Intended results*	Indicators *Evidence of achievement of outcomes*
Teens take risks in their art making	■ Portfolio demonstrates an evolving/changing use of a variety of materials, mediums, and art-making techniques ■ Identifies a new (surprising or unusual for the teen) art-making tool(s) or technique(s) s/he learned ■ Provides a specific example of how a guest artist, an artist mentor, and/or another professional artist's work inspired him/her to try something new when making art ■ Thoughtfully and logically explains the decision-making process for taking risks in art-making
Teens feel supported as part of a diverse community of teens who are producing artwork	■ Describes feeling in community among like-minded persons in the program(s) ■ Describes feeling more confident talking about art, sharing ideas, and offering critiques to fellow teens and adults than they did at the start of the program(s) ■ Regularly asks peers, mentors, and guest artists questions for feedback on their artwork and ideas ■ Stays connected with other teens after the program(s)

3. WALK-IN TEEN VISITORS

Outcomes *Intended results*	Indicators *Evidence of achievement of outcomes*
Teens feel welcome, comfortable, and curious at The Contemporary Austin	■ Participates freely and actively during museum visit ■ Chooses to make art during their museum visit ■ Expresses a desire to return to and/or maintain an association with the museum ■ Speaks positively of their experiences at the museum to others
Teens expand their understanding of art and see art in a new and different way	■ Names a new contemporary artist and/or an art-making material, medium, or technique they learned about during their museum visit ■ Describes something about contemporary art s/he has never thought of before ■ Explains that you can appreciate art without identifying as an artist or creator

Table A.2.   Capitol Visitor Center, Washington, DC

CAPITOL VISITOR CENTER'S EXHIBITION HALL AND ORIENTATION FILM IMPACT-PLANNING FRAMEWORK

MISSION What CVC does	Working together for Congress to inform, involve, and inspire every visitor to the United States Capitol.
IMPACT Ultimate effect of CVC's Exhibition Hall and Orientation Film on audiences	Audiences of the Capitol Visitor Center's Exhibition Hall and Orientation Film recognize the significance of Congress to everyday life, the role of citizens in a democratic process, and the evolving understanding of "We the People."
OUTCOME for all target audiences	Audiences recognize that in a democracy many voices play a part in the ongoing pursuit of a more perfect union.
AUDIENCES Whom CVC's Exhibition Hall and Orientation Film primarily serve	1. Eighth-grade and twelfth-grade students 2. American adult visitors 3. International visitors
DISTINCT QUALITIES What makes CVC's Exhibition Hall and Orientation Film unique	▪ Display authentic historical objects that awe audiences ▪ Dynamically place the past in situ with the present ▪ Show the growth of the Capitol and surrounding area over time ▪ Focus on the history of Congress ▪ Demonstrate relevant connections between Congress and the people

(continued)

Table A.2. *(continued)*

DISCUSSION TOOL Use this tool to ensure exhibition/program ideas support the impact statement, some outcome for all audiences, and some outcomes for individual audiences.	1. Audience: Who is the target audience/s for the proposed program/exhibition? Which aspects of the program/exhibition strongly align with the target audience? Which do not?
	2. Mission/Impact/Outcomes: Does the proposed program/exhibition support mission *and* impact? How does the program/exhibition inform, involve, and ultimately inspire your target audience to recognize the significance of Congress to everyday life, the role of citizens in a democratic process, and the evolving understanding of "We the People?" Which do not? Which outcomes does the program/exhibition support?
	3. Distinct Qualities: Does the proposed program/exhibition accentuate three or more of the Exhibition Hall's and/or Orientation Film's distinct qualities? Which ones and in what ways?
	4. Collaboration: Does the program/exhibition encourage internal/external collaboration? With whom and in what ways?
	5. Resources: How will you fund the proposed program/exhibition? Does it require new resources or resource realignment?
	6. Staff: Does the program/exhibition require additional staff or staff realignment? Which staff need to be directly involved? How does the initiative need to be communicated to staff overall?

**OUTCOMES &
INDICATORS**
Outcomes = intended results
Indicators = evidence of
achieving outcomes

EIGHTH-GRADE AND TWELFTH-GRADE STUDENTS

1. **Students recognize a connection between Congress and their everyday lives**

   A. Identify one or more acts of Congress that affects them or their community

   B. Identify one or more ways to engage their members of Congress

   C. Identify one or more acts of civic engagement in which they could participate

2. **Students deepen their understanding of Congress and the legislative process**

   A. Describe how the Capitol building's growth relates to the idea of "representation"

   B. Describe the work of Congress and the legislative process as complex, recognizing they involve debate, conflict, compromise

   C. Identify the significance of key facts about Congress, i.e., the "why" behind them

   D. Select one or more stories in Exhibition Hall and describe its (or their) importance

3. **Students are inspired to learn more about the Capitol building, Congress, and the legislative process**

   A. Identify one or more ideas or experiences from the Exhibition Hall/Orientation Film that inspire them

   B. Discuss their experiences with others after their visit

   C. Identify an action they could take to learn more about the Capitol building, Congress, and/or the legislative process, such as:

   - keeping or purchasing a memento of their visit;

   - seeking out more information about something or someone they saw in Exhibition Hall or the Orientation Film;

   - seeking out more information related to the Capitol building, Congress, and/or the legislative process; and

   - becoming more involved with the Capitol building, Congress, and/or the legislative process.

(continued)

Table A.2. *(continued)*

| OUTCOMES & INDICATORS
Outcomes = intended results
Indicators = evidence of achieving outcomes	AMERICAN ADULT VISITORS
	1. Adults see the connection between Congress and their everyday lives
	A. Identify one or more acts of Congress
	B. Identify one or more ways to engage their members of Congress
	C. Identify one or more acts of civic engagement in which they could participate
	2. Adults appreciate the responsibilities of Congress and the complexities of the legislative process
	A. Name something new or surprising they learned about Congress and/or the legislative process
	B. Describe an increased appreciation for the role of Congress
	3. Adults are interested in learning more about Congress and the legislative process
	A. Share their experiences with others after the experience
	B. Identify an action they could take to learn more about Congress and the legislative process such as:
	▪ keeping or purchasing a memento of their visit to the CVC;
	▪ seeking out more information related to the Capitol building, Congress, and/or the legislative process in general; and
	▪ becoming more involved with the Capitol building, Congress, and/or the legislative process

| OUTCOMES & INDICATORS
Outcomes = intended results
Indicators = evidence of achieving outcomes	INTERNATIONAL VISITORS
	1. International visitors enhance their knowledge of American government
	A. Learn something new or surprising about American government and why it is significant
	B. State similarities and differences between their government and American government
	C. Recognize the high level of access that Americans (and visitors) have to their government
	D. Describe how American government affects international policy
	E. Provide one or more examples of how the American government has influenced or been influenced by world events.
	F. Describe how an historical event depicted in Exhibition Hall or Orientation Film compares to their country's perspective of that same event
	G. Request more information during their visit to Exhibition Hall or Orientation Film

Table A.3. Creative Discovery Museum, Chattanooga, Tennessee

CREATIVE DISCOVERY MUSEUM (CDM) IMPACT-PLANNING FRAMEWORK

MISSION What CDM will do	To inspire all children to explore, innovate, create, and play
IMPACT The result of CDM on audiences	**Children and families engage in playful experiences that spark new passions, expand their curiosity, and deepen connections to their community and world**
PASSIONS Common passions for CDM	▪ Providing children opportunities to explore and discover the world around them through play ▪ Offering fun experiences that celebrate childhood and foster a love of learning ▪ Introducing children and their adult providers to new experiences not available at home or in school ▪ Offering accessibility options to all children and families ▪ Developing relationships—between children and caring adults, and between the community and the museum ▪ Bettering the Chattanooga community and beyond
DISTINCT QUALITIES How CDM is distinct	▪ CDM believes every learner is full of potential ▪ CDM creates unique rich experiences by integrating arts, science, and other literacies ▪ CDM uses research to create learning opportunities that are developmentally appropriate ▪ CDM attracts and invests in staff who are passionate, resourceful, proactive, and have a wide variety of expertise
INTENTIONAL AUDIENCES Whom CDM will intentionally serve	▪ Children in K–3 facilitated school programs ▪ Early childhood child and care-giving adult pairs ▪ Families with children 5–8 years old ▪ Teens in the museum apprentice program

Table A.3. *(continued)*

CREATIVE DISCOVERY MUSEUM
AUDIENCE OUTCOMES *(INTENDED RESULTS)* AND INDICATORS *(EVIDENCE OF ACHIEVING OUTCOMES)*

Children in the K–3 facilitated school programs will:

Deepen classroom learning through museum experiences
- Child vividly recalls an activity from a CDM experience and explains how it relates to classroom learning
- Child applies language or concepts from a CDM experience in the classroom
- Teacher describes children as more enthusiastic about a topic after their CDM experience

Develop/exercise their curiosity
- Child asks questions to understand the connection between one idea/situation and another during a CDM experience
- Child uses trial and error and experiments even after experiencing success during a program
- Child manipulates and plays with materials in unintended and/or unusual ways during a program
- Child seeks out materials and/or information after leaving CDM experience about something learned during a program

Develop interpersonal/collaborative skills
- Child listens intently, focuses their attention (leaning in toward and eyes on) on CDM staff and classmates during program
- Child speaks to peers during the program
- Child cheerfully shares responsibility and materials with other children during the program
- Child takes on a variety of roles during the program (followers become leaders, leaders become followers)
- Child easily shares ideas during the program

Early childhood child and care-giving adult pairs will:

Adults understand the importance of play in childhood development

- Adult encourages/engages in child-directed play
- Adult describes a way CDM has enhanced their understanding of their child's development and/or interests
- Adult shares an example of something they saw their child learn while playing at CDM

Adults cultivate skills to be their child's first teacher

- Adult practices school readiness activities modeled at CDM at home (for example, counting, singing, sorting)
- Adult spends time reading and exploring books with their child
- Adult creates opportunities for activities at home that were experienced at CDM (for example, re-creates play spaces and/or activities such as a kitchen or water table)
- Adult uses language and concepts experienced at CDM to enhance child's literacy and language abilities

Children develop socioemotional skills

- Child displays executive functions (e.g., sharing, taking turns, positive interactions with children and adults)
- Child explores through role playing during CDM visit
- Child notices and reacts to others' feelings and emotions (demonstrates empathy)

(continued)

Table A.3. *(continued)*

Families with children 5–8 years old will:

Develop/exercise an attitude of curiosity
- Family asks questions to explore connections between one idea/situation found in CDM to another
- Family fully explores the areas/materials at CDM and spends extended time in exhibition spaces
- Family uses trial and error and experiments completing an activity
- Family asks questions of each other/amongst themselves about exhibit content
- Family seeks out information or materials related to their CDM experience

Celebrate childhood and create memories together
- Family takes photos that demonstrate the fun and playfulness they experienced at CDM
- Family eagerly shares their experience at CDM with others, either in person or on social media
- Adult plays with/collaborates with/coaches the child in an activity at CDM
- Family discusses CDM experiences after their visit and recalls/describes the best parts of their visit

Experience/gain exposure to a diversity of content
- Family describes being surprised by a new experience they had at CDM
- Family interacts with content experts at CDM, which gives them an authentic experience that expands their worldview
- Family applies concepts/content from CDM to their everyday life
- Adult describes learning about or being surprised by one of their child's interests from their time at CDM

Value learning through play
- Adult encourages playful behavior
- Adult lets children explore at their own pace
- Adult shares an example of something they saw their child learn while playing at CDM

Teens in the museum apprentice program will:

Develop new skills (social, professional, customer service, teamwork, leadership)

- Teen describes/gives examples of skills they have improved as a result of participating in the program
- Teen describes a difficult situation/customer-service challenge they experience while in the program and how they resolved it
- Teen demonstrates capacity for new skills
  - Social skills: interacts with people of all ages whom they didn't know before the program, including CDM staff
  - Professional skills: is proactive, reliable, and punctual during the program
  - Teamwork skills: demonstrates collaboration skills (e.g., delegates/shares responsibility, participates in activities, discusses ideas on the teen advisory board)
  - Leadership skills: describes a time they took on a leadership role during the apprentice program

Increase their levels of self-confidence

- Teen applies for the next level of the apprentice program
- Teen takes feedback/criticism well
- Teen demonstrates confidence in their skills after participating in the apprentice program
- Teen demonstrates comfort being themselves (personal identity) after participating in the apprentice program

Feel a sense of ownership/responsibility for CDM

- Teen describes the mission of CDM and knows how they fit in
- Teen volunteers to mentor new teens coming into the apprentice program
- Teen seeks out and develops relationships with staff at CDM
- Teen provides suggestions to improve the apprentice program
- Teen easily accesses resources (human or materials) at CDM

Table A.4.   The Wild Center, Tupper Lake, New York

THE WILD CENTER: IMPACT-PLANNING FRAMEWORK

WHAT What we do (aka mission)	Ignite an enduring passion for the natural world and the Adirondacks—the place and its story—where people are learning to respect nature so both can thrive and offer an example for the world
HOW How we approach our work	Our deep respect for nature *and* people drives the methodology in all we do—from igniting curiosity about the natural world, to learning from nature's intelligence, to convening so people use their personal passion to work on nature's behalf. We learn alongside whom we seek to serve. We serve others to serve nature by: ■ Continuing to reimagine what a museum is and what museum-like entities can do for a community and a region ■ Taking risks in our work and seeking to learn from our work ■ Taking on big ideas despite our small size, and inspiring many to carry out important work ■ Relinquishing authority and valuing other perspectives and ways of knowing the natural world ■ Practicing humility
WHY Why we do this work (aka purpose/benefit/impact)	People deepen their connection to nature and consider their role in sustaining their natural world for future generations
WHO Target market and how we meet their needs (aka positioning statement)	To inquisitive minds of all ages, The Wild Center is the science-based community that cultivates and enriches your connection to nature so you can actively engage in a future where people and nature can thrive together

THE WILD CENTER: SIGNATURE PROGRAMS AND AUDIENCE OUTCOMES

Youth Climate Summit *Teens will:*	Visual Thinking Strategies *4th–6th grade students will:*	Maple Project *Tupper Tappers will:*	Building a Greener Adirondacks *Contractors will:*	Exhibitions/programs *Tourist families who experience TWC campus will:*
Become lifelong climate stewards	Learn that observation is a basic science skill	Feel a connection with the Tupper community, TWC, and other Tappers	Become aware of green building practices, products, tools, and technologies	Spend more time exploring nature after visiting TWC than they did before visiting TWC
Become climate-action leaders in their schools/communities	Ask questions about their observations and seek information accordingly	Learn about the sugaring process—from collecting sap to the newest technology for boiling sap	Learn about the efficiencies of green approaches	Slow down to take notice of nature
Implement their climate plans in schools/communities	Realize that different observers have different responses	Develop a deepened respect for this place—the Adirondacks—its land and its culture	Implement sustainable building practices in the Adirondacks	Begin to realize that they are part of nature
Lead others to act on climate change	Analyze observations to learn about the natural world	Feel proud to participate in a local Adirondack tradition	Communicate the virtues of sustainable building practices to their clients and peers	Try new experiences in nature while at TWC
Find purpose in their active citizenship	Know that their and others' observations are valid			Share positive memories of their family enjoying the natural world
	Respectfully share ideas about their observations with their peers			

Table A.5. North Carolina Museum of Natural Sciences, Raleigh, North Carolina

NORTH CAROLINA MUSEUM OF NATURAL SCIENCES
IMPACT-PLANNING FRAMEWORK FOR THE NATURE RESOURCE CENTER (NRC)

MISSION
What the NCMNS does

To illuminate the interdependence of nature and humanity

IMPACT
The ultimate result of the NRC on audiences

Audiences appreciate the process that scientists use to study our world—past, present, and future—and contemplate the countless ways they can engage with others in the scientific enterprise.

Adult Learners
Adults visiting alone or in social/family groups who identify as lifelong learners

Outcomes (intended results) and indicators (evidence of achieving outcomes):

1. **See the relevance of science to their daily lives**
   Describe at least one example of the way science, as presented in the NRC, relates personally to their lives
   Share with friends and family something learned or experienced at the NRC
   Identify at least one example from NRC of why science matters to them or to humankind generally

2. **Have an increased appreciation for the interdependence of nature and humanity**
   Provide an example from the NRC of the ways humans and nature affect one another
   Provide an example of actions they can take to increase conservation
   Affiliate with conservation causes and organizations

3. **Feel comfortable with scientists and science content**
   Actively participate (ask questions, converse) in public science programs at the NRC (like Science Café)
   Access more science content (through books, articles, TV shows)

4. **Participate in opportunities to do science**
   Join a citizen science project
   Volunteer in the NRC and/or labs
   Participate in science-based social media

5. **Develop critical thinking skills to take action and make decisions based on an understanding of scientific evidence**
   Question the science they hear about in the media
   Discern the difference between "pseudo-science" and authentic science
   Make personal behavioral decisions based on evidence-based science (e.g., immunize their children)

Middle-School-Aged Children
Children ages 10 to 14 visiting in family or school groups

Outcomes (intended results) and indicators (evidence of achieving outcomes)**:**

1. **See the relevance of science to their daily lives**
   Describe at least one example of the way science, as presented in the NRC, relates personally to their lives
   Share with friends and family something learned or experienced at the NRC
   Identify at least one example from NRC of why science matters to them or to humankind generally

2. **Perceive science as a cool way to explore a personal interest in something not known (through curiosity, discovery, solving problems)**
   Give an example of the way a scientist has explored his or her interest
   Give an example of an interest, passion, or question they want to explore through science
   Describe how they will use science to explore an interest, question, or curiosity (questioning, testing, trial and error, etc.)

3. **Perceive science and scientists as exciting, fun, and accessible**
   Actively participate (ask questions, converse with scientists, volunteers, and staff) in the NRC
   Describe feeling personally connected to and comfortable with scientists and volunteers in the NRC

4. **Appreciate important scientific concepts**
   Explain (or demonstrate through actions) a scientific concept
   Explain (or demonstrate through actions) a scientific procedure

5. **Become aware that a career in science may be relevant to common societal issues/questions**
   Describe a common issue that scientists from diverse disciplines are working on together and explain the unique contribution of each scientist
   Name ways that scientists collaborate in their work

(continued)

Table A.5. *(continued)*

Academic Community
Educators and students representing local universities

Outcomes (intended results) and indicators (evidence of achieving outcomes):

1. **Have an increased awareness of the museum's research collections as a resource**
   Deposit voucher specimens into the museum's research collection
   Use the museum's research collection (borrow from or search the database)
   Report the ways using the research collection has positively affected their work

2. **Recognize the value of two-way communication with the public and involving the public in research**
   Participate in science communication training and positively respond to feedback
   Volunteer (and are mentored) in the research lab and give X number of presentations per week
   Actively participate with the museum's programming (Daily Planet, Science Café)
   Describe how public communication has enhanced their work as scientists

3. **Value the museum as a research and public engagement partner**
   Diversify the ways they partner with the museum (e.g., programming, grants, conferences, events)
   Describe how partnering with the museum has enhanced their work as scientists

Appendix B
Proposed Schedule for Intentional-Practice Work

INTENTIONAL-PRACTICE WORKSHOPS and core-team meetings can create a rhythm to the museum's intentional practice. You will see in the schedule below (table B.1) that intentional-practice workshops are interspersed across a span of eighteen months. Intermingling a museum's daily work with intentional-practice work creates much-needed time for ideas to settle and for staff to reflect and consider its micro work with its macro work. Additionally, spacing out workshops provides opportunities to reinforce intentional-practice ideas, which sometimes can be difficult to retain. As noted throughout the book, a museum's intentional practice is ongoing—as long as it strives to achieve its intended impact.

Table B.1. Proposed Schedule for Intentional-Practice Work

Months after Start	Task
Month 1	Core team meets to plan for first workshop (determines who will attend, identifies community members to invite, selects three or four target audiences)
Month 2.5	**First workshop** (exploring passions, identifying distinct qualities, envisioning outcomes)
Month 3	Core team analyzes data from workshop and writes draft impact statement and outcomes for vetting in next workshop
Month 5	**Second workshop:** vetting impact statement and outcomes and prioritizing outcomes
Month 6	Core team revises impact statement and outcomes

(continued)

Table B.1. *(Continued)*

Months after Start	Task
Month 8	**Third workshop:** developing indicators (if evaluation is part of the museum's intentional-practice work)
Months 9–13	Conducting evaluation or basic audience research (includes planning time)
Month 15	**Fourth workshop:** reflecting on data (if data are not available, staff can reflect on their museum's organizational practices)
Month 16	**Fifth workshop:** aligning the museum's work to achieve its intended impact
Month 18	**Sixth workshop:** reflecting on the museum's intentional practice

Glossary

Alignment (in intentional practice): when all the people in the organization—from leadership to frontline staff and volunteers—are working together to achieve the intended impact of the museum as per the Impact Framework.

Alignment exercises (in intentional practice): when staff examine their work in the context of achieving impact and expending resources (time and dollars) and discuss how to improve their work from impact and resource perspectives.

Evaluation: systematic assessment of the merit of a project according to a set of predetermined criteria. In the context of intentional practice, merit is determined by the museum's ability to achieve its intentions, and the criteria are the impact statement and associated outcomes.

Holistic intentionality: when all museum staff work together to continually clarify and pursue the impact the museum wants to achieve.

Impact: the overarching result of a museum's work on target audiences and what a museum will achieve when it fulfills its mission.

Impact evaluation (in intentional practice): examines the effectiveness of the entire museum's work through the lenses of the impact statement and associated outcomes on specified target audiences, as identified during planning.

Impact Framework: a draft or living document that concisely presents the organization's mission, impact statement, distinct qualities, target audiences, and outcomes for target audiences (and sometimes indicators for target audience outcomes).

Impact statement: one sentence that describes the overall effect of a museum on target audiences. It balances aspiration with realism, and by design, reflects staff members' passion for their work, the museum's distinct qualities, and what is relevant to audiences.

Indicators: observable and measurable evidence that an outcome is achieved.

Intentionality: When an idea formed in the mind through careful deliberation and reflection directs a person/entity toward it (a goal or thing). In intentional practice, the goal or thing is the impact statement, supporting outcomes, and specified audiences as the beneficiaries of the museum's impact.

Intentional planning: part of an organization's intentional-practice work whereby staff identify their passions, the museum's distinct qualities, and experiential outcomes for target audiences and use those elements to guide their work and decisions.

Intentional practice: a holistic way of thinking and working that includes collaborating with colleagues from across the organization to articulate the organization's intended impact so it can do the following: plan the organization's work to achieve impact; evaluate the ways in which the organization is achieving impact based on its intentions; reflect on the results of the evaluation and the organization's actions for the purpose of learning and improving; and analyze its work with the goal of strengthening alignment between what it does and its intended impact.

Mission: describes what an organization does. A museum's mission often includes verbs such as collect, preserve, interpret, and educate.

Outcomes: explicit measurable results on specified audiences including attitudes, knowledge, understanding, skills, and behaviors.

Outputs: products that a museum might create, such as an exhibition; the number of people who visited the exhibition.

Reflection: the active process of deliberately stepping back to look closely at an experience, a thought, or a thing with the intent of exploring it in great depth.

Notes

Preface

1. Stephen E. Weil, "Can and Do They Make a Difference?" in *Making Museums Matter,* 55–74 (Washington, DC: Smithsonian Books, 2002), 63.

2. Douglas Worts, "Planning for Cultural Relevance: A Systems Workshop at the Georgia O'Keeffe Museum," in *Systems Thinking in Museums: Theory and Practice,* ed. Yuha Jung and Ann Rowson Love, 81 (New York: Rowman & Littlefield, 2017).

3. Oxford Economics, "Museums as Economic Engines: A National Report" (Washington, DC: American Alliance of Museums, 2017).

Chapter 1

1. T. Crane, "Intentionality," in the *Oxford Companion to Philosophy,* ed. Ted Honderich (Oxford: Oxford University Press, 2005), 438.

2. Pierre Jacob, "Intentionality," in *The Stanford Encyclopedia of Philosophy* (Winter 2014 edition), ed. Edward N. Zalta (Stanford University, 1997–), accessed January 18, 2017, https://plato.stanford.edu/entries/intentionality/.

3. Barry Smith, "Franz Brentano I: On Mind and Its Objects," in *Austrian Philosophy: The Legacy of Franz Brentano,* chap. 2 (Chicago: Open Court Publishing Company, 1994), accessed January 18, 2017, http://ontology.buffalo.edu/smith/book/austrian_philosophy/CH2.pdf.

4. Crane, "Intentionality," 438.

5. Throughout this book, when I talk about results (e.g., particular end) or ask "To what end?" I always mean on the public the museum serves. Results, from my perspective, are not a program or an exhibition—they are means to an end. The public experience is the end result.

6. See George E. Hein, "Dewey's Debt to Barnes," *Curator: The Museum Journal* 54, no. 2 (2011): 123–39.

7. George E. Hein, *Progressive Museum Practice: John Dewey and Democracy* (Walnut Creek, CA: Left Coast Press, 2012), 11.

8. Ibid.

9. Ibid., 26–27.

10. John Cotton Dana, *The New Museum: Selected Writings by John Cotton Dana*, ed. William A. Peniston (Washington, DC: Newark Museum Association and the American Alliance of Museums, 1999), 65 and 102.

11. "Public value" is a term coined by Harvard professor Mark Moore. For an in-depth discussion, see Mark Moore, *Creating Public Value: Strategic Management in Government* (Cambridge, MA: Harvard University Press, 1997).

12. Bonnie Pitman and Ellen Hirzy, *New Forums: Art Museums & Communities* (Washington, DC: American Association of Museums, 2004).

13. Emlyn Koster, "The Relevant Museum: A Reflection on Sustainability," *Museum News* 85, no. 3 (2006): 67–70, 85–87; David Fleming, "Museums Campaigning for Social Justice," the Fifth Stephen Weil Memorial Lecture, Shanghai, China, November 2010. http://www.intercom.museum/documents/5thWeilLectureShanghaiNov2010.pdf; Janes, Robert and Gerald T. Conaty. 2005. *Looking Reality in the Eye: Museums and Social Responsibility*. Calgary, Alberta: University of Calgary Press.

14. Randi Korn, "Self Portrait: First Know Thyself, Then Serve Your Public," *Museum News* 83, no. 1 (2004): 32–35, 50–52.

15. Dana, *The New Museum*, 101–2.

16. Stephen E. Weil, "Can and Do They Make a Difference?" In *Making Museums Matter* (Washington, DC: Smithsonian Books, 2002), 55–56.

17. Ibid., 63.

18. Ibid.

19. Ibid., 60.

20. Stephen E. Weil, "From Being about Something to Being for Somebody," in *Making Museums Matter* (Washington, DC: Smithsonian Books, 2002), 28–52.

21. Ibid., 47.

22. Stephen E. Weil, "Romance versus Realism," in *Making Museums Matter* (Washington, DC: Smithsonian Books, 2002), 102–8.

23. Ibid., 106.

24. Stephen E. Weil, "Museums: Can and Do They Make a Difference?" in *Making Museums Matter* (Washington, DC: Smithsonian Institution, 2002), 61–62.

25. Randi Korn, "The Case for Holistic Intentionality," *Curator: The Museum Journal* 50, no. 2 (2007): 255–64.

26. Evaluative thinking is defined in an article by Jane Buckley et al., as follows: "Evaluative thinking is critical thinking applied in the context of evaluation, motivated by an attitude of inquisitiveness and a belief in the value of evidence, that involves identifying assumptions, posing thoughtful questions, pursuing deeper understanding through reflection and perspective taking, and informing decisions in preparation for action." Jane Buckley et al., "Defining and Teaching Evaluative Thinking: Insights from Research on Critical Thinking," *American Journal*

of Evaluation 36, no. 3 (2015): 375–88, accessed March 23, 2017, http://www
.socialresearchmethods.net/research/2015/2015%20-%20Buckley%20et%20
al%20-%20Evaluative%20Thinking.pdf.

27. Stephen E. Weil, "A Success/Failure Matrix for Museums," *Museum News*
84, no. 1 (2005): 36.

28. Ibid., 38.

29. Ibid., 39.

30. Ibid.

31. Many business authors have written about organizational learning and
change, most notably Peter Senge, who wrote *The Fifth Discipline* in 1990 (New
York: Doubleday/Currency).

32. Hallie S. Preskill and Rosalie T. Torres, *Evaluative Inquiry for Learning in
Organizations* (Thousand Oaks, CA: Sage Publications, 1999), xxi.

33. Korn, "The Case for Holistic Intentionality."

34. Preskill and Torres, *Evaluative Inquiry for Learning in Organizations,* 1–2.

35. Ibid., 2.

36. Ibid., 23.

37. Ibid., 184.

38. Ibid.

39. Ibid., 185.

40. Ibid.

41. Weil, "A Success/Failure Matrix for Museums," 36.

Chapter 2

1. Jack Kemp, "The Politics of the Impossible," the Heritage Lectures 511, November 1994, Washington, DC, http://thf_media.s3.amazonaws.com/1994/pdf/
hl511.pdf; Laurence Jarvik, "Ten Good Reasons to Eliminate Funding for the National Endowment for the Arts," *Backgrounder*, no. 1110 (1997), http://thf_media
.s3.amazonaws.com/1997/pdf/bg1110.pdf; and Rachel Greszler, "Show Me the
Math: How to Achieve a Leaner Federal Government," the Heritage Foundation,
March 28, 2017, http://www.heritage.org/budget-and-spending/commentary/
show-me-the-math-how-achieve-leaner-federal-government.

2. Gaea Leinhardt, Karen Knutson, and Kevin Crowley, "Museum Learning
Collaborative Redux," *Journal of Museum Education* 28, no. 1 (2003): 23.

3. Institute of Museum and Library Services, *True Needs True Partners: Museums
Serving Schools, 2002 Survey Highlights*, 2002, https://www.imls.gov/sites/default/
files/publications/documents/trueneedstruepartners98highlights_0.pdf.

4. Robert Janes, *Museums in a Troubled World* (New York: Routledge, 2009);
John W. Jacobson, *Measuring Museum Impact and Performance: Theory and Practice*
(New York: Rowman & Littlefield, 2016).

5. Government Performance and Results Act of 1993, Cong. Rec., 103rd
Cong. (1993) https://www.dol.gov/ocfo/media/regs/GPRA.pdf.

6. Stephen E. Weil and Peggy D. Rudd, *Perspectives on Outcome Based Evaluation for Libraries and Museums*, Institute of Museum and Library Studies, 2000. https:// www.imls.gov/sites/default/files/publications/documents/perspectivesobe_0.pdf.

7. Alan Friedman, ed., *Framework for Evaluating Impacts of Informal Science Education Projects*. Report from a National Science Foundation Workshop, March 12–13, 2008, Arlington, VA: National Science Foundation. http://www.informalscience .org/framework-evaluating-impacts-informal-science-education-projects.

8. Ibid., 8–9.

9. John Falk and Beverley Sheppard, *Thriving in the Knowledge Age* (Lanham, MD: AltaMira Press, 2006), 239.

10. American Evaluation Association, "American Evaluation Association Guiding Principles for Evaluators," 2013, http://www.eval.org/p/cm/ld/fid=51.

11. Visitor Studies Association, "Evaluator Competencies for Professional Development," Visitor Studies Association, accessed May 30, 2017, http://www .visitorstudies.org/evaluator-competencies.

12. Kevin F. McCarthy, Elizabeth H. Ondaatje, Laura Zakaras, and Arthur Brooks, *Gifts of the Muse: Reframing the Debate about the Benefits of the Arts* (New York: Wallace Foundation, 2004), http://www.wallacefoundation.org/knowledge -center/Documents/Gifts-of-the-Muse.pdf.

13. Ibid., xi.

14. Ibid., 37.

15. Increasingly, museums that seek funding from IMLS, NEH, and NEA ask for assistance from evaluators to support their grant applications as well as to conduct program evaluations. IMLS provides online tools to guide staff in their work with evaluators (see https://www.imls.gov/research-evaluation/evaluation-resources); NEH provides guidance on reporting requirements, which includes evaluation (see https://www.neh.gov/grants/manage/performance-reporting-requirements). IMLS also evaluates entire grant programs, such as Museum for America (for example, see https://www.imls.gov/sites/default/files/publications/documents/mfaevalexec summary_0.pdf). NSF has always required evaluation, which I discuss later in this chapter. Increasingly, some private foundations that fund museums also require and expect that their grantees conduct evaluations. Some, such as the Irvine Foundation, offer an external evaluator to support their grantees in their evaluation efforts.

16. McCarthy et al., *Gifts of the Muse*, xiv.

17. Ibid., xiv–xv.

18. Philippe de. Montebello, "Art Museums, Inspiring Public Trust," in *Whose Muse: Art Museums and the Public Trust*, ed. James Cuno, 151–69 (Princeton, NJ: Princeton University Press and Harvard Art Museums, 2004).

19. Selma Holo, *Beyond the Turnstile: Making the Case for Museums and Sustainable Values* (Lanham, MD: AltaMira Press, 2009), xv.

20. Mihaly Csikszentmihalyi, and Rick E. Robinson, *The Art of Seeing: An Interpretation of the Aesthetic Encounter* (Los Angeles: J. Paul Getty Museum, 1990).

21. Ibid., 68.

22. James Cuno, ed., *Whose Muse: Art Museums and the Public Trust* (Princeton, NJ: Princeton University Press and Harvard Art Museums, 2004).

23. Association of Art Museum Directors, "Association of Art Museum Directors Issues Art Museums by the Numbers 2016," released January 9, 2017, accessed April 8, 2017, https://www.aamd.org/for-the-media/press-release/association-of-art-museum-directors-issues-art-museums-by-the-numbers-0.

24. McCarthy et al., *Gifts of the Muse*, 5.

25. Ibid., xv.

26. See National Endowment for the Arts, "Arts Participation," accessed April 14, 2017, https://www.arts.gov/artistic-fields/research-analysis/arts-quadrants/arts-participation.

27. Alan Brown, 2006. "An Architecture of Value." *Grantmakers in the Arts Reader* 17 no. 1: 18.

28. David A. Ucko, "The *Learning Science in Informal Environments* Study in Context," *Curator: The Museum Journal* 53, no. 2 (2010): 129–36.

29. See Valerie Crane, Heather Nicholson, Milton Chen, and Stephen Bitgood, eds., *Informal Science Learning: What the Research Says about Television, Science Museums, and Community-Based Projects* (Dedham, MA: Research Communications, 1994).

30. See COSMOS Corporation, "A Report on the Evaluation of the National Science Foundation's Informal Science Education Program" (Arlington, VA: National Science Foundation, 1998).

31. Divisions within government agencies often change names. Previously, Informal Science Education (ISE) was the Public Understanding of Science program; now it is called Advancing Informal STEM Learning (AISL), and it is within the Division of Research on Learning in Formal and Informal Settings.

32. See Gaea Leinhardt, Kevin Crowley, and Karen Knutson, *Learning Conversations in Museums* (Mahwah, NJ: Lawrence Erlbaum Associates Publishers, 2002); Gaea Leinhardt and Karen Knutson, *Listening In on Museum Conversations* (Walnut Creek, CA: AltaMira Press, 2004).

33. See Philippe Bell, Bruch Lewenstein, Andrew W. Shouse, and Michael A. Feder, eds., *Learning Science in Informal Environments: People, Places, and Pursuits* (Washington, DC: National Research Council of the National Academies, 2009).

34. Zahava D. Doering and Martin Storksdieck, eds., Special Issue on Science, *Curator: The Museum Journal* 53, no. 2 (2010).

35. Importantly, *Learning Science in Informal Environments* added strands 1 and 6 to four previously identified strands that appeared in *Taking Science to School: Learning and Teaching Science in Grades K–8*. See Richard A. Duschl, Heidi A. Schweingruber, and Andrew W. Shouse, eds., *Taking Science to School: Learning and Teaching Science in Grades K–8* (Washington, DC: The National Academies Press, 2007).

36. David A. Ucko, *NSF Influence on the Field of Informal Science Education.* Informal Science Education, 2010, accessed June 7, 2017. http://www.informalscience.org/sites/default/files/NSFImpactonISE.pdf.

37. Leonard Krishtalka, "Natural History Museums as Sentinel Observatories of Life on Earth: A Public Trust," in *Beyond the Turnstile: Making the Case for Museums and Sustainable Values*, ed. Selma Holo, 12–15 (Lanham, MD: AltaMira Press, 2009), 13.

38. Emlyn Koster, "From Apollo into the Anthropocene: The Odyssey of Nature and Science Museums in an Externally Responsible Context," in *Museums, Ethics and Cultural Heritage*, ed. B. Murphy, 228–41 (New York: Routledge and International Council of Museums, 2016).

39. Emlyn Koster, E. Dorfman, and T. Myambe, "A Holistic Ethos for Nature-Focused Museums in the Anthropocene," in *The Future of Natural History Museums*, ed. E. Dorfman, 29–48 (New York: Routledge, 2018).

40. Bill Watson, and Shari Rosenstein Werb, "One Hundred Strong: A Colloquium on Transforming Natural History Museums in the Twenty-First Century," *Curator: The Museum Journal* 56, no. 2 (2013): 255–65.

41. Ibid., 260.

42. Personal conversation, April 12, 2017.

43. Humanities Indicators, "Historic Site Visits," American Academy of Arts and Sciences, accessed April 14, 2016. http://www.humanitiesindicators.org/content/indicatorDoc.aspx?d=101&hl=historic+site+visits&m=0.

44. Ibid.

45. Max van Balgooy, "NEA Survey Reveals Patterns in Historic Site Visitation," Engaging Places, March 5, 2013, https://engagingplaces.net/2013/03/05/nea-survey-reveals-patterns-in-historic-site-visitation/.

46. Max van Balgooy, "Hot Topics," Engaging Places, accessed April 18, 2017, https://engagingplaces.net/hot-topics/.

47. Roy Rosenzweig and David Thelen, *Presence of the Past: Popular Uses of History in American Life* (Columbia, NY: Columbia University Press, 1998), 32.

48. Ibid., 106.

49. Ibid., 105.

50. Ibid., 107.

51. Lois Silverman, "Making Meaning Together: Lessons from the Field of American History," *Journal of Museum Education* 18, no. 3 (1993): 7–11.

52. Lois Silverman, "Visitor Meaning-Making in Museums for a New Age," *Curator: The Museum Journal* 38, no. 3 (1995): 162.

53. Silverman, "Making Meaning Together," 7.

54. International Coalition of Sites of Conscience, "Home," accessed April 18, 2017, http://www.sitesofconscience.org/en/home/.

55. McCarthy et al., *Gifts of the Muse*, 4.

56. Elaine Gurian, *Civilizing the Museum: The Collected Writings of Elaine Heumann Gurian* (New York: Taylor and Francis, 2006), 89.

57. Elaine Gurian, "What Is the Object of This Exercise? A Meandering Exploration of the Many Meanings of Objects in Museums," *Daedalus* 128, no. 3 (1999): 163–64.

58. Ibid., 165–66.

59. Watson Laetsch, "A Basis for Better Public Understanding of Science," in *Communicating Science to the Public*, ed. David Evered and Maeve O'Connor. Proceedings of the Conference on the Communication of Science, held at the CIBA Foundation, London, October 14–16, 1987 (New York: Wiley, 1987), 8–9.

60. Ibid., 9.

61. Daisy Yuhas, "Curiosity Prepares the Brain for Better Learning," *Scientific American*, October 2, 2014, https://www.scientificamerican.com/article/curiosity-prepares-the-brain-for-better-learning/.

62. Carol Kaesuk Yoon, "Stephen Jay Gould, 60, Is Dead; Enlivened Evolutionary Theory," *New York Times*, May 21, 2002, http://www.nytimes.com/2002/05/21/us/stephen-jay-gould-60-is-dead-enlivened-evolutionary-theory.html.

63. Deborah Perry, *What Makes Learning Fun?: Principles for the Design of Intrinsically Motivating Museum Exhibits* (Lanham, MD: AltaMira Press, 2012), 97.

64. Mihaly Csikszentmihalyi and Kim Hermanson, "Intrinsic Motivation in Museums: Why Does One Want to Learn?" in *Public Institutions for Personal Learning*, ed. John Falk and Lynn Dierking, 67–77 (Washington, DC: American Association of Museums, 1995).

65. Susanna Sirefman, "Formed and Forming: Contemporary Museum Architecture," *Daedalus* 128, no. 3 (1999): 297–320.

66. John Wetenhall, "Why Not to Run Your Museum 'More like a Business.'" *Museum* 96, no. 3 (2017): 37–42.

67. See Randi Korn, "The Case for Holistic Intentionality," *The Museum Journal* 50, no. 2 (2007): 256.

68. Robert Janes and Gerald Conaty, *Looking Reality in the Eye: Museums and Social Responsibility* (Calgary, Alberta: University of Calgary Press, 2005), 9.

69. Montebello, "Art Museums, Inspiring Public Trust," 158.

70. Stephen J. Gould, "Dinomania," *New York Times Review of Books*, August 1, 1993, http://www.nybooks.com/articles/1993/08/12/dinomania/.

71. Michael Kimmelman, "Museums in a Quandary: Where Are the Ideals?" *New York Times*, August 26, 2001, http://www.nytimes.com/2001/08/26/arts/art-architecture-museums-in-a-quandary-where-are-the-ideals.html.

72. Ibid.

73. Simon J. Knell, Suzanne MacLeod, and Sheila Watson, *Museum Revolutions: How Museums Change and Are Changed* (London: Routledge, 2007).

74. James C. Collins and Jerry I. Porras, *Built to Last: Successful Habits of Visionary Companies* (New York: HarperBusiness, 1997), 80.

75. Julia Halperin, "US Museums Spent $5bn to Expand as Economy Shrank," *Art News Paper*, April 4, 2016, http://theartnewspaper.com/news/news/us-museums-spent-5bn-to-expand-as-economy-shrank/.

76. Wetenhall, "Why Not to Run Your Museum 'More Like a Business.'"

77. See Associated Press, "Denver Art Museum Cuts Budget 12 Percent," *Denver Post*, January 11, 2009, http://www.denverpost.com/2009/01/11/

denver-art-museum-cuts-budget-12-percent/; Kenneth Chang, "Exploratorium Forced to Cut Back," *New York Times*, August 26, 2013, http://www.nytimes .com/2013/08/27/science/exploratorium-forced-to-cut-back.html; Jenna Lyons, "Union Supporters Rally against Layoffs at Exploratorium," SFGate, October 1, 2015, http://www.sfgate.com/bayarea/article/Rally-fights-layoffs-at-S-F-s -famed-6544127.php; Greg Adomaitis, "Please Touch Museum, $60 million in Debt, Files for Bankruptcy," *NJ.com*, September 11, 2015, http://www.nj.com/ news/index.ssf/2015/09/please_touch_musuem_60_million_in_debt_files_for_b html.

78. Halperin, "US Museums Spent $5bn to Expand as Economy Shrank."

79. Harold Skramstad, "Changing Public Expectations of Museums," paper presented at Museums for the New Millennium: A Symposium for the Museum Community, September 5–7, 1996, Washington, DC.

80. Stephen E. Weil, "From Being about Something to Being for Somebody," in *Making Museums Matter* (Washington, DC: Smithsonian Books, 2002), 39.

81. Randi Korn, "Self Portrait: First Know Thyself, Then Serve Your Public," *Museum News* 83, no. 1 (2004): 32–35, 50–52.

82. McCarthy et al., *Gifts of the Muse,* xviii.

83. José-Marie Griffiths and Donald W. King, "Interconnections: The IMLS Study on the Use of Libraries, Museums, and the Internet: Museum Survey Results," Institute of Museum and Library Services, 2008, http://www.interconnections report.org/reports/IMLSMusRpt20080312kjm.pdf.

Chapter 3

1. Paul F. McCawley, "The Logic Model for Program Planning and Evaluation." University of Idaho, 2001, https://www.cals.uidaho.edu/edcomm/pdf/ cis/cis1097.pdf.

2. Gail Anderson, ed., *Museum Mission Statements: Building a Distinct Identity* (Washington, DC: American Association of Museums Press, 1998).

3. See Anderson, *Museum Mission Statements*; American Alliance of Museums, "Developing a Mission Statement" (Arlington, VA: American Alliance of Museums, 2012), http://www.aam-us.org/docs/default-source/continuum/ developing-a-mission-statement-final.pdf?sfvrsn=4; and Jean Vergeront, "Missions that Matter," 2011, https://museumnotes.blogspot.com/2011/01/missions -that-matter.html.

4. Milton J. Bloch, "Forum: Mission as Measure: Second Thoughts." *Museum News* 84, no. 3 (2005): 37–41, 78–79.

5. See Harold Skramstad, "Changing Public Expectations of Museums," paper presented at Museums for the New Millennium: A Symposium for the Museum Community, September 5–7, 1996, Washington, DC; Randi Korn, "The Case

for Holistic Intentionality," *Curator: The Museum Studies Journal* 50, no. 2 (2007): 255–64; and Randi Korn, "Self-Portrait: First Know Thyself, Then Serve Your Public," *Museum News* 83, no. 1 (2004): 33–35, 50–52.

6. David La Piana, *The Nonprofit Strategy Revolution: Real-Time Strategic Planning in a Rapid-Response World* (Saint Paul, MN: Fieldstone Alliance, 2008).

7. *Harvard Business Review*, "The New Game Plan for Strategic Planning," Harvard Business Review Analytic Service Report, Harvard Business School Publishing, 2016, https://hbr.org/resources/pdfs/comm/anaplan/HBRASAnaplan 12.7.16.pdf.

8. La Piana, *The Nonprofit Strategy Revolution*, xiv.

9. Alan Friedman, ed., *Framework for Evaluating Impacts of Informal Science Education Projects*. Report from a National Science Foundation Workshop, March 12–13, 2008, Arlington, VA: National Science Foundation. http://www.informalscience .org/framework-evaluating-impacts-informal-science-education-projects.

10. See Korn, "The Case for Holistic Intentionality," and Korn, "Self-Portrait."

11. Mary Ellen Munley, "Evaluating Public Value: Strategy and Practice," in *Museums and Public Value: Creating Sustainable Futures*, ed. Carol Ann Scott, 45–61 (London: Routledge, 2013).

12. See Carol A. Scott, 2013, "Introduction to Museums and Public Value," in *Museums and Public Value: Creating Sustainable Futures*, ed. Carol Ann Scott, 1–13 (London: Routledge); and Munley, "Evaluating Public Value: Strategy and Practice."

13. Mark Moore, *Creating Public Value: Strategic Management in Government* (Cambridge, MA: Harvard University Press, 1997). See also his 2013 publication, *Recognizing Public Value* (Cambridge, MA: Harvard University Press).

14. Ibid.

15. Ibid.

16. Stephen E. Weil, *Making Museums Matter* (Washington, DC: Smithsonian Books, 2002), 60.

17. James C. Collins and Jerry I. Porras, *Built to Last: Successful Habits of Visionary Companies* (New York: Harper Collins, 2002).

18. Jim Collins, 2011. *Good to Great: Why Some Companies Make the Leap . . . and Some Don't* (New York: Harper Collins, 2011).

19. Jim Collins, *Good to Great and the Social Sectors: Why Business Thinking Is Not the Answer: A Monograph to Accompany Good to Great* (New York: Harper Collins, 2005).

20. Collins adapted the Greek parable about a hedgehog and a fox to illustrate the importance of focusing on one thing. For Collins, it is greatness, and in intentional practice for museums, it is impact. The parable's line "The fox knows many things, but the hedgehog knows one big thing" saves the hedgehog from the fox during its daily chase. The one thing the hedgehog knows

is to curl up into a ball to deflect the fox. The fox represents distractions that bombard us every day, and by maintaining focus on the museum's intended impact, you will have the will to deflect those distractions. For more about the fox's pursuit of the hedgehog, see http://assets.press.princeton.edu/chapters/s9981.pdf.

21. Collins, *Good to Great*.

22. Korn, "The Case for Holistic Intentionality." See also Sherene Suchy, *Leading with Passion: Change Management in the Twenty-First Century* (Lanham, MD: AltaMira Press, 2004).

23. Collins, *Good to Great*, 109.

24. Korn, "The Case for Holistic Intentionality."

25. Gloria Goodale, "Museums' New Mantra: Connect with Community," *Christian Science Monitor,* July 20, 2009, https://www.csmonitor.com/The-Culture/Arts/2009/0721/p17s01-algn.html.

26. Elaine Gurian, "Museum as Soup Kitchen." *Curator: The Museums Journal* 53, no. 1 (2010): 82.

27. Emlyn Koster, "The Relevant Museum: A Reflection on Sustainability," *Museum News* 85, no. 3 (2006): 67.

28. Gail Anderson, "Museums and Relevancy," *Journal of Museum Education* 31, no. 1 (2006): 3.

29. Cynthia Vernon and Paul Boyle, "Impact Aquarium Visit," *Connect* (April 2008): 7–9.

30. Bonnie Pitman and Ellen Hirzy, *Ignite the Power of Art: Advancing Visitor Engagement in Museums* (New Haven, CT: Yale University Press, 2010).

31. Randi Korn, Amanda Krantz, and Margaret Menninger, "Rethinking Museum Visitors: Using K-Means Cluster Analysis to Explore a Museum's Audience," *Curator: The Museum Journal* 52, no. 4 (2009): 363–74.

32. John Falk, *Identity and the Museum Visitor Experience* (Walnut Creek, CA: Left Coast Press, 2013).

33. Jane Wales, "Framing the Issue," *Stanford Social Innovation Review* (Summer 2012). https://ssir.org/articles/entry/framing_the_issue_2.

34. Ibid.

35. Mary Ellen Munley, "Museum Education and the Genius of Improvisation," *Journal of Museum Education* 21, no. 1 (1996): 19.

36. Stephen R. Covey, *The 7 Habits of Highly Effective People* (New York: Free Press, 1988).

37. If the museum's planning work is project specific, it might consider using a logic model, keeping in mind that the Cycle of Intentional Practice provides additional planning options such as reflection and alignment—elements that are absent in logic models.

38. Collins, *Good to Great*, 11.

39. Covey, *The 7 Habits of Highly Effective People*.

40. For guidance and how-to information on writing outcomes, see Innovation Network, *Logic Model Workbook*, https://www.innonet.org/media/logic_model_workbook_0.pdf; and W. H. Kellogg Foundation, *Logic Model Development Guide,* 2006, https://www.wkkf.org/resource-directory/resource/2006/02/wk-kellogg-foundation-logic-model-development-guide.

41. Beverly Serrell, *Exhibit Labels: An Interpretive Approach,* 2nd ed. (Lanham, MD: Rowman & Littlefield, 2015), 7–9.

42. There are many excellent books on how to conduct evaluations, and there are also many educational opportunities for earning a degree or certificate in evaluation; for readers interested in honing their evaluation skills, see the American Evaluation Association (http://www.eval.org/), the Evaluators' Institute (https://tei.cgu.edu/), the Visitor Studies Association (http://www.visitorstudies.org/), and the following publications: Judy Diamond, Michael Horn, and David H. Uttal, *Practical Evaluation Guide* (New York: Rowman & Littlefield, 2016); Michael Quinn Patton, *Principles-Focused Evaluation: The Guide* (New York: The Guilford Press, 2017); and Joseph S. Wholey, Harry P. Hatry, and Kathryn E. Newcomer, eds., *Handbook of Practical Program Evaluation,* 2nd ed. (San Francisco, CA: Jossey-Bass, 2004).

43. Korn, "The Case for Holistic Intentionality." See www.informalscience.org for program-specific evaluations.

44. Stephen E. Weil, "Museums: Can and Do They Make a Difference?," in *Making Museums Matter,* 55–74 (Washington, DC: Smithsonian Institution, 2002), 61–62.

45. Leonard Bickman, "Evaluation Research," in *Encyclopedia of Evaluation,* ed. Sandra Mathison (Thousand Oaks, CA: Sage Publications, 2005), 141.

46. Randi Korn, "Creating Public Value through Intentional Practice," in *Museums and Public Value: Creating Sustainable Futures,* ed. Carol Ann Scott, 31–43 (London: Routledge, 2013).

47. David Chesebrough, "Putting Public Value to the Test," ASTC Dimensions (January/February 2010): 7, 12, http://www.astc.org/Dimensions PDFS/2010/JanFeb.pdf#page=6.

48. Clare Cooper and Roanne Dods, "Mission, Models, Money—Frustration, Passion, Vision, Mission," 2006, https://www.artsprofessional.co.uk/magazine/article/mission-models-money-frustration-passion-vision-mission.

49. The Museums Association, "Sustainability and Museums: Your Chance to Make a Difference," 2008, p. 7, http://www.museumsassociation.org/download?id=16398.

50. Randi Korn, "When Less Is More," *Museum* 89, no. 5 (2010): 25–27.

51. Ibid.

52. Ibid., 26.

53. Lynda Kelly, "Measuring the Impact of Museums on their Communities: The Role of the 21st Century Museum," paper presented at Intercom

Conference 2006, Taiwan, November 2–4, 2006, http://www.intercom .museum/documents/1-2Kelly.pdf.

54. Minda Borun and Randi Korn, "The Quandaries of Audience Research," *Journal of Museum Education* 20, no. 1 (1995): 3–4. See also Arts Education Partnership's criteria for rigor at www.artsedsearch.org/about/submit-a-study.

55. Douglas Worts, "Measuring Museum Meaning: A Critical Assessment Framework," *Journal of Museum Education* 31, no. 1 (2006): 43, 49.

56. Carol A. Scott, "Museums: Impact and Value," *Cultural Trends* 15, no. 1 (March 2006): 45–75.

57. Victor S. Yocco, Joe E. Heimlich, Emily Meyer, and Pam Edwards, "Measuring Public Value: An Instrument and an Art Museum Case Study," *Visitor Studies* 12, no. 2 (2009): 152–63.

58. Barbara Soren, "Museum Experiences that Change Visitors," *Museum Management and Curatorship* 24, no. 3 (2009): 233–51.

59. Kelly, "Measuring the Impact of Museums on their Communities," 2.

60. Ibid., 9.

61. See Alessandro Bollo, "Report 3: Measuring Museum Impacts," *The Learning Museum Project*, 2013, http://online.ibc.regione.emilia-romagna.it/I/libri/ pdf/LEM3rd-report-measuring-museum-impacts.pdf; DSP-groep, "More Than Worth It: The Social Significance of Museums," 2011, Netherlands Museum Association, https://www.dsp-groep.eu/wp-content/uploads/17elmusea_The _social_signifigance_of_museums.pdf; Robin Garnett, "The Impact of Science Centers/Museums on Their Surrounding Communities: Summary Report," ASTC and ECSITE, 2001, http://www.astc.org/resource/case/Impact_Study02 .pdf; Ben Gammon, "The Impact of Science and Discovery Centres: A Review of Worldwide Studies," UK Association for Science and Discovery Centres, http:// sciencecentres.org.uk/reports/downloads/impact-of-science-discovery-centres -review-of-worldwide-studies.pdf; and Jody Evans, Kerrie Bridson, and Joanna Minkiewicz, "Demonstrating Impact—Four Case Studies of Public Art Museums," Asia Pacific Social Impact Leadership Centre, Melbourne Business School, 2013, http://www.pgav.org.au/cms/tinymce/filemanager/library/Demonstrating %20Impact%20in%20Public%20Art%20Museums%20Report.pdf.

62. See Lori Marino, Scott O. Lilienfeld, Randy Malamud, Nathan Nobis, and Ron Brogliod, "Do Zoos and Aquariums Promote Attitude Change in Visitors? A Critical Evaluation of the American Zoo and Aquarium Study," *Society and Animals: Journal of Human-Animal Studies* 18 (2010): 126, http://www.animals andsociety.org/wp-content/uploads/2016/04/marino.pdf; and John H. Falk, Eric M. Reinhard, Cynthia L. Vernon, Kerry Bronnenkant, Joe E. Heimlich, and Nora L. Deans, "Why Zoos and Aquariums Matter: Assessing the Impact of a Visit to a Zoo or Aquarium," Silver Spring, MD: Association of Zoos and Aquariums, 2007, https://www.scribd.com/document/29860905/Why-Zoos -and-Aquariums-Matter.

63. Joy Amulya, "What Is Reflective Practice?" The Center for Reflective Community Practice at MIT, 2004, www.itslifejimbutnotasweknowit.org.uk/files/whatisreflectivepractice.pdf.

64. Susan Glasser, "The Forgotten Audience," *Museum* 87 no. 3 (2008): 70–75.

65. Donald A. Schön, *The Reflective Practitioner: How Professionals Think in Action* (New York: Basic Books, 1983).

66. Donald A. Schön, *Educating the Reflective Practitioner: Towards a New Design for Teaching and Learning in the Professions* (San Francisco, CA: Jossey-Bass, 1987).

67. Jenny Moon, "PDP (Professional Development Planning) Working Paper 4: Reflection in Higher Education Learning." LTSN Generic Centre, 2001, http://citeseerx.ist.psu.edu/viewdoc/download?doi=10.1.1.503.5288&rep=rep1&type=pd.

68. Ibid.

69. Ibid.

70. Ibid.

71. Joseph A. Raelin, "'I Don't Have the Time to Think!' Versus the Art of Reflective Practice," *Reflections* 4, no. 1 (2002): 66–75.

72. See Raelin, "'I Don't Have the Time to Think!'"; Peter Senge, C. Otto Scharmer, Joseph Jaworski, and Betty Sue Flowers, *Presence: Exploring Profound Change in People, Organizations, and Society* (New York: Society for Organizational Learning, 2004); and C. Otto. Scharmer, *Theory of U: Leading from the Future as It Emerges* (Cambridge, MA: Society for Organizational Learning, 2004).

73. For more information on Serrell's approach using questions to reflect on exhibitions, see Beverly Serrell, *Judging Exhibitions: A Framework for Assessing Excellence* (Walnut Creek, CA: Left Coast Press, 2006).

74. Raelin, "'I Don't Have the Time to Think!'"

75. Edgar Schein, "Commentary," *Reflections* 4, no. 1 (2002): 79.

76. Raelin, "'I Don't Have the Time to Think!'"

77. Sandy Richardson, "Why Organizational Alignment Should Matter to You (and How to Get It)," *The SFO Blog,* August 2, 2011, http://sfo-blog.typepad.com/sfo-blog/2011/08/why-organizational-alignment-should-matter-to-you-and-how-to-get-it.html.

78. Carolyn P. Blackmon, Theresa K. LaMaster, Lisa C. Roberts, and Beverly Serrell, *Open Conversations: Strategies for Professional Development in Museums* (Chicago, IL: Field Museum of Natural History, 1988).

79. Korn, "The Case for Holistic Intentionality" (see note 5); see www.informalscience.org for program-specific evaluations.

80. Peter Samis and Mimi Michaelson, *Creating the Visitor-Centered Museum* (New York: Routledge, 2017).

81. Stephen E. Weil, "A Success/Failure Matrix for Museums," *Museum News* 84, no. 1 (2005): 36.

82. Senge, Scharmer, Jaworski, and Flowers, *Presence.*

83. See this reading list: http://aspire.surrey.ac.uk/lists/CFA35ABC-EB08
-F05E-B387-0943D316689C/bibliography.html.

Chapter 4

1. Stephen E. Weil, "Museums: Can and Do They Make a Difference?," in *Making Museums Matter* (Washington, DC: Smithsonian Books, 2002), 61.

2. George Labovitz and Victor Rosansky, *Rapid Realignment: How to Quickly Integrate People, Processes, and Strategy for Unbeatable Performance* (New York: McGraw Hill, 2012), 14.

3. Ibid.

4. Ibid.

5. See Beverly Serrell, *Judging Exhibitions: A Framework for Assessing Excellence* (Walnut Creek, CA: Left Coast Press, 2006).

6. Osvaldo Néstor Feinstein, "Evaluation as a Learning Tool," in *Evaluation Voices from Latin America: New Directions for Evaluation*, ed. Saville Kushner and E. Rotondo, No. 134 of J-B PE Single Issue (Program) Evaluation Series (Somerset, NJ: John Wiley and Sons, 2012): 103–12; Emily Hoole and Tracy E. Patterson, "Voices from the Field: Evaluation as Part of a Learning Culture," in "Nonprofits and Evaluation," ed. Joanne G. Carman and Kimberly A. Fredericks. Special issue, *New Directions for Evaluation* 2008, no. 119: 93–113; and Hallie S. Preskill and Rosalie T. Torres, "The Learning Dimension of Evaluation Use," in "The Expanding Scope of Evaluation Use," ed. Valerie J. Caracelli and Hallie Preskill. Special issue, *New Directions for Evaluation* 2000, no. 88, 25–37.

7. Jenny Moon, "PDP (Professional Development Planning) Working Paper 4: Reflection in Higher Education Learning," LTSN Generic Centre, May 10, 2001, https://www.cumbria.ac.uk/media/university-of-cumbria-website/content-assets/public/er/documents/admissions/interviewdocs/Moon2001 ReflectivePracticeInterview-1.pdf.

8. Carol Rodgers, E. Spalding, and A. Wilson have summarized these ideas from John Dewey's book, *How We Think*. See Carol Rodgers, "Defining Reflection: Another Look at John Dewey and Reflective Thinking," *Teachers College Record* 104 no. 4 (2002): 842–66; and E. Spalding and A. Wilson, "Demystifying Reflection: A Study of Pedagogical Strategies that Encourage Reflective Journal Writing," *Teachers College Record* 104 no. 7 (2002): 1393–421.

9. Simon Sinek, *Start with Why: How Great Leaders Inspire Everyone to Take Action* (New York: Penguin Group, 2009).

10. Labovitz and Rosansky, *Rapid Realignment*.

11. Presented in Labovitz and Rosansky, *Rapid Realignment*.

12. Heidi K. Gardner and Herminia Ibarra, "How to Capture Value from Collaboration, Especially If You're Skeptical about It," *Harvard Business Review*, May 2, 2017, https://hbr.org/2017/05/how-to-capture-value-from-collaboration-especially-if-youre-skeptical-about-it.

13. Herminia Ibarra and Morten T. Hansen, "Are You a Collaborative Leader?," *Harvard Business Review*, July–August 2001, 72.

14. Ibid.

15. Suzanne M. Donovan, John D. Bransford, and James W. Pellegrino, eds., *How People Learn: Bridging Research and Practice* (Washington, DC: National Academy Press, 1999).

16. Susan Sternberg, "The Art of Participation," in *Museum Education: History, Theory, and Practice*, ed. Nancy Berry and Susan Mayer, 154–71 (Reston, VA: National Art Education Association, 1989).

17. Joshua P. Gutwill and Sue Allen, *Group Inquiry at Science Museum Exhibits* (San Francisco, CA: Exploratorium, 2010).

18. Beverly Serrell, *Exhibit Labels: An Interpretive Approach* (New York: Rowman & Littlefield, 2015).

19. George Hein, "John Dewey's 'Wholly Original Philosophy' and Its Significance for Museums," *Curator: The Museum Journal* 49 no. 2 (2006): 196.

20. Labovitz and Rosansky, *Rapid Realignment,* 48.

21. Amy Jen Su and Muriel Maignan Wilkins, "What Gets in the Way of Listening," *Harvard Business Review,* April 14, 2014, https://hbr.org/2014/04/what-gets-in-the-way-of-listening.

22. Melissa Daimler, "Listening Is an Overlooked Leadership Tool," *Harvard Business Review,* May 25, 2016, https://hbr.org/2016/05/listening-is-an-overlooked-leadership-tool.

23. Jen Su and Wilkins, "What Gets in the Way of Listening."

24. Ram Charan, "The Discipline of Listening," *Harvard Business Review,* June 21, 2012, https://hbr.org/2012/06/the-discipline-of-listening.

25. Robert J. Stahl, "Using 'Think-Time' and 'Wait-Time' Skillfully in the Classroom," *ERIC Digest*, May 1994, https://www.ericdigests.org/1995-1/think.htm.

26. George Ambler, "Leadership Develops When You Escape Your Comfort Zone," *GeorgeAmbler.com,* May 10, 2015, http://www.georgeambler.com/leadership-develops-when-you-escape-your-comfort-zone/.

27. David Linden, *The Compass of Pleasure* (New York: Penguin Books, 2011).

28. Daniel Pink, *Drive: The Surprising Truth about What Motivates Us* (New York: Riverhead Books, 2011).

29. Ron Ashkenas, "Basecamp's Strategy Offers a Useful Reminder: Less Is More," *Harvard Business Review,* February 10, 2014, https://hbr.org/2014/02/basecamps-strategy-offers-a-useful-reminder-less-is-more.

30. Matthew May, "Zen and the Art of Simplicity," *Rotman Magazine* (Fall 2011): 39, https://matthewemay.com/wp-content/uploads/2011/10/zenandtheartofsimplicity.pdf.

31. Ashkenas, "Basecamp's Strategy."

32. Peter Drucker, "The Theory of the Business," *Harvard Business Review,* September–October 1994, https://hbr.org/1994/09/the-theory-of-the-business.

33. Jim Collins, *Good to Great: Why Some Companies Make the Leap . . . and Others Don't* (New York: HarperCollins, 2001), 139.

34. Carlin Flora, "The Hardest Word," *Psychology Today,* September 5, 2017, https://www.psychologytoday.com/articles/201709/the-hardest-word; Alexandra Samuel, "This Year, Say Yes to Saying No," *Harvard Business Review,* January 8, 2010, https://hbr.org/2010/01/say-yes-to-saying-no.

35. Jonathan Becher, "6 Quotes to Help You Understand Why It Is Important to Say No," *Forbes,* August 12, 2015, https://www.forbes.com/sites/sap/2015/08/12/quotes-on-saying-no/#50d8100a5555.

36. Elizabeth Grace Saunders, "Accomplish More by Committing to Less," *Harvard Business Review,* January 30, 2015, https://hbr.org/2015/01/accomplish-more-by-committing-to-less.

37. Serrell, *Exhibit Labels.*

Chapter 5

1. See Yayasan IDEP, "Workshop Resources 1: Creative Facilitation Techniques," in *Permaculture Facilitator's Resource Book for Training and Assessment* (Bali, Indonesia: IDEP Foundation, 2006), http://www.teindia.nic.in/files/teacher_trg_module/8_creative_facilitation_techniques.pdf; MindTools, "The Role of a Facilitator," MindTools.com, accessed March 13, 2018, https://www.mindtools.com/pages/article/RoleofAFacilitator.htm; and Sam Kaner, *Facilitator's Guide to Participatory Decision-Making,* 3rd ed, Jossey-Bass Business and Management Series (San Francisco, CA: Jossey-Bass, 2014).

2. See MindTools, "5 Whys: Getting to the Root of a Problem Quickly," MindTools.com, accessed March 13, 2018, https://www.mindtools.com/pages/article/newTMC_5W.htm; and James C. Collins and Jerry I. Porras, *Built to Last: Successful Habits of Visionary Companies* (New York: HarperBusiness, 1997), 80.

3. There are many excellent how-to books on conducting research, and I urge readers to seek them out for a thorough presentation on the topic. See, for example, Arlene Fink, 2017. *How to Conduct Surveys: A Step-by-Step Guide* (Washington, DC: Sage Publications, 2017); Lesley Andres, *Designing and Doing Survey Research* (Washington, DC: Sage Publications, 2012); and Floyd J. Fowler Jr., *Survey Research Methods* (Washington, DC: Sage Publications, 2014).

4. David Kolb, *Experiential Learning: Experience as the Source for Learning and Development,* 2nd ed. (Upper Saddle River, NJ: Pearson Education, Inc., 2012); and Saul McLeod, "Kolb: Learning Styles," SimplyPsychology.com, 2017, https://www.simplypsychology.org/learning-kolb.html.

5. Though intentional practice is ongoing, reflecting on results from a study may have a natural end point.

6. Peter Senge, *The Fifth Discipline* (New York: Doubleday/Currency, 1990).

7. Stephen E. Weil, "A Success/Failure Matrix for Museums," *Museum News* 84, no. 1 (2005): 36.

8. Senge, *The Fifth Discipline,* 3.

Chapter 6

1. Children's Museum Research Network, Association of Children's Museums, accessed April 10, 2018, http://www.childrensmuseums.org/children-s-museum-research-network.

2. Special thanks to Sarah Barr, director of the Center for Community Engagement at Amherst College, for sharing this resource. Deborah Mashek and Michael Nanfito, "People, Tools, and Processes That Build Collaborative Capacity," The Teagle Foundation, November 2015, accessed April 25, 2018, http://www.teaglefoundation.org/Library-Resources/Faculty-Planning-and-Curricular-Coherence/People,-Tools,-and-Processes-that-Build-Collaborat.

3. Emlyn H. Koster and John H. Falk, "Maximizing the External Value of Museums," *Curator: The Museum Journal* 50, no. 2, (2007): 193.

4. Ibid., 193–94.

Chapter 7

1. Peter M. Senge, *The Fifth Discipline* (New York: Doubleday, 1990), 1.

2. Business Dictionary, accessed April 16, 2018, http://www.businessdictionary.com/definition/organizational-learning.html.

3. See Hallie Preskill and Rosalie Torres, *Evaluative Inquiry for Learning in Organizations* (Thousand Oaks, CA: Sage Publications, 1999) for a more thorough discussion about the why, how, and what of organizational learning.

Bibliography

Adomaitis, Greg. 2015. "Please Touch Museum, $60 million in Debt, Files for Bankruptcy." *NJ.com*, September 11. http://www.nj.com/news/index .ssf/2015/09/please_touch_musuem_60_million_in_debt_files_for_b.html.

Ambler, George. 2015. "Leadership Develops When You Escape Your Comfort Zone." *GeorgeAmbler.com,* May 10. http://www.georgeambler.com/leadership -develops-when-you-escape-your-comfort-zone/.

American Alliance of Museums. 2012. "Developing a Mission Statement." Arlington, VA: American Alliance of Museums. http://www.aam-us.org/docs/ default-source/continuum/developing-a-mission-statement-final.pdf?sfvrsn=4.

American Evaluation Association. 2013. "American Evaluation Association Guiding Principles for Evaluators." American Evaluation Association. Accessed May 30, 2017. http://www.eval.org/p/cm/ld/fid=51.

Amulya, Joy. 2004. "What Is Reflective Practice?" The Center for Reflective Community Practice at MIT. www.itslifejimbutnotasweknowit.org.uk/files/ whatisreflectivepractice.pdf.

Anderson, Gail, ed. 1998. *Museum Mission Statements: Building a Distinct Identity.* Washington, DC: American Association of Museums Press.

———. 2006. "Museums and Relevancy." *Journal of Museum Education* 31, no. 1: 3–6.

Andres, Lesley. 2012. *Designing and Doing Survey Research.* Washington, DC: Sage Publications.

Ashkenas, Ron. 2014. "Basecamp's Strategy Offers a Useful Reminder: Less Is More." *Harvard Business Review,* February 10. https://hbr.org/2014/02/ basecamps-strategy-offers-a-useful-reminder-less-is-more.

Associated Press. 2009. "Denver Art Museum Cuts Budget 12 Percent." *Denver Post*, January 11. http://www.denverpost.com/2009/01/11/denver-art -museum-cuts-budget-12-percent/.

Association of Art Museum Directors. 2017. "Association of Art Museum Directors Issues Art Museums by the Numbers 2016." Released January 9. https://www .aamd.org/for-the-media/press-release/association-of-art-museum-directors -issues-art-museums-by-the-numbers-0.

Balgooy, Max van. 2013. "NEA Survey Reveals Patterns in Historic Site Visitation." Engaging Places. March 5. https://engagingplaces.net/2013/03/05/nea -survey-reveals-patterns-in-historic-site-visitation/.

———. 2017. "Hot Topics." Engaging Places. Accessed April 18. https://engaging places.net/hot-topics/.

Becher, Jonathan. 2015. "6 Quotes to Help You Understand Why It Is Important to Say No." *Forbes*, August 12. https://www.forbes.com/sites/sap/ 2015/08/12/quotes-on-saying-no/#50d8100a5555.

Bell, Philippe, Bruch Lewenstein, Andrew W. Shouse, and Michael A. Feder, eds. 2009. *Learning Science in Informal Environments: People, Places, and Pursuits*. Washington, DC: National Research Council of the National Academies.

Bickman, Leonard. 2005. "Evaluation Research." In *Encyclopedia of Evaluation*, edited by Sandra Mathison, 141. Thousand Oaks, CA: Sage Publications.

Blackmon, Carolyn P., Theresa K. LaMaster, Lisa C. Roberts, and Beverly Serrell. 1988. *Open Conversations: Strategies for Professional Development in Museums*. Chicago, IL: Field Museum of Natural History.

Bloch, Milton J. 2005. "Forum: Mission as Measure: Second Thoughts." *Museum News* 84, no. 3: 37–41, 78–79.

Bollo, Alessandro. 2013. "Report 3: Measuring Museum Impacts." *The Learning Museum Project*. http://online.ibc.regione.emilia-romagna.it/I/libri/pdf/ LEM3rd-report-measuring-museum-impacts.pdf.

Borun, Minda, and Randi Korn. 1995. "The Quandaries of Audience Research." *Journal of Museum Education* 20, no. 1: 3–4.

Brown, Alan. 2006. "An Architecture of Value." *Grantmakers in the Arts Reader* 17 no. 1: 18–23.

Buckley, Jane, et al. 2015. "Defining and Teaching Evaluative Thinking: Insights from Research on Critical Thinking," *American Journal of Evaluation* 36, no. 3: 375–88. http://www.socialresearchmethods.net/research/2015/2015%20-%20 Buckley%20et%20al%20-%20Evaluative%20Thinking.pdf.

Business Dictionary. Accessed April 16, 2018. http://www.businessdictionary.com/ definition/organizational-learning.html.

Chang, Kenneth. 2013. "Exploratorium Forced to Cut Back." *New York Times*, August 26. http://www.nytimes.com/2013/08/27/science/exploratorium -forced-to-cut-back.html.

Charan, Ram. 2012. "The Discipline of Listening." *Harvard Business Review*. June 21. https://hbr.org/2012/06/the-discipline-of-listening.

Chesebrough, David. 2010. "Putting Public Value to the Test." ASTC Dimensions (January/February): 7, 12. http://www.astc.org/DimensionsPDFS/2010/ JanFeb.pdf#page=6.

Children's Museum Research Network, Association of Children's Museums. Accessed April 10, 2018. http://www.childrensmuseums.org/children-s-museum-research-network.

Collins, James C., and Jerry I. Porras. 2002. *Built to Last: Successful Habits of Visionary Companies*. New York: HarperBusiness.

Collins, Jim. 2005. *Good to Great and the Social Sectors: Why Business Thinking is Not the Answer: A Monograph to Accompany Good to Great*. New York: Harper Collins.

———. 2011. *Good to Great: Why Some Companies Make the Leap . . . and Others Don't*. New York: Harper Collins.

Cooper, Clare, and Roanne Dods. 2006. "Mission, Models, Money—Frustration, Passion, Vision, Mission." https://www.artsprofessional.co.uk/magazine/article/mission-models-money-frustration-passion-vision-mission.

COSMOS Corporation. 1998. "A Report on the Evaluation of the National Science Foundation's Informal Science Education Program." Arlington, VA: National Science Foundation.

Covey, Stephen R. 1988. *The 7 Habits of Highly Effective People*. New York: Free Press.

Crane, T. 2005. "Intentionality." In the *Oxford Companion to Philosophy*, edited by Ted Honderich, 438. Oxford: Oxford University Press.

Crane, Valerie, Heather Nicholson, Milton Chen, and Stephen Bitgood, eds. 1994. *Informal Science Learning: What the Research Says about Television, Science Museums, and Community-Based Projects*. Dedham, MA: Research Communications.

Csikszentmihalyi, Mihaly, and Kim Hermanson. 1995. "Intrinsic Motivation in Museums: Why Does One Want to Learn?" In *Public Institutions for Personal Learning*, edited by John Falk and Lynn Dierking, 67–77. Washington, DC: American Association of Museums.

Csikszentmihalyi, Mihaly, and Rick E. Robinson. 1990. *The Art of Seeing: An Interpretation of the Aesthetic Encounter*. Los Angeles: J. Paul Getty Museum.

Cuno, James, ed. 2004. *Whose Muse: Art Museums and the Public Trust*. Princeton, NJ: Princeton University Press and Harvard Art Museums.

Daimler, Melissa. 2016. "Listening Is an Overlooked Leadership Tool." *Harvard Business Review*, May 25. https://hbr.org/2016/05/listening-is-an-overlooked-leadership-tool.

Dana, John Cotton. 1999. *The New Museum: Selected Writings by John Cotton Dana*, edited by William A. Peniston. Washington, DC: Newark Museum Association and the American Alliance of Museums.

Diamond, Judy, Michael Horn, and David H. Uttal. 2016. *Practical Evaluation Guide*. New York: Rowman & Littlefield.

Doering, Zahava, D. 1999. "Strangers, Guests or Clients? Visitor Experiences in Museums." Washington, DC: Smithsonian Studies Office.

Doering, Zahava D., and Martin Storksdieck, eds. 2010. Special Issue on Science. *Curator: The Museum Journal* 53, no. 2.

Donovan, Suzanne M., John D. Bransford, and James W. Pellegrino, eds. 1999. *How People Learn: Bridging Research and Practice.* Washington, DC: National Academy Press.

Drucker, Peter. 1994. "The Theory of the Business." *Harvard Business Review,* September–October. https://hbr.org/1994/09/the-theory-of-the-business.

DSP-groep. 2011. "More Than Worth It: The Social Significance of Museums." Netherlands Museum Association. https://www.dsp-groep.eu/wp-content/uploads/17elmusea_The_social_signifigance_of_museums.pdf.

Duschl, Richard A., Heidi A. Schweingruber, and Andrew W. Shouse, eds. 2007. *Taking Science to School: Learning and Teaching Science in Grades K–8.* Washington, DC: The National Academies Press.

Egan, Sara, Emily Jennings, and Chelsea Emelie Kelly. 2017. "Intentionality and the Role of the Museum Educator: Letter from the Editors." *Viewfinder* 4. https://medium.com/viewfinder-reflecting-on-museum-education/viewfinder-issue-4-intentionality-and-the-role-of-the-museum-educator-letter-from-the-editors-fb06f85b58c6#.bhxed97rr.

Evans, Jody, Kerrie Bridson, and Joanna Minkiewicz. 2013. "Demonstrating Impact—Four Case Studies of Public Art Museums." Asia Pacific Social Impact Leadership Centre, Melbourne Business School. http://www.pgav.org.au/cms/tinymce/filemanager/library/Demonstrating%20Impact%20in%20Public%20Art%20Museums%20Report.pdf.

Falk, John. 2013. *Identity and the Museum Visitor Experience.* Walnut Creek, CA: Left Coast Press.

Falk, John H., Eric M. Reinhard, Cynthia L. Vernon, Kerry Bronnenkant, Joe E. Heimlich, and Nora L. Deans. 2007. "Why Zoos & Aquariums Matter: Assessing the Impact of a Visit to a Zoo or Aquarium." Silver Spring, MD: Association of Zoos and Aquariums. https://www.scribd.com/document/29860905/Why-Zoos-and-Aquariums-Matter.

Falk, John, and Beverley Sheppard. 2006. *Thriving in the Knowledge Age.* Lanham, MD: AltaMira Press.

Feinstein, Osvaldo Néstor. 2012. "Evaluation as a Learning Tool." In *Evaluation Voices from Latin America: New Directions for Evaluation,* edited by Saville Kushner and E. Rotondo, 103–12. No. 134 of J-B PE Single Issue (Program) Evaluation Series. Somerset, NJ: John Wiley and Sons.

Fink, Arlene. 2017. *How to Conduct Surveys: A Step-by-Step Guide.* Washington, DC: Sage Publications.

Fleming, David. 2010. "Museums Campaigning for Social Justice." The Fifth Stephen Weil Memorial Lecture, Shanghai, China, November 2010. http://www.intercom.museum/documents/5thWeilLectureShanghaiNov2010.pdf.

Flora, Carlin. 2017. "The Hardest Word." *Psychology Today,* September 5. https://www.psychologytoday.com/articles/201709/the-hardest-word.

Foley, Cindy Meyers, and Rachel Trinkley. 2014. "Intentionality and the Twenty-First Century Museum." In "Intentionality and the Twenty-first

Century Museum," special issue. Edited by Cindy Meyers Foley and Rachel Trinkley. *Journal of Museum Education* 39, no. 2: 125–31.

Fowler, Floyd J., Jr. 2014. *Survey Research Methods.* Washington, DC: Sage Publications.

Friedman, Alan, ed. 2008. *Framework for Evaluating Impacts of Informal Science Education Projects.* Report from a National Science Foundation Workshop. March 12–13. Arlington, VA: National Science Foundation. http://www.informalscience.org/framework-evaluating-impacts-informal-science-education-projects.

Gammon, Ben. n.d. "The Impact of Science & Discovery Centres: A Review of Worldwide Studies." UK Association for Science and Discovery Centres. http://sciencecentres.org.uk/reports/downloads/impact-of-science-discovery-centres-review-of-worldwide-studies.pdf.

Gardner, Heidi K., and Herminia Ibarra. 2017. "How to Capture Value from Collaboration, Especially If You're Skeptical about It." *Harvard Business Review,* May 2. https://hbr.org/2017/05/how-to-capture-value-from-collaboration-especially-if-youre-skeptical-about-it.

Garnett, Robin. 2001. "The Impact of Science Centers/Museums on Their Surrounding Communities: Summary Report." ASTC and ECSITE. http://www.astc.org/resource/case/Impact_Study02.pdf.

Glasser, Susan. 2008. "The Forgotten Audience." *Museum* 87 no. 3: 70–75.

Goodale, Gloria. 2009. "Museums' New Mantra: Connect with Community." *Christian Science Monitor,* July 20. https://www.csmonitor.com/The-Culture/Arts/2009/0721/p17s01-algn.html.

Gould, Stephen J. 1993. "Dinomania." *New York Times Review of Books*, August 1. http://www.nybooks.com/articles/1993/08/12/dinomania/.

Government Performance and Results Act of 1993, Cong. Rec., 103rd Cong. (1993).

Greszler, Rachel. 2017. "Show Me the Math: How to Achieve a Leaner Federal Government." The Heritage Foundation. March 28. http://www.heritage.org/budget-and-spending/commentary/show-me-the-math-how-achieve-leaner-federal-government.

Griffiths, José-Marie, and Donald W. King. 2008. "Interconnections: The IMLS Study on the Use of Libraries, Museums, and the Internet: Museum Survey Results." Institute of Museum and Library Services. http://www.interconnectionsreport.org/reports/IMLSMusRpt20080312kjm.pdf.

Gurian, Elaine. 1999. "What Is the Object of This Exercise? A Meandering Exploration of the Many Meanings of Objects in Museums." *Daedalus* 128, no. 3: 163–83.

———. 2006. *Civilizing the Museum: The Collected Writings of Elaine Heumann Gurian.* New York: Taylor and Francis.

———. 2010. "Museum as Soup Kitchen." *Curator: The Museum Journal* 53, no. 1: 71–85.

Gutwill, Joshua P., and Sue Allen. 2010. *Group Inquiry at Science Museum Exhibits.* San Francisco, CA: Exploratorium.

Halperin, Julia. 2016. "US Museums Spent $5bn to Expand as Economy Shrank."
    Art News Paper, April 4. http://theartnewspaper.com/news/news/us-museums
    -spent-5bn-to-expand-as-economy-shrank/.
Harvard Business Review. 2016. "The New Game Plan for Strategic Planning." Har-
    vard Business Review Analytic Service Report, Harvard Business School Pub-
    lishing. https://hbr.org/resources/pdfs/comm/anaplan/HBRASAnaplan12.7.16
    .pdf.
Hein, George E. 2006. "John Dewey's 'Wholly Original Philosophy' and Its
    Significance for Museums." *Curator: The Museum Journal* 49 no. 2: 181–203.
———. 2011. "Dewey's Debt to Barnes." *Curator: The Museum Journal* 54, no.
    2: 123–39.
———. 2012. *Progressive Museum Practice: John Dewey and Democracy*. Walnut
    Creek, CA: Left Coast Press.
Holo, Selma. 2009. *Beyond the Turnstile: Making the Case for Museums and Sustain-
    able Values*. Lanham, MD: AltaMira Press.
Hoole, Emily, and Tracy E. Patterson. 2008. "Voices from the Field: Evaluation
    as Part of a Learning Culture." In "Nonprofits and Evaluation." Edited by
    Joanne G. Carman and Kimberly A. Fredericks. Special issue, *New Directions
    for Evaluation* 2008, no. 119: 93–113.
Humanities Indicators. 2016. "Historic Site Visits." American Academy of Arts and
    Sciences. Accessed April 14. http://www.humanitiesindicators.org/content/
    indicatorDoc.aspx?d=101&hl=historic+site+visits&m=0.
Ibarra, Herminia, and Morten T. Hansen. 2001. "Are You a Collaborative
    Leader?" *Harvard Business Review*, July–August: 69–74.
Innovation Network. *Logic Model Workbook*. Innovation Network. https://www
    .innonet.org/media/logic_model_workbook_0.pdf.
Institute of Museum and Library Services. 2002. *True Needs True Partners: Museums
    Serving Schools, 2002 Survey Highlights*. Accessed May 16, 2017. https://www
    .imls.gov/sites/default/files/publications/documents/trueneedstruepartners
    98highlights_0.pdf.
International Coalition of Sites of Conscience. 2017. "Home." Accessed April 18.
    http://www.sitesofconscience.org/en/home/.
Jacob, Pierre. 2014. "Intentionality." In *The Stanford Encyclopedia of Philosophy*,
    edited by Edward N. Zalta. Stanford University, 1997– . Accessed January 18,
    2017. https://plato.stanford.edu/entries/intentionality/.
Jacobson, John W. 2016. *Measuring Museum Impact and Performance: Theory and
    Practice*. New York: Rowman & Littlefield.
Janes, Robert. 2009. *Museums in a Troubled World*. New York: Routledge.
Janes, Robert, and Gerald Conaty. 2005. *Looking Reality in the Eye: Museums and
    Social Responsibility*. Calgary, Alberta: University of Calgary Press.
Jarvik, Laurence. 1997. "Ten Good Reasons to Eliminate Funding for the Na-
    tional Endowment for the Arts." *Backgrounder*, no. 1110. http://thf_media
    .s3.amazonaws.com/1997/pdf/bg1110.pdf.

Jen Su, Amy, and Muriel Maignan Wilkins. 2014. "What Gets in the Way of Listening." *Harvard Business Review*, April 14. https://hbr.org/2014/04/what -gets-in-the-way-of-listening.

Kaner, Sam. 2014. *Facilitator's Guide to Participatory Decision-Making*, 3rd ed. Jossey-Bass Business and Management Series. San Francisco, CA: Jossey-Bass.

Kelly, Lynda. 2006. "Measuring the Impact of Museums on their Communities: The Role of the 21st Century Museum." Paper presented at Intercom Conference 2006, Taiwan, November 2–4. http://www.intercom.museum/ documents/1–2Kelly.pdf.

Kemp, Jack. 1994. "The Politics of the Impossible." The Heritage Lectures 511, November 1994, Washington, DC. Accessed May 30, 2017. http://thf_media .s3.amazonaws.com/1994/pdf/hl511.pdf.

Kimmelman, Michael. 2001. "Museums in a Quandary: Where Are the Ideals?" *New York Times*, August 26. http://www.nytimes.com/2001/08/26/arts/art -architecture-museums-in-a-quandary-where-are-the-ideals.html.

Knell, Simon J., Suzanne MacLeod, and Sheila Watson. 2007. *Museum Revolutions: How Museums Change and Are Changed*. London: Routledge.

Kolb, David. 2012. *Experiential Learning: Experience as the Source for Learning and Development*, 2nd ed. Upper Saddle River, NJ: Pearson Education, Inc.

Korn, Randi. 2004. "Self Portrait: First Know Thyself, Then Serve Your Public." *Museum News* 83, no. 1: 32–35, 50–52.

———. 2007. "The Case for Holistic Intentionality." *Curator: The Museum Journal* 50, no. 2: 255–64.

———. 2010. "When Less Is More." *Museum* 89, no. 5: 25–27.

———. 2013. "Creating Public Value through Intentional Practice." In *Museums and Public Value: Creating Sustainable Futures*, edited by Carol Ann Scott, 31–43. London: Routledge.

Korn, Randi, Amanda Krantz, and Margaret Menninger. 2009. "Rethinking Museum Visitors: Using K-Means Cluster Analysis to Explore a Museum's Audience." *Curator: The Museum Journal* 52, no. 4: 363–74.

Koster, Emlyn. 2006. "The Relevant Museum: A Reflection on Sustainability." *Museum News* 85, no. 3: 67–70, 85–87.

———. 2016. "From Apollo into the Anthropocene: The Odyssey of Nature and Science Museums in an Externally Responsible Context." In *Museums, Ethics and Cultural Heritage*, edited by B. Murphy, 228–41. New York: Routledge and International Council of Museums.

Koster, Emlyn, E. Dorfman, and T. Myambe. 2018. "A Holistic Ethos for Nature-Focused Museums in the Anthropocene." In *The Future of Natural History Museums*, edited by E. Dorfman, 29–48. New York: Routledge.

Koster, Emlyn, and John H. Falk. 2007. "Maximizing the External Value of Museums." *Curator: The Museum Journal* 50, no. 2: 191–96.

Krishtalka, Leonard. 2009. "Natural History Museums as Sentinel Observatories of Life on Earth: A Public Trust." In *Beyond the Turnstile: Making the Case for*

Museums and Sustainable Values, edited by Selma Holo, 12–15. Lanham, MD: AltaMira Press.

La Piana, David. 2008. *The Nonprofit Strategy Revolution: Real-Time Strategic Planning in a Rapid-Response World*. Saint Paul, MN: Fieldstone Alliance.

Labovitz, George, and Victor Rosansky. 2012. *Rapid Realignment: How to Quickly Integrate People, Processes, and Strategy for Unbeatable Performance*. New York: McGraw Hill.

Laetsch, Watson. 1987. "A Basis for Better Public Understanding of Science." In *Communicating Science to the Public*, edited by David Evered and Maeve O'Connor. Proceedings of the Conference on the Communication of Science, held at the CIBA Foundation, London, October 14–16. New York: Wiley.

Leinhardt, Gaea, Kevin Crowley, and Karen Knutson. 2002. *Learning Conversations in Museums*. Mahwah, NJ: Lawrence Erlbaum Associates Publishers.

Leinhardt, Gaea, and Karen Knutson. 2004. *Listening In on Museum Conversations*. Walnut Creek: AltaMira Press.

Leinhardt, Gaea, Karen Knutson, and Kevin Crowley. 2003. "Museum Learning Collaborative Redux," *Journal of Museum Education* 28, no. 1: 23–31.

Linden, David. 2011. *The Compass of Pleasure*. New York: Penguin Books.

Lyons, Jenna. 2015. "Union Supporters Rally against Layoffs at Exploratorium." SFGate, October 1. http://www.sfgate.com/bayarea/article/Rally-fights-layoffs-at-S-F-s-famed-6544127.php.

Marino, Lori, Scott O. Lilienfeld, Randy Malamud, Nathan Nobis, and Ron Brogliod. 2010. "Do Zoos and Aquariums Promote Attitude Change in Visitors? A Critical Evaluation of the American Zoo and Aquarium Study." *Society and Animals: Journal of Human-Animal Studies* 18: 126. http://www.animalsandsociety.org/wp-content/uploads/2016/04/marino.pdf.

May, Matthew. 2011. "Zen and the Art of Simplicity." *Rotman Magazine* (Fall): 37–41. https://matthewemay.com/wp-content/uploads/2011/10/zenandtheartofsimplicity.pdf.

McCarthy, Kevin F., Elizabeth H. Ondaatje, Laura Zakaras, and Arthur Brooks. 2004. *Gifts of the Muse: Reframing the Debate about the Benefits of the Arts*. Wallace Foundation: New York. http://www.wallacefoundation.org/knowledge-center/Documents/Gifts-of-the-Muse.pdf.

McCawley, Paul F. 2001. "The Logic Model for Program Planning and Evaluation." University of Idaho. https://www.cals.uidaho.edu/edcomm/pdf/cis/cis1097.pdf.

McLeod, Saul. 2017. "Kolb: Learning Styles." SimplyPsychology.com. https://www.simplypsychology.org/learning-kolb.html.

MindTools. n.d. "5 Whys: Getting to the Root of a Problem Quickly." Mind Tools.com. Accessed March 13, 2018. https://www.mindtools.com/pages/article/newTMC_5W.htm.

———. "The Role of a Facilitator." MindTools.com. Accessed March 13, 2018. https://www.mindtools.com/pages/article/RoleofAFacilitator.htm.

Montebello, Philippe de. 2004. "Art Museums, Inspiring Public Trust." In *Whose Muse: Art Museums and the Public Trust*, edited by James Cuno, 151–69. New Jersey: Princeton University Press and Harvard Art Museums.

Moon, Jenny. 2001. "PDP (Professional Development Planning) Working Paper 4: Reflection in Higher Education Learning." LTSN Generic Centre. May 10. https://www.cumbria.ac.uk/media/university-of-cumbria-website/content -assets/public/er/documents/admissions/interviewdocs/Moon2001Reflective PracticeInterview-1.pdf.

Moore, Mark. 1997. *Creating Public Value: Strategic Management in Government.* Cambridge, MA: Harvard University Press.

———. 2013. *Recognizing Public Value.* Cambridge, MA: Harvard University Press.

Munley, Mary Ellen. 1996. "Museum Education and the Genius of Improvisation." *Journal of Museum Education* 21, no. 1: 18–20.

———. 2013. "Evaluating Public Value: Strategy and Practice." In *Museums and Public Value: Creating Sustainable Futures*, edited by Carol Ann Scott, 45–61. London: Routledge.

The Museums Association. 2008. "Sustainability and Museums: Your Chance to Make a Difference." http://www.museumsassociation.org/download ?id=16398. 7.

National Endowment for the Arts. 2017. "Arts Participation." Accessed April 14, 2017. https://www.arts.gov/artistic-fields/research-analysis/arts-quadrants/arts -participation.

Oxford Economics. 2017. "Museums as Economic Engines: A National Report." Washington, DC: American Alliance of Museums.

Patton, Michael Quinn. 2017. *Principles-Focused Evaluation: The Guide.* New York: The Guilford Press.

Perry, Deborah. 2012. *What Makes Learning Fun?: Principles for the Design of Intrinsically Motivating Museum Exhibits.* Lanham, MD: AltaMira Press.

Pink, Daniel. 2011. *Drive: The Surprising Truth about What Motivates Us.* New York: Riverhead Books.

Pitman, Bonnie, and Ellen Hirzy. 2004. *New Forums: Art Museums & Communities.* Washington, DC: American Association of Museums.

———. 2010. *Ignite the Power of Art: Advancing Visitor Engagement in Museums.* New Haven, CT: Yale University Press.

Preskill, Hallie S., and Rosalie T. Torres. 1999. *Evaluative Inquiry for Learning in Organizations.* Thousand Oaks, CA: Sage Publications.

———. 2000. "The Learning Dimension of Evaluation Use." In "The Expanding Scope of Evaluation Use," edited by Valerie J. Caracelli and Hallie Preskill. Special issue, *New Directions for Evaluation* no. 88: 25–37.

Raelin, Joseph A. 2002. "'I Don't Have the Time to Think!' Versus the Art of Reflective Practice." *Reflections* 4, no. 1: 66–75.

Richardson, Sandy. 2011. "Why Organizational Alignment Should Matter to You (and How to Get It)." *The SFO Blog.* August 2. http://sfo-blog.typepad.com/

sfo-blog/2011/08/why-organizational-alignment-should-matter-to-you-and
-how-to-get-it.html.

Rodgers, Carol. 2002. "Defining Reflection: Another Look at John Dewey and
Reflective Thinking." *Teachers College Record* 104 no. 4: 842–66.

Rosenzweig, Roy, and David Thelen. 1998. *Presence of the Past: Popular Uses of
History in American Life.* New York: Columbia University Press.

Samis, Peter, and Mimi Michaelson. 2017. *Creating the Visitor-Centered Museum.*
New York: Routledge.

Samuel, Alexandra. 2010. "This Year, Say Yes to Saying No." *Harvard Business
Review,* January 8. https://hbr.org/2010/01/say-yes-to-saying-no.

Saunders, Elizabeth Grace. 2015. "Accomplish More by Committing to Less."
Harvard Business Review, January 30. https://hbr.org/2015/01/accomplish
-more-by-committing-to-less.

Scharmer, C. Otto. 2004. *Theory of U: Leading from the Future as It Emerges.* Cambridge, MA: Society for Organizational Learning.

Schein, Edgar H. 2002. "Commentary." *Reflections* 4, no. 1: 79.

Schön, Donald A. 1983. *The Reflective Practitioner: How Professionals Think in Action.*
New York: Basic Books.

———. 1987. *Educating the Reflective Practitioner: Towards a New Design for Teaching
and Learning in the Professions.* San Francisco, CA: Jossey-Bass.

Scott, Carol A. 2006. "Museums: Impact and Value." *Cultural Trends* 15, no. 1:
45–75.

———. 2013. "Introduction to Museums and Public Value." In *Museums and
Public Value: Creating Sustainable Futures,* edited by Carol Ann Scott, 1–13.
London: Routledge.

Senge, Peter. 1990. *The Fifth Discipline.* New York: Doubleday/Currency.

Senge, Peter, C. Otto Scharmer, Joseph Jaworski, and Betty Sue Flowers. 2004.
Presence: Exploring Profound Change in People, Organizations, and Society. New
York: Society for Organizational Learning.

Serrell, Beverly. 2006. *Judging Exhibitions: A Framework for Assessing Excellence.*
Walnut Creek, CA: Left Coast Press.

———. 2015. *Exhibit Labels: An Interpretive Approach,* 2nd ed. Lanham, MD:
Rowman & Littlefield.

Silverman, Lois. 1993. "Making Meaning Together: Lessons from the Field of
American History." *Journal of Museum Education* 18, no. 3: 7–11.

———. 1995. "Visitor Meaning-Making in Museums for a New Age." *Curator:
The Museum Journal* 38, no. 3: 161–70.

Sinek, Simon. 2009. *Start with Why: How Great Leaders Inspire Everyone to Take
Action.* New York: Penguin Group.

Sirefman, Susanna. 1999. "Formed and Forming: Contemporary Museum Architecture." *Daedalus* 128, no. 3: 297–320.

Skramstad, H. 1996. "Changing Public Expectations of Museums." Paper presented at Museums for the New Millennium: A Symposium for the Museum
Community, September 5–7, 1996, Washington, DC.

Smith, Barry. 1994. "Franz Brentano I: On Mind and Its Objects." In *Austrian Philosophy: The Legacy of Franz Brentano*. Chicago: Open Court Publishing Company. Accessed January 18, 2017. http://ontology.buffalo.edu/smith/book/austrian_philosophy/CH2.pdf.

Soren, Barbara. 2009. "Museum Experiences that Change Visitors." *Museum Management and Curatorship* 24, no. 3: 233–51.

Spalding, E., and A. Wilson. 2002. "Demystifying Reflection: A Study of Pedagogical Strategies that Encourage Reflective Journal Writing." *Teachers College Record* 104 no. 7: 1393–1421.

Stahl, Robert J. 1994. "Using 'Think-Time' and 'Wait-Time' Skillfully in the Classroom." *ERIC Digest*. May. https://www.ericdigests.org/1995–1/think.htm.

Sternberg, Susan. 1989. "The Art of Participation." In *Museum Education: History, Theory, and Practice*, edited by Nancy Berry and Susan Mayer, 154–71. Reston, VA: National Art Education Association.

Suchy, Sherene. 2004. *Leading with Passion: Change Management in the Twenty-First Century*. Lanham, MD: AltaMira Press.

Ucko, David A. 2010. "The *Learning Science in Informal Environments* Study in Context." *Curator: The Museum Journal* 53, no. 2: 129–36.

———. 2010. *NSF Influence on the Field of Informal Science Education*. Informal Science Education. Accessed June 7, 2017. http://www.informalscience.org/sites/default/files/NSFImpactonISE.pdf.

Vergeront, Jean. 2011. "Missions that Matter." https://museumnotes.blogspot.com/2011/01/missions-that-matter.html.

Vernon, Cynthia, and Paul Boyle. 2008. "Impact Aquarium Visit." *Connect* (April): 7–9.

Visitor Studies Association. 2017. "Evaluator Competencies for Professional Development." Accessed May 30, 2017. http://www.visitorstudies.org/evaluator-competencies.

W. H. Kellogg Foundation. 2006. *Logic Model Development Guide*. https://www.wkkf.org/resource-directory/resource/2006/02/wk-kellogg-foundation-logic-model-development-guide.

Wales, Jane. 2012. "Framing the Issue." *Stanford Social Innovation Review* (Summer). https://ssir.org/articles/entry/framing_the_issue_2.

Watson, Bill, and Shari Rosenstein Werb. 2013. "One Hundred Strong: A Colloquium on Transforming Natural History Museums in the Twenty-First Century." *Curator: The Museum Journal* 56, no. 2: 255–65.

Weil, Stephen E. 2002. "From Being about Something to Being for Somebody." In *Making Museums Matter*, 28–52. Washington, DC: Smithsonian Books.

———. 2002. *Making Museums Matter*. Washington, DC: Smithsonian Books.

———. 2002. "Museums: Can and Do They Make a Difference?" In *Making Museums Matter*, 55–74. Washington, DC: Smithsonian Institution.

———. 2002. "Romance versus Realism." In *Making Museums Matter*, 102–8. Washington, DC: Smithsonian Books.

————. 2005. "A Success/Failure Matrix for Museums," *Museum News* 84, no. 1: 36.

Weil, Stephen E., and Peggy D. Rudd. 2000. *Perspectives on Outcome Based Evaluation for Libraries and Museums*. Institute of Museum and Library Studies. https://www.imls.gov/sites/default/files/publications/documents/perspectivesobe_0.pdf.

Wetenhall, John. 2017. "Why Not to Run Your Museum 'More Like a Business.'" *Museum* 96, no. 3: 37–42.

Wholey, Joseph S., Harry P. Hatry, and Kathryn E. Newcomer, eds. 2004. *Handbook of Practical Program Evaluation*, 2nd ed. San Francisco, CA: Jossey-Bass.

Worts, Douglas. 2006. "Measuring Museum Meaning: A Critical Assessment Framework." *Journal of Museum Education* 31, no. 1: 49.

————. 2017. "Planning for Cultural Relevance: A Systems Workshop at the Georgia O'Keeffe Museum." In *Systems Thinking in Museums: Theory and Practice*, edited by Yuha Jung and Ann Rowson Love, 81. New York: Rowman & Littlefield.

Yayasan IDEP. 2006. "Workshop Resources 1: Creative Facilitation Techniques." In *Permaculture Facilitator's Resource Book for Training and Assessment*. Bali, Indonesia: IDEP Foundation. http://www.teindia.nic.in/files/teacher_trg_module/8_creative_facilitation_techniques.pdf.

Yocco, Victor S., Joe E. Heimlich, Emily Meyer, and Pam Edwards. 2009. "Measuring Public Value: An Instrument and an Art Museum Case Study." *Visitor Studies* 12, no. 2: 152–63.

Yoon, Carol Kaesuk. 2002. "Stephen Jay Gould, 60, Is Dead; Enlivened Evolutionary Theory." *New York Times*, May 21. Accessed April 17, 2017. http://www.nytimes.com/2002/05/21/us/stephen-jay-gould-60-is-dead-enlivened-evolutionary-theory.html.

Yuhas, Daisy. 2014. "Curiosity Prepares the Brain for Better Learning." *Scientific American*, October 2. https://www.scientificamerican.com/article/curiosity-prepares-the-brain-for-better-learning/.

Index

Page references for figures, tables, and textboxes are italicized.

About the Author

Randi Korn is founding director of RK&A, a company that partners with all types of cultural organizations to plan and evaluate their work around achieving impact. Prior to starting RK&A in 1988, Randi had held a variety of positions in museums, including executive director at a history museum; exhibition designer at a natural history museum; interpretive planner and writer at a botanic garden; and an audience researcher and evaluator at an art museum. These multidisciplinary experiences strengthened her understanding of museum work and heightened her sensitivities about what different museums afford the public.

With a passion for museums and desire to strengthen the relationship between museums and the public, Randi's most recent work focuses on helping museums plan for and achieve their intended impact for the public good. Intentional practice, which grew from her evaluation experience, uses an impact-based approach to planning that is designed to encourage staff to collaboratively articulate their intended impact, evaluate their achievement of impact, reflect on what they learned from evaluation, and align their resources and programs to deepen their organization's intended impact.

Randi was editor of *The Gauge*, a past newsletter for the American Alliance of Museums' Committee on Audience Research and Evaluation, served on the editorial board of *Museums and Social Issues* and as a reviewer for *Curator: The Museum Journal* and *International Journal of Museum Management and Curatorship*. She received a Certificate of Design Excellence in recognition for her interpretive writing in the exhibition *Plant/People Partnership* and was the recipient of the Southeastern Museum Education Division Museum Educator of the Year award from the National

Art Education Association (NAEA). She taught evaluation at the George Washington University for eighteen years, has lectured at the University of Maryland, Johns Hopkins University, and University of Washington, and was a visiting scholar at the University of Michigan. She served on the board of Museum Education Roundtable, the Visitor Studies Association twice since its founding, and as a research commissioner for the NAEA.